THE UPPER ROOM

Disciplines

2012

UPPER
ROOM BOOKS®
NASHVILLE

AN OUTLINE FOR SMALL-GROUP USE OF DISCIPLINES

Here is a simple plan for a one-hour, weekly group meeting based on reading Disciplines. One person may act as convener every week, or the role can rotate among group members. You may want to light a white Christ candle each week to signal the beginning of your time together.

OPENING

Convener: Let us come into the presence of God.

Others: Lord Jesus Christ, thank you for being with us. Let us hear your word to us as we speak to one another.

SCRIPTURE

Convener reads the scripture suggested for that day in Disciplines. After a one- or two-minute silence, convener asks: What did you hear God saying to you in this passage? What response does this call for? (Group members respond in turn or as led.)

REFLECTION

- What scripture passage(s) and meditation(s) from this week was (were) particularly meaningful for you? Why? (Group members respond in turn or as led.)
- What actions were you nudged to take in response to the week's meditations? (Group members respond in turn or as led.)
- Where were you challenged in your discipleship this week? How did you respond to the challenge? (Group members respond in turn or as led.)

PRAYING TOGETHER

Convener says: Based on today's discussion, what people and situations do you want us to pray for now and in the coming week? Convener or other volunteer then prays about the concerns named.

DEPARTING

Convener says: Let us go in peace to serve God and our neighbors in all that we do.

Adapted from *The Upper Room* daily devotional guide, January–February 2001. © 2000 The Upper Room. Used by permission.

THE UPPER ROOM DISCIPLINES 2012

The Upper Room Web site: http://www.upperroom.org

Cover design: Left Coast Design, Portland, Oregon

Cover photo: Brother John, OEF

ISBN: 978-0-8358-1020-3

Printed in the United States of America

CONTENTS

FOREWORD

*Your word is a lamp to my feet
and a light to my path.*

—Psalm 119:105

This verse from scripture speaks a deep and timeless truth for me. It captures the guidance, discernment, and clarity that the Bible imparts to me now and has imparted to me throughout my life. Indeed, the words are stamped on my heart, and my memory is filled with moments in which scripture provided needed light to my path.

September 1978. I was eighteen years old and sitting on my sheetless bed the first day at college, having just bravely waved good-bye to my parents as they headed toward home—three hours away. I suddenly realized how alone I was, on a campus with twenty-five thousand strangers. I turned in prayer to God and began reading Psalm 139; I realized that I wasn't really alone and the psalmist's words comforted me: "Your hand shall lead me, and your right hand shall hold me fast" (v. 10).

March 1988. I was twenty-eight, single, pregnant, and scared. Having transgressed my own moral code, I felt awash in guilt and fear. Could I still know God's blessing in my life? And how would I view this young life I carried inside of me? In the early months of my pregnancy, I read with new understanding the words of Ecclesiastes 3:1-2: "For everything there is a season, and a time for every matter under heaven: a time to be born, and a time to die." This scripture spoke courage and brought light to my heart, reminding me of the paradoxical blessing and intention of God. Somehow, I sensed God in this situation. I could hold my head high as a single mother-to-be, anticipating the birth of my child.

September 11, 2001. Fear gripped me the day I heard the horrible, unbelievable news that terrorists had flown planes into the World Trade Center, the Pentagon, and a field in Pennsylvania. I felt afraid for our world, for our country, and for my kids and their future. Now a forty-one-year-old married mother of three, I held tight to the simple, yet comforting words of Psalm 56:3, which became a constant prayer for me: "When I am afraid, I put my trust in you."

December 24, 2010. Family issues, wayward young-adult children, anxiety—I carried all of these burdens with me into the church candlelight service. Our pastor's creative reading of Luke 1:26-38 centered on Mary's troubled first response to Gabriel's news, "How can this be?" (v. 34). Mary's question echoed the pain and questions in my own heart: *Why has life happened like this? What can I do to fix it? Will things ever get better?* And then I heard those first words of Mary's response: "Let it be" (v. 38). That Christmas Eve, as I let the light of acceptance seep into my tense muscles and weary heart, I began to see possibilities or at least next steps. God's word became "a lamp to my feet."

The Bible has become a light to my path as I've learned, over the course of a lifetime, to heed the admonition of Colossians 3:16: "Let the word of Christ dwell in you richly." By regularly immersing myself in scripture, I open myself to the grace and light of God. *Upper Room Disciplines* facilitates the daily practice of Bible reading with guidance from spiritual leaders around the world. For tens of thousands of daily readers, reading scripture with *Disciplines* is a trusted and meaningful way to allow "the word of Christ to dwell in [them] richly."

May you find this year, through the daily practice of reading the scripture and meditations in *Disciplines*, that you are becoming a dwelling place for the word of Christ and that this word is becoming a light to your path.

—ROBIN PIPPIN
Editorial Director • Upper Room Books

After the Birth

JANUARY 1, 2012 • NATALIE A. HANSON

SUNDAY, JANUARY 1 ~ *Read Isaiah 60:1-6*

We begin the year with a love song from God to the family in exile. "Arise," God says. "Shine."

As a college student I spent two summers leading work teams at a cooperative parish in West Virginia. I first visited the parish as a high school volunteer and then as a young adult counselor. On the second visit, the director of the parish looked me up and down, took me aside, handed me a tool box and a pencil drawing, and said, "I want you to take these kids over to that trailer and build Mrs. Love a new set of steps." I protested that I had no idea how to build steps. He looked at me again and finally said, "It's high time you began to see in yourself what others see in you. I see something like a carpenter, something like a leader. You'd best get out there and see for yourself." Riding his confidence, I figured out how to read his pencil sketch and build those steps. I learned how to work concrete and to organize a team. I learned how to sit down and appreciate the folks for whom and with whom I was working. Because he called me out, something in me began to rise and shine.

We catch light from one another; God models it. We're given the great privilege of helping ignite other lives. We catch light from each other—or darkness. That's the way it works. With Joseph and Mary, with Boaz and Naomi, with a wise old nurse and a courageous old couple, with Simeon and Anna, with Thomas Merton and Dorothy Day, we are all invited by God-in-Christ to help one another rise and shine, redeemed to be redeemers.

Love made flesh, be truly born in and among us, that love may be borne by and through us for all the world. Amen.

Senior Pastor, Christ First United Methodist Church, Jamestown, New York

When God Speaks

JANUARY 2-8, 2012 • JOEY FAUCETTE

MONDAY, JANUARY 2 ~ *Read Genesis 1:1-2*

Parents have a way of getting their point across to their children without ever saying a word. I still recall my mother's smile of approval across the room after I made a speech as a fifth grader. Upon occasion her piercing stare across the sanctuary caused me to sit up straight and pay attention to the preacher.

"Nonverbal cues" the experts call them. You create and communicate your message without ever saying a word. That's how God began creating. "The Spirit of God was moving over the face of the waters" (RSV). God's movement creates a message that permeates the chaos and unveils an order of a magnitude that previously did not exist.

When your life mirrors the chaos of earth's beginnings—with no form and void of purpose or meaning—you most likely pray. As you pray, perhaps you set aside your lists and litanies long enough to listen. But do you merely listen for words with your ears?

Or, do you employ other senses and listen to your life with your eyes? How often do you peer into the darkness, watching for a flicker of movement that creates a message that communicates order, not chaos; purpose, not puzzle; vitality, not void? God's nonverbal cues are as much a part of our reality as were my mother's smiles and stares. What is God speaking into your life without ever saying a word on this second day of the new year? How are you listening with your eyes?

God, we find order arising from our chaos, not so much in what you say but in what you do. Amen.

Speaker and author who coaches people to listen to life and make a life, not just a living at www.ListentoLife.org; Dry Fork, Virginia

TUESDAY, JANUARY 3 ~ *Read Genesis 1:3-5*

In the part of the world where I live, at this time of year the daylight hours are very short. In fact, when I'm not traveling and find myself working from my office, the sun has set when I pull into my garage.

Frankly, this isn't my favorite time of year. I really enjoy being outdoors in the sunlight. I want to ride horses with my wife, but until we get our horses to leave the flashlights taped to their heads, we can't.

And yet I know that this time of year is a part of God's intended purpose. These days are necessary to create balance in my life, a rhythm that moves beyond the frenetic activity of long daylight hours into a hibernating time of darkness. "Then God said, 'Let there be light.' . . . And God saw that the light was good; and God separated the light from the darkness."

When God speaks, God's voice balances the rhythm of our lives. Yes, the light is good. Times of activity and productivity form a vital part of our making a life and a living. The goodness of such experiences comes in their perpetuation of the light. However, the light is separate from the darkness. Just as music is a series of sounds and silence in rhythm, so our lives must be a series of light and darkness, activity and rest, work and sabbath.

Embrace this season of your life and God's created daily work-and-rest rhythm. Such percussive movement is a part of our purpose and God's plan.

When God speaks, balance discovers its rhythm in our lives.

O God, thank you for separating the light from the darkness. May its visual cues remind us of our lives' rhythms that bring us balance in a world that often seems off-center. Amen.

My wife and I live on a small farm. She enjoys raising and playing with our yellow Labrador retrievers. She enjoys our pets so much that she boards other people's pets also. On any given occasion, we may have ten dogs at our home. When these dogs begin barking at a squirrel or at our cat, you can imagine the noise. To me, it is just noise; but to my wife, each dog has a distinctive voice. Lucy yelps. Jake has a deep-throated "Whoof." Dutchess, always the first to bark, alerts the others. Down the list of dogs she goes, reciting the unique nuances of each bark.

In today's reading, the psalmist cites the unique nuances of "the voice of the LORD." As in Genesis, movement reflects God's power and rule. Natural experiences such as thunderstorms booming and flashing across a lake, cedars breaking in the wind, and oak leaves swirling in the gusts until they separate from their branches are more than just video footage for weather cable channels. They are creative expressions of God's voice. The "flood" of verse 10 calls to mind the waters of chaos over which God prevailed "in the beginning." "The voice of the LORD" embodies power and majesty; our God communicates, instructs, and redeems.

God, sovereign over all, employs such powerful strength that all of nature bows down; and God strengthens the people. "May the LORD give strength to his people!" God's voice strengthens and sustains us in all our life experiences, even the stormy ones.

O God, the stormy noises of this life distract us with their crashing waves of worry, breaking trees of terror, flashing signs of fear, and swirling winds of separation. They would cause us to skip like immature believers away from you. Give us your strength to distinguish the noise from your voice. Amen.

Each spring a mother bird builds a nest atop a column on our porch. This column is adjacent to the door through which we come and go many times each day. The opportunities for her to be frightened, interrupted, and irritated to the point of leaving are multiple as we open and shut the door going to and from the garage, welcoming people into our home, and shouting "I love you!" to one another. However, she focuses on her task at hand, whether building her nest twig by twig or hunkering down on her eggs until they hatch or bringing delicacies to feed her fledglings. In a situation potentially filled with peril, she discovers peace. Her peace allows her to focus on and achieve positive results.

The psalmist describes a frightening storm that not only interrupts routine but must have been irritating to no end. He sees past the fear to hear God's voice, sensing God's strength in the storm. Then, once the storm passes, he declares that the Lord blesses the people with peace. Not only does quiet precede the storm, but peace follows it. Our God who speaks and creates out of nothingness also speaks peace following our storms.

Think back on a time of fear for you. How did God bless you with peace following your storm? Recall an experience of chronic interruption when you believed you would never finish the task at hand. In what way did God's peace emerge after the delay? Relive a point of irritation with someone or some situation. Where did God's peace surface?

God's voice brings peace that blesses following the storms of our lives.

O God, in the storms we discern your voice. Speak peace that calms our anxiety, keeps us on task, and relieves our irritations. Not just for our own comfort but for your glory. Amen.

Being the father of two daughters, I would slam and lock the door, dial 9-1-1, and grab a baseball bat if someone looking like John showed up at my door to take either of them on a date. Clad in camel's hair and a leather belt and smelling of desert locusts and honey, he would not be welcome at our house.

My judgment of him might end there were it not for his words, "I am not worthy to stoop down and untie the thong of his sandals." John's clothing and his words are traveling companions. His humility takes us aback when compared with those who use dress and words to toot their own horns.

"He that tooteth not his own horn, the same doth not get tooted." I repeated to my wife those words of encouragement that someone once spoke to me.

"The problem with tooting your own horn," she replied, "is that it's usually off-key."

God's voice humbles us. God's pitch-perfect voice by which we tune our lives is muted by this world, which devalues humility. So we toot along with the others, off-key though we may be, settling for less than we could be and do.

John could have tooted his own horn as the harbinger of the Messiah. But he wore camel's hair and a leather girdle instead of a purple robe and golden sash. He ate locusts and honey instead of filet and asparagus. He said, "I am not worthy" instead of "Look at me!"

God's voice humbles us. I suppose I should *listen* to who shows up at my door before I slam and lock it.

O God, forgive our egotistical exaggerations of our own abilities. Speak to us. Humble us. May we find you in others. Amen.

SATURDAY, JANUARY 7 ~ *Read Acts 19:1-7*

You don't know what you don't know. The speed limit changes; you miss the signs. The police officer doesn't. The swirling lights tell the story. You misplace your debit card. Someone finds and uses it. The overdrawn account tells the story. You study all night but miss the part of the syllabus that details the final exam. Your professor does not. The final course grade tells the story.

You don't know what you don't know, do you? If you knew, you could do something about it, right? If you knew, your behavior would have been different, true? If you knew, your story would sound better, correct?

But you didn't know.

Paul asked these disciples in Corinth, "Did you receive the Holy Spirit when you became believers?" And they replied, "No, we have not even heard that there is a Holy Spirit."

Paul baptizes them in the name of the Lord Jesus and the Holy Spirit comes upon them. They begin to prophesy and speak in tongues. Before, they did not know the Holy Spirit; now they do. We also know. So what will be different?

God speaks through messengers like Paul to close the gap between what we know and what we don't know we don't know. God's voice completes.

Whom has God sent to you as a clarion voice of knowledge? Who has spoken boldly into your ignorance and enlightened you to the ways of the Spirit?

Since we don't know what we don't know, let us praise God for those who in this new year will speak God's reality into our lives. God's voice completes us.

O God, save us from our ignorance. Send us a Paul. Speak to us that we may be complete. Amen.

SUNDAY, JANUARY 8 ~ *Read Mark 1:8-11*

BAPTISM OF THE LORD

We all long to hear "Well done!" or "Way to go, girl!" or "Atta-boy!"—especially when we're undertaking a new venture in our lives. Each of us desires to hear, "I see you." We crave validation.

We seek that validation in many forms, most of them insubstantial. In my experience, only one of them truly fulfills. Such validation happens when *God* speaks into our lives and grants divine approval. Something like, "You are my Son, the Beloved; with you I am well pleased." What a poignant picture of parental support!

Jesus accepts his earthly mission by slipping beneath the baptismal waters of the muddy Jordan River, guided by John's hands and preparatory journey. He emerges, dripping with the newness of this mission, to hear God speak words of validation, a cosmic "Atta-boy!" that resounds for eternity.

Divine validation creates an unbreakable bond of parental approval that withstands all manner of temptation, such as, "If you are the Son of God . . . " (Luke 4:3). No, nothing can separate us from such a love.

God's voice approves. Not of our imperfections as we seek validation at idol altars. Not of our vainglorious attempts at self-validation through power and prestige. Not of our choosing our life mission instead of receiving it.

God's voice approves of us because our ultimate validation emerges with us, dripping wet with baptismal water, in our relationship with God. We too are God's beloved. May God be equally well pleased with us.

God, may we find our true validation in relationship with you. Amen.

When God Speaks

The Word and Our Words

JANUARY 9–15, 2012 • MARILYN BROWN ODEN

MONDAY, JANUARY 9 ~ *Read 1 Samuel 3:10-20*

This week we'll ponder whether our words—the ones we speak and think—reflect *the* Word. Today *the* Word shows Samuel's connection with God: he listened; the Lord was with him; none of Samuel's words fell to the ground; and all Israel acknowledged him as the Lord's trustworthy prophet.

What connects you to God? The *sounds* of nature? music? The *touch* of a rose petal? a wooden cross? those you love? The *sight* of a sunrise? a dome of stars in the night sky? The *aroma* of a spring rain? freshly mown grass? a trellis of honeysuckle? The *taste* of Communion wine? cotton candy? a potluck dinner with friends?

Do you connect to God in solitude and silence? What sacred space or place calls to your soul? For me it is high in the San Juan Mountains. I stacked wood there recently, trying to fit the logs together so they wouldn't roll off. I recalled how none of Samuel's words fell to the ground—unlike my logs. As the woodpile grew, I thought about stacking words and how many we stack in a week—talking, texting, e-mailing—and how many fall to the ground. Each word we stack is chosen. When we step back and look at our wordpile, does it reflect God's love and grace?

Only vanity would suggest that we are trustworthy prophets like Samuel and that none of our words falls to the ground. But not all of them do. Sometimes we follow Jesus' teachings. We connect with God and neighbor, grow in faithfulness, serve and listen, practice spiritual disciplines, do no harm and do good— remaining conscious of stacking a wordpile pleasing to God.

Holy Present One, help us to grow in faith, to reflect your love to others, and to stack a wordpile pleasing to you. Amen.

Award-winning author of 11 books; Santa Fe, New Mexico

Today's Word tells us that Jesus said, "Follow me." Philip follows, engaging heart and feet. For me, Jesus' invitation to follow is multidimensional. It affects not only where our feet go but also what our mouths say, what our minds think, and our attitude when we face the unknown. It includes following the disciplines in order to journey more faithfully; in other words, trying to become more centered and connected becomes the basis for the rest. Doing that calls us to breathe in and breathe out: to connect with the mystery of the sacred through a daily personal time and also to connect with others, reflecting the love and compassion Jesus taught us.

Though it sounds contradictory, I've begun to think of my daily set-apart time as connection time. These sacred moments offer a concentrated period to connect with the loving Holy One, with the scriptures, and with ancient and contemporary spiritual writings. This time also provides an opportunity to connect with other people through intercessory prayer and to take it seriously when I feel drawn toward a specific person.

For example, one morning during this set-apart time, I felt a strong pull toward a particular friend—too strong simply to jot down the name on my ever-undone to-do list. I realized that when we feel powerfully drawn to someone, our immediate written or verbal communication is not an interruption of this sacred time; it is a skipping-rock gesture that is part of it, rippling in wider and wider circles. That morning my set-apart time became connection time.

We can view all of our connections from a spiritual perspective; that awareness changes our relationships. We remember Jesus' love for others and acknowledge that our words—thought and spoken—can echo his love and compassion.

Loving Holy One, help us to grow closer to you in our journey and to reflect your love to others. Amen.

The Word today offers praise and thanks: "For so many marvels I thank you; a wonder am I, and all your works are wonders" (NJB). G. K. Chesterton speaks of taking things with gratitude instead of taking them for granted. To live more gratefully is to live more fully.

A few years ago I began noting a gift each day, followed by a whispered thank-you. Anticipating the gift of the day is like walking on tiptoe, aware of God's presence. Attentiveness to little daily gifts helps us respond to life with gratitude. The gifts are simple—a smile from a child, a kind word, lunch with a dear friend, a single white rose outside a winter window that hangs on despite the snow, promising endurance to become the first rose of summer. These simple gifts signify the fullness of life. Our difficulty comes not in discovering a daily gift but in deciding which one to record, for many await our notice and unwrapping. God's gifts abound, calling forth gratitude.

Researchers have found that grateful persons tend to have more vitality; are more positive, empathic, generous, and helpful; are less depressed and stressed; and place less importance on material possessions. They note that gratitude encourages a positive cycle of reciprocal kindness among people.

Noticing God's little gifts and responding gratefully can transform us. The moment our feet hit the floor we are alert to God's presence and lean into the day with anticipation, the psalmist's words of praise on our lips: "For so many marvels I thank you; a wonder am I, and all your works are wonders."

Giving God, we thank you for your abundant gifts. Amen.

The Word today tells us about Samuel and Eli, and we also see our own words. The Word of the Lord is "precious" (ASV). Eli's eyes have grown dim. The Word is not yet revealed to Samuel. He hears his name, thinks Eli is calling, and runs to him saying, "Here I am." Eli finally realizes the Lord is calling and tells Samuel the words of response: "Your servant is listening."

The "precious" Word affirms that God's loving, grace-filled presence is always with us. We know, however, that our awareness of God's presence waxes and wanes. Often we don't even notice it; our eyes, like Eli's, are dim.

Like Samuel we experience moments when we distinctly hear a call. Sometimes we too become confused and run in the wrong direction, offering "Here I am" to the wrong person or project or purpose. Sometimes we need help from another to discern the right direction. If so, do we look for someone like Eli who has been on the faith journey longer? Or someone we trust whose daily living reflects God's love and grace?

This scripture makes clear our response: "Your servant is listening." "Your *servant*"—an image that leaves no place for arrogance, egotism, pomposity—"is *listening*." Listening to the God of love and grace and listening to others who, like us, are struggling for discernment or perhaps simply to be heard and shown care. Our appropriate response is not to advise or exhort but to listen. Sometimes faith calls not for our words but for our silence, our attentive silence. How do we discern when to offer loving, grace-filled words and when to offer loving, grace-filled silence?

O God, may your light shine on our discernment as we examine our responses to you and to others. Amen.

Today we read that when Philip tells Nathanael about Jesus, Nathanael reveals his bias by asking if anything good can come out of Nazareth. Philip responds, "Come and see." Those three simple words can change our lives.

We suffer from the tinted-window syndrome. Our family, culture, background, church, and location lend a hand in mixing the tint that coats our window on the world. When we look through it, we miss a lot. Flannery O'Connor related a man's comment after a peacock's magnificent display of beauty: "Never saw such long ugly legs." How easy it is to miss the beauty of those in our "Nazareth" bias and trip over their spindly legs. We tend to see the things we expect to see and to ignore realities that don't fit our perceptions, perspectives, and positions. But like Nathanael, Jesus issues an invitation for us to come and see—to look up close with new eyes and broaden our view.

If Jesus knows of Nathanael's disparagement, he doesn't reciprocate. He compliments him as a person without "deceit" and says he remembers seeing him under the fig tree. Nathanael sees Jesus through new eyes. (Perhaps we too take a second look when someone we've disparaged compliments and remembers us.) We don't know whether this conversation alters Nathanael's Nazareth bias; perhaps like most of us, he keeps his bias and sees Jesus as an exception—but even that scrapes a bit of tint off the window. His eyes open enough to see who Jesus really is.

Jesus tells Nathanael that he will see greater things than these. Might we see greater things if we weren't satisfied with our tinted view of the world? We can gradually and intentionally become conscious of these tints and how they affect us, reconsider our worldview and our "Nazareth" biases, and prayerfully journey toward clarity of vision. Come and see!

God of grace, who loves us even with our tints and biases, transform us. Strengthen us to come and see. Amen.

The Word addresses the behavior of Christian believers and gives expression to a "full-bodied" spirituality. This passage advises restraint, but self-restraint is a contemporary countercultural concept. I think of marketing ads: buy this or pursue that "because you can." Paul says that not all things are "beneficial," and he will not allow anything to dominate him. True freedom includes restraint—both in actions and words. Paul is united to the Lord, one in spirit with him.

Unlike Paul, we and the Corinthians find ourselves divided within. Our spirit loses ground to cultural assumptions and expectations. We fear losing power, prestige, position. So we go forth, in Parker Palmer's words, "masked and armored."

The Corinthian Christians express a disconnect between their spiritual selves redeemed by Christ and the actions of their bodily selves. Paul reminds them that the temple of the Holy Spirit is within. That image evokes a sense of reverence. But in our dividedness, we speak words to and about others unfit for a temple. We do things that desecrate it, take it places not good for the spirit. But we hide our reverence behind our masks and armor.

In London a pleasant automated voice reminds people exiting the tube to "mind the gap" (between the train and the platform). A gap stands between the expedient words we say and the faithful words we long to say. Christ invites us to a global Table, to sit around it together in his name. If we look across the Table directly at the others, instead of through our tinted window, we might even see that the temple of the Holy Spirit is within us—and also within all those around us.

Let's mind the gap between *the* Word and *our* words, between the temple within and our outer masks and armor.

Gracious God, grant us self-restraint and a sense of reverence for the temple of the Holy Spirit within us. Amen.

SUNDAY, JANUARY 15 ~ *Read Psalm 139:1-6*

The psalm tells us that God discerns our thoughts, is acquainted with all our ways, and knows our words before we speak them. No division here! No faking with masks or hiding behind armor.

Our words are known by God: our words that use, abuse, and misuse, as well as our words that offer love and kindness and compassion. How we yearn for our words to be more faithful to *the* Word!

God is acquainted with our ways, our habits and patterns and purposes, that bring harm as well as the ones that bring good. How we yearn for our ways to be more pleasing to God!

God discerns our thoughts, our silent mental commentaries that flow continuously. They can roar down a destructive track with the power to persuade us that our actions are someone else's fault or that a goal motivated by our self-interest is a moral cause or that dehumanizing certain groups is a reasonable, necessary option. But we are not doomed to these thoughts. We can change our train of thought, take it down another track, and offer second thoughts that form something beautiful for God.

The psalm celebrates God's inescapability; "such knowledge is too wonderful for me." The sacred abounds! May we grow in our connection to God; deepen our awareness of what it means to follow Jesus; live with gratitude in our hearts and on our lips; discern when to say, "Here I am"; clear away our Nazareth biases and see greater things; practice restraint and mind the gap between *the* Word and *our* words. May we have the courage to be one with God and others, training our thoughts and words to celebrate our loving, inescapable God!

O God, help us cleanse our thoughts and words and the stains in our worldview. Amen.

God Calls

JANUARY 16–22, 2012 • CECIL MURPHEY

MONDAY, JANUARY 16 ~ *Read Mark 1:14-15*

Jesus firmly calls his listeners to make the supreme life decision: "Repent, and believe in the good news." He doesn't ask them to ponder or to go home and consider. His message carries demand and urgency. Jesus has come and *now*—this minute—is the time to turn and embrace the message. These words signal his first call or invitation. We don't know how many responded, but we read of the four fishermen who join him. I assume many listeners turned to Jesus.

But not everyone.

Even today, the first call of the gospel means nothing to some. They reject the first call because they haven't seen the godly life in those who profess to follow Jesus. They turn away because they've known too many who didn't show the spirit of Christ to others.

And what about us? We listened to our first call and turned to God. We know how to point others to Jesus Christ. However, our lifestyles may unintentionally block the message so that others can't hear the call. Because they don't see us living a life of love, compassion, and understanding, they turn away.

For some of us, *now* is a good time to heed Jesus' words as direct messages from God to us, the committed followers. We not only listen but undertake serious self-examination. Maybe we, the committed, are the ones who need to hear afresh Jesus' words so we can live as he demands: "Repent and believe."

God, in responding to the first call, teach me to live so I can show you at work in me. Amen.

Ordained minister of the gospel, Presbyterian Church (USA), full-time author, former missionary; living in Decatur, Georgia

Jesus issues his first call, which his words, "Follow me" reinforce. Four fishermen respond to his challenging first call and move into a new area of endeavor: fishing for people. And it was a quick turnaround! Jesus "immediately" calls, and they "immediately" follow.

I used to feel guilty about the disciples' ready willingness to "fish for people." I'm not an evangelist, and it's not easy for me to challenge strangers with the gospel.

Yet my friend Joe can do it. At lunch, I introduced him to three businessmen. Within minutes Joe, in an easy, nonpushy way, talked to them about following Jesus. I marveled at his ability to talk so readily. When I asked how he did that, Joe said he didn't know. I wondered why he could do it and I couldn't. Joe has a gift—a special gift—and he can talk to people, even strangers.

I have my own spiritual gifts. My wife says that though I'm now a full-time writer, I'm still a pastor at heart. She's probably right. I want to establish a relationship with people and listen to them. I willingly respond by pointing them to God.

So what gifts did Jesus see in those first disciples? What did they see in Jesus that enabled them to leave their livelihood for a new career on the road? Perhaps some of the understanding comes in Jesus' words: "The kingdom of God has come near" (Mark 1:15). With no promise of answers or security, those first disciples step out in faith and find themselves empowered to do the work of the kingdom. Joe evangelizes, and I listen—both of us empowered by the call to follow and the hope of doing kingdom work. Both of us have answered God's call to serve.

Lord Jesus, you call us to follow you. Help us recognize the nearness of the kingdom and to employ our gifts to your service. Amen.

World War II called for sacrifice on the battlefields, and at home governments imposed restrictive demands on civilians. Most countries began rationing programs. No one built new houses, and many people ate meat only once a week. In 1929, our modern world plunged into what many call the Great Depression. In these instances, people had little choice. They had to give up luxuries, vacation plans, and put off buying expensive cars. They economized because of job loss. They made sacrifices. That's not answering a radical call—only surviving in tough economic times.

If we consider the historical context of Paul's words, his teaching doesn't seem so negative. The apostle wrote at a time when he believed the end of the world was near; therefore, he wanted his readers to focus on a radical, self-denying lifestyle.

It's as if Paul says, "We're almost out of time, so don't delay or get involved in other things. I want all of you to be prepared for Jesus' return. Set aside all distractions—even the good things of this life—and concentrate on being ready."

Answering God's extreme, uncompromising call requires that we look at our world and ask, "Is this the way I want to live the rest of my life? How may I best serve God?"

The kingdom of God has come near, and the "present form of this world is passing away," Paul wrote. The current form is still passing away, and God still issues a radical call: "Live as if these are your last days. Be prepared for my coming."

All-wise God, may my life reflect my commitment to you. Amen.

Jonah ran from God the first time; the second time he obeyed God's call. He preached to the people of Nineveh, probably because he feared the consequences of not obeying. Being imprisoned once inside the large fish was enough.

The prophet refused at first because he knew God was merciful; Jonah wasn't, and he wanted Israel's enemies destroyed. (See Jonah 4:1-2.) Many of us are like Jonah—although perhaps not as hard-hearted. We hear the call but ignore it or run from it.

Our calls to serve aren't as dramatic as the prophet's. God doesn't usually tell us to go thousands of miles from home and preach divine destruction that will arrive in forty days.

Our calls may seem minor, such as visiting the sick, ushering at church, and helping the poor. We may not see dramatic turn-arounds as Jonah did. After he preached, the Ninevites believed. Then God "changed his mind about the calamity that he had said he would bring upon them; and he did not do it."

Jonah obeyed God—finally. And perhaps that's the tarnished testimony of many: "I obeyed God—finally." Extreme measures brought about Jonah's obedience. For some of us today it may take financial loss, marital breakup, the loss of a job, or grief over the death of a loved one before we begin to obey.

Even when he obeyed, Jonah found no delight in God's will. The book closes with the prophet being rebuked for his attitude. He did the right thing but with reluctance. Although it's good to respond the second time (or third or fourth), it's even better to cry out with joy the first time, "Yes, Lord, here I am." Jonah didn't obey with alacrity, and we may assume that he missed out on many divine blessings.

Lord, you call me to serve. Forgive me for holding back. Help me to serve joyfully the first time you call. Amen.

People testify of running from God until they reach the place of full surrender. Others attain success only to find it meaningless, so they leave everything and serve the Lord.

Calls to serve don't come just to professionals—pastors, missionaries, and chaplains. God calls and endows all of us with abilities to serve. For example, Gary's parents were missionaries and his brother was a pastor. "What about you?" I asked.

Gary wrapped his arms around his computer and said, "This is my ministry." Gary knew his call.

But what about the cost of not obeying the call of God? Jonah didn't obey the first time and almost died until he heard God the second time. One friend almost died from cancer before he left a lucrative public relations job to work with refugees in Rwanda. Others hang on to jobs they dislike rather than obey God's call.

If we answer God's call—regardless of what it is—we will pay a price. Our lives will change, and we'll be different. It may mean we'll have to undergo training that lasts a long time. We may have to study long hours and push ourselves to learn more. When I became a believer, I lost my close friends because they thought I had become a fanatic.

If God has called us and we pay the price, the good news is that we look back and thank God for the privilege of service. And we realize that the biggest cost is to surrender control of our lives.

I wonder if that's not the heaviest price: to willingly, joyfully, say, "God you know better than I do, so I surrender." When we talk about commitment, it may not sound like much, but it is costly to answer God's call.

Loving God, teach me to surrender to your call to serve, regardless of what it is, and may I do it joyfully. Amen.

In 2007, my family's house burned; we lost everything. As I watched it burn, I heard myself say, "I've been preparing for this." I didn't mean I expected a tragedy, but I had learned to be at peace no matter what happened.

I don't know when, like the psalmist, I started to trust in God at all times and without anxiety. I know it happened gradually, the result of a long-term relationship with the Lord. I can recall several seemingly terrible experiences where God intervened and made them special times of victory:

- During my student days we had no food and no money. We told no one, but someone brought us a large box of groceries.
- My wife lay in the emergency room after a head-on collision; the doctor didn't expect her to live. She walked out of the hospital in less than a week.

Such experiences taught me that I can endure hardships with quietness and calm. Even when current circumstances seemingly belie God's presence and involvement, "I shall not be shaken." The psalmist knew his deliverance was certain, and I can echo his words. Like him, I can sit silently and wait for God to act. Because I remember what the Lord did in the past, I take my rest in the present.

Verse 8 of Psalm 62 links two important words: *trust* and *heart*—the psalmist pours out his heart in prayers of petition. He urges us to trust God and pray. I can do that because God has been teaching me to trust. Where do you set your heart?

Sovereign God, help me to live in readiness. Whenever you call and for whatever you call, may I always trust, regardless of the circumstances, because I know you are with me. Amen.

Clearly these verses imply that a possible deterrent to finding peace in God alone could be wealth. Those of "low estate" and "high estate" fare alike: "they are together lighter than a breath." Extortion and robbery provide means to get money. Riches and wealth can lull us into thinking that we are self-sufficient, that we can take care of ourselves, thank you very much. We can learn to trust and rely on our own resources rather than on God's power. Once again the psalmist raises the issue of the heart: where we set our hearts, where we place our security.

But consider these words of the psalmist: "You repay to all according to their work." Whether we are rich or poor, an ultimate payday awaits each of us.

I like being appreciated; it makes me feel good. Most of us hold that value. Yet when we talk about God, we're slow to admit that we relish God's appreciation. A few people remind me that we don't do good so we can be rewarded. "We do good," they say, "because it's the right thing to do." I don't argue with them, but I want to ask, "What's wrong with doing good and *also* receiving a reward?"

As students we can work hard and find our reward in our grades. Vocationally we may reap the reward of knowledge and relationships. Those are rewards, and we joyfully accept them.

God's steadfast love can allow us to focus on the good things that lie ahead for us. We hear God's call and respond, "Yes, God, I'll serve you. I know that one day I'll enjoy a glorious payday when you make all things right."

Dear God, may I be faithful to you today, tomorrow, and every day I live. May I set my heart on you. Amen.

Words of Authority

JANUARY 23–29, 2012 • NELL NOONAN

MONDAY, JANUARY 23 ~ *Read Deuteronomy 18:15-20*

Over the decades I have listened to hundreds of sermons, most containing some nugget of God's truth for me that day. Today's reading from Deuteronomy is part of a long sermon. Its recording takes up almost the entire fifth and final book of the Torah. Its speaking lasts over one day, the last in the life of Moses when he addresses the Israelites as they prepare to cross the Jordan to take possession of Canaan. The preaching has a three-part theme: (1) what God will do, (2) God's expectation of the people's response, and (3) what God proposes for their future if they are found faithful.

What will God do? God will raise up a prophet like Moses who will speak the commands and words of the Lord to the chosen. What does God expect? The Lord wants the people to listen and heed the prophet's words. Obedience to God's commands as spoken by the prophet will ensure a hopeful future.

The formula seems so simple I can fit it on a sticky note for my bathroom mirror as a minisermon: *remember, obey, behold.* Remember God's gracious deeds and steadfastness; obey God's words in unswerving loyalty; and behold what God has in store for the beloved. The future will bring an even greater prophet who will not only speak the Lord's words but will also be the one who *is* the Word.

O God, teach us to recall your goodness and to live our lives in gratitude for what you have done for us. Amen.

Church educator, librarian, Stephen minister, author; Arlington, Texas

Today's scripture is located midpoint in the section of Deuteronomy known as "the Law Book" (12:1–26:15). These six verses suggest that the prophet's role is instrumental in the survival of God's people. The legacy of biblical prophets provides a key to understanding the dimensions of Jesus who came to fulfill the Law and the Prophets. (See Matthew 5:17.)

A true prophet is one called by Yahweh to be speaker, messenger, and voice for God's words and to make known God's will for the people. Both people and prophet acknowledge this as an avenue of spiritual insight that will come no other way.

Formula phrases such as "Thus says the LORD," "the word of Yahweh," and "I will put my words in [his] mouth" indicate that the authority lies not in the prophets themselves, their opinions, or their personal religious experiences. Their authority originates with the One who speaks through them; therefore, the people are to heed their instruction.

God's people (in both Testaments) are admonished to beware of false prophets. These verses imply both enticement of the people and the seduction of the prophet toward idolatry. Several requirements are laid out. Prophets are to be "from among your own people" (a native Israelite) and be "like Moses" (teaching in accord with the words and spirit of Moses). How are we to know who they are? Perhaps the plumb line to the authenticity of a prophet is this: Is the message in accord with what we understand about God? Is the message both loving and just?

O God, may we hear your message through your prophets and respond with our lives. Amen.

Psalms 111–118 are called hallelujah psalms (hallelujah, Hebrew for "praise the Lord"). What causes the people to shout and sing joyous accolades? Beginning with this first psalm in the cluster, we discover the reasons: the works of God's hands, deeds of deliverance and covenant, the precepts and laws, God's glorious wonders to behold and ponder. The deeds of God confirm the people's understanding of God's very nature.

The priest has called the congregation to praise; God's mighty works have been recited and recalled. Now the people can affirm that "the fear of the LORD is the beginning of wisdom; all those who practice it have a good understanding." The term *fear* suggests an all-encompassing stance of both worship and obedience for building a holy relationship with God. The world rings with praise because what God has done evokes eloquence and passion. The deeds inspire a turning, a recapturing of a sense of wonder, a deepening of piety that cultivates a desire to lead a faith-filled life.

My husband is currently in a nursing home after complications from hip replacement surgery. This ordeal has slipped from days into weeks. He deeply misses Molly, a little sheltie he rescued five years ago. Late Sunday afternoon, I took her to see Bob. She jumped on his bed, crawled over him, and put her nose in his face. They were happy.

We moved to a courtyard gazebo. The weather, in the 90s with oppressive humidity, did not lend itself to outdoor visiting. Suddenly the sky shifted to half sunny and half dark rain clouds. A vigorous wind kicked up; cool rain began to spray our sweaty faces. I looked up and saw the rainbow. Hallelujah, praise the Lord!

O God, with reverence we thank you for reminders of your provision and grace. Amen.

One afternoon a young minister decided to make an introductory call on a ninety-year-old member of his new church. She resided in an assisted living facility twenty-five miles away, so this trip was a major commitment of time and resources. The conversation went well until she abruptly said, "You know, young man, you need to go on a diet. You are fat. You'd better do something quick. I'm telling you this for your own good." The young man left with bowed head.

I thought about that incident when I read these verses written by Paul to the church in Corinth with its factions. Clearly some in the church at Corinth seemed to have ready answers related to appropriate behavior—both for themselves and for others. Paul states, "Knowledge puffs up, but love builds up." Some members boasted of secret spiritual knowledge, while others smugly claimed privileged Holy Spirit experiences. Yet Paul affirms a unity among the community's diversity based on "one God, the Father, from whom are all things and for whom we exist." Paul emphasizes the well-being of the entire body.

Some Christians today act like those Corinthians with ready answers to all life's dilemmas. Or like the older woman in the example above, they feel they know what is best for everyone. They arrogantly flaunt their special knowledge. Yet faith rests not on human wisdom but springs from relationship with a God who loves. Paul encourages the church, then and now, to focus on what encourages and builds up the Christian community.

Gracious God, may we walk humbly with you. Forgive our foolish spiritual pride and arrogance. Unite us that others may know us by our love. Amen.

In Paul's day, people came to the many temples of their gods to offer sacrifices. The animals were killed, cooked, and became the main course for the family meal. Leftover meat might be offered to temple visitors or taken by temple officials to the market where it was sold with other meats. The believers in Corinth raise the question about eating meat sacrificed to idols.

Some teachers allowed new Christians to eat the sacrificial meat, implying that Christians aren't affected by anything so trivial as eating food offered to idols. Meat is meat.

Other Christians criticized those who ate the food. They meticulously bought meat in nonritual shops, ate only unsanctified animals, and were careful in which homes they dined. They became judgmental moralists, trapped by their squeamish concerns.

Though Paul agrees with those who eat the meat (8:8), he did not insist on eating it himself. He abstains not only if it offends others in the group but if his action might cause those less mature in the faith to imitate him. For him, the issue centers on respect and love. He disciplines himself to be faithful while encouraging unity. The definitive "knowing" or knowledge comes in God's knowing of us. This love claims us for God and encourages our love for others. The members at Corinth are to make choices that do not harm others who are more susceptible to influence. Paul desires to build up the church as the body of Christ, made up of a variety of opinions and gifts, but working together in love and harmony. How we treat and value one another matters, if we claim to be part of the body of Christ.

Lord God, may our faith communities seek unity amid diversity for the sake of the gospel. Amen.

The Gospel of Mark wastes no time. By verse 21 of the first chapter, John has announced and baptized Jesus. Jesus has dealt with the temptations and called disciples. In today's verses, he arrives in Capernaum, which becomes the hub of his operational ministry.

Jesus and his first four disciples, being loyal Jews, go to the synagogue on the sabbath. Unlike the Temple in Jerusalem where people worshiped and made sacrifices, the synagogue was primarily a teaching institution, although without a permanent or professional preacher/teacher. The synagogue was a place of prayer and instruction. Its service consisted of prayer, the reading of God's word, followed by exposition. What a perfect setup from which to launch a campaign.

This passage contrasts Jesus' teaching with that of the scribes (those professionally trained in the interpretation and application of scripture and the oral traditions handed down by generations of rabbis). The method and character of Jesus' teaching are electric and new. In contrast to the scribes, he cites no authorities and quotes no experts. Instead he teaches out of his own "authority" (*exousia* means literally "out of one's being") with forthright certainty of the voice of God.

Jesus has already announced, "The kingdom of God has come near; repent, and believe in the good news" (Mark 1:15). He not only proclaims the new reign, the new way of living; he ushers it in. The people are astounded. What good news do you need to hear? What good news would you find amazing?

Great Teacher, may we also hear and be astounded by your words. Make us instruments in the building of your kingdom. Amen.

If Jesus' words amaze the people in the synagogue that day, his action leaves them totally dumbfounded. A man, caught in the grip of an unclean spirit, creates a disturbance. And Jesus moves from authoritative teaching to authoritative action.

We know nothing about the man who enters the scene: his background, whether he is faithful or faithless—only that he is possessed by an unclean spirit. In a few brief verses, the man's unclean spirit addresses Jesus by name and acknowledges him as "the Holy One of God." Jesus commands the unclean spirit to leave the man. The spirit leaves; the man convulses; the onlookers stand in amazement. We learn no more. The man's appearance is less about the man and more about Jesus' authority and command over unclean spirits.

Some exorcists of the day claimed to cast out demons using spells, incantations, and magical rites. Here Jesus exorcises the unclean spirit from the man with clear, simple, concise words of authority—no spell, formula, rite, or incantation. The power resides in Jesus himself. The incredulous people, buzzing with bewilderment, ask, "What is this? A new teaching—with authority!"

Even today people remain baffled by this scene and want to know what sort of man can possibly possess the insight and authority Mark attributes to Jesus. What's going on here?

This new teaching does what it says. These words and deeds are kingdom signs. How does this new reign break down barriers between heaven and earth? between conditions that separate people? between sabbath rules and compassionate healing? To the writer of the Gospel of Mark, Jesus is not simply one man among many; he is God among humankind.

God, you boggle our minds and ask us to believe in impossibilities. Love asks that of us. I believe; help my unbelief. Amen.

Rediscovering God's Presence

JANUARY 30–FEBRUARY 5, 2012 • DION FORSTER

MONDAY, JANUARY 30 ~ *Read Isaiah 40:21-28*

In the region of KwaZula Natal, shops are few and far between. In between planned visits, you learn to rely on neighbors if you run out of milk, sugar, or flour. Early one morning Mrs. Khumalo woke her young son. She handed him a tin cup and told him to go to his uncle's home to get sugar. While the uncle lived only a mile or two away, the young boy had to pass over a hill and through a valley to get there. The young man set out, but before long he stopped to look back at his mother standing in the door of their hut. He needed reassurance of her presence. She smiled and called to him, "I can see you from here! Keep going; you're doing just fine!" It gave him courage to complete the journey—he was not alone.

Isaiah 40 speaks words of comfort and encouragement to Jerusalem. The Israelites fear that God has forgotten them; they feel alone in a valley of despair. As they turn to God they hear the reassuring words: "Do you not know? Have you not heard? The LORD is the everlasting God, the Creator of the ends of the earth. He does not faint or grow weary."

Like the young boy, you may sometimes be afraid, feeling alone in a valley far from comforting and familiar surroundings; perhaps like the Israelites you need a gentle reminder that God watches over you. Isaiah reassures us of God's glory and power and then reminds us that this powerful God keeps watch over our lives.

Lord God, I listen for your reassuring voice on my journey today. Keep me mindful of your watchful care. Amen.

Methodist minister, author, and theologian; Somerset West, South Africa

Irecently had to drive home from a conference on unfamiliar rural roads at night. The roads had no streetlights. All I had was a clear sense of my final destination and the light created by my car's headlights. That was enough to allow me to move ahead through the dark. Within a few hours I was safely home.

Isaiah 40 offers the Israelites a similar hope. First, the author reminds them God has set out a final destination for them, a return from exile to the Promised Land. That is their hope, the direction in which they travel. Second, however, he offers them a beam of light to guide them through the darkness toward their goal. While the road home may be uncertain, God's loving care, sustaining power, and life-giving grace are certainties upon which they can rely. As long as they "hope in the LORD" (NIV), they will find their strength renewed.

Be assured that God has a glorious destination in mind for you just as God did for the Israelites. But as you travel daily toward that goal, it may not be entirely visible. At times you may feel like you're driving into the dark. In those moments let God's promise of strength, provision, and care illuminate enough of your path so that you can move ahead with confidence and in safety. The promise from Isaiah 40:30-31 offers great encouragement: "Those who hope in the LORD will renew their strength. They will soar on wings like eagles; they will run and not grow weary, they will walk and not be faint" (NIV).

Loving God, illuminate my path by the light of your love that I may face this day with confidence, moving ever closer to the glorious destination you have in mind. Amen.

Cape Town is a city frequented by many movie stars and celebrities. I recently heard about a young woman who went into an ice-cream store near the Cape Town Waterfront. She placed her order at the counter and paid. As she turned around she was astonished to see the actor Brad Pitt standing behind her! She felt her knees buckle a little; but she pulled herself together, stepped out of his way, and walked toward the door only to realize that she did not have her ice cream in hand. As she returned to the counter to get her order, Mr. Pitt smiled and said, "You put the ice cream into your handbag with your change."

As I thought about this event I was struck by the fact that inconsequential things often impress me—like a famous person—yet I miss the greatest miracles all around me. I miss the glory of God's might in creation. I fail to thank God for my daily provision. I find rain irritating, and the only time I notice the grass is when I need to mow my lawn. The psalmist states that God "determines the number of the stars and calls them each by name" (NIV). That should make our knees buckle!

Psalm 147 fits into a group of five psalms (146–150), each of which begins and ends with a simple instruction: "Praise the LORD!" Today's psalm strongly reminds us to look around with eyes open to the wonder and awe of God's power in creation. It reminds us that the Lord "delights in those who fear him, who put their hope in his unfailing love" (NIV).

When did your knees last buckle at the wonder and glory of God's power in creation?

Mighty God, open my eyes to see your glory in creation today. Let my knees buckle at the beauty of your wonderful work, and I will praise you, Lord. Amen.

For almost twenty years I served as a Methodist pastor in Southern Africa. Some years ago the Methodist Church of Southern Africa tapped me to pioneer a new work as a corporate chaplain, working primarily among business people. While I still counsel, encourage prayer initiatives, develop leadership, and manage projects, I no longer preach regularly. I still preach some Sunday services but not to my "workplace congregation." Between Monday and Saturday I spend most of my time in meetings and offices working with small groups and individuals. In the business setting, the primary question is not What does the gospel *sound* like? but rather What does the gospel *look* like?

Proclaiming God's good news was central to Paul's ministry. Yet he always wanted to underscore his words with deeds. The Corinthians, while struggling to balance word and deed, have allowed their actions to compromise their message.

So Paul tries to help the church at Corinth understand the importance of its witness. The gospel becomes the shaper of Christian identity. Paul, a Hebrew of Hebrews and born in Tarsus as a Roman citizen and a free man, writes, "Though I am free with respect to all, I have made myself a slave to all, so that I might win more of them." Sometimes the method is as important as the message.

Today you will meet people and encounter systems that deserve the touch of the gospel of Christ. In some situations you may use a familiar method; in others you will need to be more creative to adapt to the context. The key comes in finding ways to leave behind in every daily encounter and with every person you meet an undeniable measure of God's good news.

Pray about the people and situations you will encounter today. Ask God to give you creative ways to express the gospel in each setting.

Jesus never seems to get a break. He leaves the synagogue after teaching and healing for a respite with friends—only to find Simon's mother-in-law in bed with a fever. He heals her, and by sundown word has spread such that people are bringing the sick and demon-possessed to him for healing.

And Jesus "cured many who were sick with various diseases, and cast out many demons; and he would not permit the demons to speak." What struck me was the phrase "he would not permit the demons to speak." He silenced the demons. Some contend that Jesus silenced the demons to protect his anonymity and guard his messianic secret.

Yet a greater truth lies hidden beneath this simple statement. First, it assumes that the demons can speak. Second, it clearly shows that when the demons speak, they intend to cause harm. Third, it demonstrates Jesus' power to quiet the demons' destructive voices.

Jesus silences the demons.

In my ministry I have had the privilege to help individuals and communities take authority over the destructive voices that are intent on causing them harm. For some this involves silencing the unwarranted criticism of a loved one. For others it has required silencing the untrue narrative associated with their gender, age, or race.

Jesus has the power to silence the demons that seek to destroy us with their words. What demons need to be silenced in your life and in the life of your community?

Lord Jesus, you know my struggles and needs. Silence the demons that seek to speak evil and destructive words in my life. Amen.

Jesus is in demand. He takes an early-morning break to pray. Simon's desperate words interrupt his time away: "Everyone is looking for you!" (NIV). It must have been tough for Jesus to hear those words. I'm sure that he was acutely aware of how precious his time, energy, and presence were during his earthly ministry. Yet, Jesus took time to be alone.

Mark's Gospel is the shortest of the four Gospels and offers a straightforward collection of the sayings and deeds of Jesus during his ministry. Luke and Matthew seemed to feel a little more freedom to include additional narratives and explanations in their Gospels. Mark, however, only includes what he believes to be most critical to convey his message. And here it is, a few precious verses carefully tucked within Mark's narrative to remind the reader of the importance of taking time in solitude to pray.

Perhaps this simple event, retold in the years after Jesus' death, left an impression on the early Christians: "You will always face demands and a need to manage expectations. In order to do so, you have to make time for silence and prayer. It is great to be needed and wanted. But these desires can easily become unhealthy, driving you to do things for the wrong reasons and even to become taxed and burdened by doing good."

Mark's Gospel reminds us, as it has done for centuries, that even Jesus found a solitary place to meet with God. This encounter helped him maintain balance and find the right perspective, pace, direction, and intention for his daily life and ministry.

Loving God, I choose to withdraw from the demands and expectations of my daily life to be alone with you. Give me the courage to seek you and your will first. Guide my thoughts and actions today. Amen.

Simon and his companions have hunted for Jesus, and they find him in prayer. Simon's words pull him back to the location and events of the previous day. However, Jesus, having spent time in prayer, answers his urgent statement with these words: "Let us go somewhere else" (NIV).

Jesus could stay near the home of Simon and Andrew. He has already healed many in that area and is sure to be well-received among the people. Yet, Jesus tells his disciples that it is time to go to different places, to move beyond the comfort of familiarity toward the areas of need, the unreached towns and villages.

When I served as a pastor, I encouraged my church members to get involved in the local congregation. But in my new job capacity, I have been encouraging pastors and members of congregations to "go somewhere else." I have realized the massive need to go to other places. Every day Christians in large numbers go into one of the least-reached regions of the world. What is this region? It is the world of work. Millions of Christians spend hours in offices, corporate buildings, schools, and hospitals each day; but few of us view these places as mission fields.

In my local church I would often pray for teams of members who would travel to far-off places in the world to build churches, work in hospitals, and teach in schools. Yet I seldom prayed for the builders, nurses, and teachers who would go into the areas surrounding our community on Monday to do the very same thing! Somehow we had fallen into the trap of thinking that certain undertakings are ministry, and the others are just plain work. Today I can hear Jesus saying, "Let's go somewhere else." Perhaps that is somewhere you go every day of the week!

Lord, open my eyes to see the work that you want done in the places I am this week. Give me the courage to make my work life an action of ministry. Amen.

"I Do Choose"

FEBRUARY 6–12, 2012 • RICHARD B. WILKE

MONDAY, FEBRUARY 6 ~ *Read Psalm 30:1-5*

The psalm begins with "I" and is saturated with one person's tears. The psalmist rejoices that God has "restored me to life." Clearly he would affirm that it's OK to cry! Some people, especially men, think that crying signals weakness. Not so! When life throws a curve at us—when we place our beloved mother or father in the grave, when a son is killed in war, when we've made a grievous, irrevocable mistake—it's good to cry.

I grew up in my father's funeral home. As a boy, I helped set up the chairs in the chapel before the funeral. One time I noticed Dad going over to a seldom-used cabinet, reaching for something. "What are you getting, Dad?" I asked. "Smelling salts, Son," he replied. "A lady coming to this service usually needs them."

So, at the funeral, I watched. When the time came to view the body, a woman lurched forward, wailing, weeping. I saw Dad move forward; then another man got up. As the lady stood before the casket, she screamed and began sinking to her knees. The two men caught her and eased her down as she fainted. After a few seconds, Dad put the smelling salts to her nose and she returned to her seat, quiet and relaxed. I will always recall what Dad said to me after the service. "Well, Son, she'll never have to visit a psychiatrist."

We never need to be ashamed of crying. Weeping will pass, and it can bring healing. Crying joins us with others who suffer. It does not last forever. "Weeping may linger for the night, but joy comes with the morning."

Dear Lord, as we weep, be near us and heal us. Amen.

Bishop-in-residence, Southwestern College, Winfield, Kansas; co-author with his wife, Julia, of the Disciple Bible Study series

TUESDAY, FEBRUARY 7 ~ *Read Psalm 30:6-12*

In Psalm 30, the brokenhearted person not only quits crying but rejoices, for God has stood by. When the Jews celebrated the feast of Hanukkah in 164 CE, they then could worship freely. They sang, feasted, and danced. *Praise* is the key word. "O LORD, my God, I will give thanks to you forever."

Some people mishandle crying persons. An immediate inclination is to say, "Don't cry; everything's going to be all right" or "You shouldn't cry." Those words only add guilt to an already troubled soul. No, there is a time to weep.

As a pastor, I learned the hard way that weeping people need a quiet friend, a person who will simply stand by and listen. One day I was called to the hospital. A middle-aged woman in our church had died suddenly and unexpectedly. Her husband was in the hospital room, angry, upset, weeping. "How could this have happened? She was getting better. I was preparing to take her home!" I put my arm on his shoulder and listened. Then we sat down, and between sobs, he told me what a wonderful wife she was. I just sat and listened as he recalled the years of their lives together. It lasted a couple of hours.

Later, at the funeral, the man seemed calm. Soon he became a faithful leader in the church. Then he thrilled my pastoral heart when, one day, he said to me, "You were a great help to me when she passed away. Thank you for listening."

Thank God for loving friends who simply, lovingly, stand by and listen. That helps us move through grief, through the "valley of the shadow." Thank the Lord for listening lovingly. "You have turned my mourning into dancing; you have taken off my sackcloth and clothed me with joy."

Lord, thank you for listening. Thank you for those folks who lovingly listen when we cry. Amen.

"I Do Choose"

In the Hebrew Bible, First and Second Kings are part of the former prophets—Joshua, Judges, and Samuel. They comprise a prophetic interpretation of four hundred years of Israel's history. So Naaman's healing has spiritual significance.

Naaman was a big shot—too big for his britches, my dad would say. He served as commander in chief of the army and was the right-hand man of the king of Aram. He expected to be treated with dignity and respect. The only problem was, he had leprosy, a form of flesh-deteriorating disease that people feared tremendously.

This story demonstrates God's power to heal, but I love its appeal for humility. First, the slave girl, a young little nobody, suggests that the mighty general go to a Hebrew prophet for healing—what a comedown! Then, with top-flight credentials in hand, Naaman goes to the king of Israel. This king tears his robe, thinking a terrible war might come of this.

But the climax comes when Naaman goes to the hut where Elisha lives. The prophet will not come out of the house but suggests that Naaman go wash seven times in the nearby Jordan, a modest little stream. High and mighty Naaman throws a fit, but a humble servant advises that since it's a simple thing, why not do it. Coming off his high horse, the mighty general takes off his clothes, washes seven times in the gentle stream, and is completely healed.

How often we reject the simple! The doctor says to eat fruit and vegetables and exercise, but we continue to gain weight. The pastor says, "Come and kneel here at the altar," but we smile and go our way. Too simple for us. As the servant said, if it were big, expensive, complicated, we would do it. Why not do the humble things God requires?

Dear Lord, help me to be humble and willing to do the simple things that bring health and happiness. Amen.

For the Hebrew people, history is a radical up-and-down story from the end of King Solomon's reign until the fall of Jerusalem to the Babylonians in 587 CE. The story tells of enemy neighbors, constant strife, and warfare—and God's interaction. The Arameans were border-neighbors with a long history of dispute, conflict, and fear.

This account begins with leprosy and ends with healing. And between the beginning and the end runs a narrative of miscommunication and assumption. As human beings, we tend to view some people as outsiders. A Mexican farm worker walks into the restaurant, and a customer makes disparaging remarks to his friends. A black man parks beside a car, and the car's occupants wait until he leaves before getting out of our car. A teenage girl comes to church with jeans cut too low, shirt cut too high, and members wonder who let her in.

Naaman receives advice from a young Israelite woman captive. He might be willing to discount her advice based on nationality, gender, and youth. The king of Aram sends a letter to the king of Israel asking for the healing of Naaman's leprosy. The king does not turn to a prophet for healing but, out of his own bias, to a man of power. His assumption does not further Naaman's wellness. Naaman, a foreigner, and a feared and hated enemy, hesitates to seek help in Israel.

And then, Naaman, in his own arrogance and prejudice, asserts the rivers of Damascus to be far more curative than all the waters of Israel. Our biases, prejudices, and perceptions of others as outsiders can, as with Naaman, affect our health. Healing comes from unlikely sources. Our openness to others—even the enemy—may be our first step down the path to wholeness.

O Lord, may I view all people through your eyes. May I welcome the outsider with warmth and acceptance. Amen.

Sometimes in the church we stress, "Come forward if you want to become a Christian." Or, "Raise your hand if you want to be saved." And that's good. "A journey of a thousand miles begins with a single step." We have to start somewhere.

But Jesus said, "Not everyone who says to me 'Lord, Lord' will enter the kingdom of heaven, but only the one who does the will of my Father" (Matt. 7:21). Again he insisted, "I am the way" (John 14:6). The Christ-walk entails a day-by-day faithful lifestyle. Discipleship is not an emotional binge but a journey of faithful obedience and service to the Lord Jesus.

Paul loved Corinth—a huge seaport city with Jews and Gentiles, slaves and free, rabbis and sailors. Paul enjoyed watching Greek sporting events. Paul was a scholar, not an athlete, but he knew the training and discipline an athlete had to undertake. Paul shouts, "Run in such a way that you may win it." Keep your eye on the goal (on Jesus), and don't falter.

I was never a fast runner. I tried to keep up with my friend, Paul, who was a champion in the mile run. In practice, he always beat me, but I ran as best I could, always making it to the finish line. I'm now retired—but not from being a Christian. Folks my age visit the shut-ins, deliver meals-on-wheels, invite neighbors to church, lead Disciple Bible studies. One lady, in her nursing home bed, reads the scriptures and prays for others on a daily basis. She is still running the race.

Notice that Paul doesn't want us to run aimlessly, to flounder, to "box as though beating the air." We can rest but not tarry; we can take a breath but not follow a false trail. Paul's words encourage us to run the race: to make new disciples, teach the children, support the youth. As long as we have life and breath, we must "walk the walk"—run in such a way that we will win.

Lord, help us to run on the Jesus way, always—to the finish line. Amen.

By the time Paul writes back to Corinth, he has endured hardship, hunger, beatings, even imprisonment. He knows firsthand the steady disciplines that loyal discipleship requires. Even though he is a free man with civil rights, he understands that his spiritual obligation requires a steadfastness. People are waiting to be saved; no time to waste.

Paul not only wants us to run the discipleship race with joy, looking for the finish line; he also issues a negative warning. He doesn't want us to pound our fists in the air, wasting our time, fooling around in fruitless activity.

Paul is not talking about rest. As a Jewish Christian, he believed in sabbath rest. Nor is Paul decrying recreation. He traveled, read books, visited with friends, worked as a tent-maker. Different activity sometimes energizes us, sometimes gives us rest for our bodies and for our souls.

My doctor wants me to exercise at the gym for a half hour or so each day. I play tennis once a week. But beating our fists in the air, dilly dallying, just wasting time, equates to weak discipleship. So, without being frenetic, never resting, always on the go, ask yourself if you could be more fruitful. Might you use some of your spare time more creatively in your faith journey, in your spiritual discipleship run?

Could you commit to using your spare time to read a chapter of scripture each night before sleeping? Might you phone a friend who is recuperating from surgery? Could you take a plate of food to a neighbor woman who has just lost her husband? Could you read *The Upper Room* daily devotional guide at breakfast while you finish your coffee? Could you invite someone to drink a cup of coffee and offer your faith story?

Paul wants us to run all the way to the finish line.

Dear Lord, give us creative rest to save us from wasting life and energy. Amen.

Leprosy in antiquity referred to a variety of skin diseases, but by Jewish law, all of them made victims "unclean." They couldn't even go to worship! No one dared touch a leper, so Jesus' action—he "stretched out his hand and touched him"—is all the more remarkable.

Jesus heals! In our day we experience Jesus' healing power through dedicated doctors and nurses. At fourteen, I was sick unto death with acute nephritis. My dedicated doctor, frustrated by failure, heard about a new drug. He drove to a nearby city, obtained it, and within days I was well. Think of hospitals around the world—Catholic, Protestant, Pentecostal, and countless missionary medical centers—all healing because Jesus was a healer.

I think too of prayer. Often I have prayed with and for the sick. Once I asked a famous cancer doctor if prayer made a difference. He looked at me and laughed, "Are you kidding," he said. "I go into a room where a patient has serious cancer. Persons around the bed are singing hymns, saying prayers, laughing. The patient is getting better. I go into another room. I find the patient alone, bitter, complaining. No faith. No prayers. This patient with less severe cancer is dying."

So Jesus still heals. The leper approaches Jesus with full confidence in his ability to heal but unsure of Jesus' willingness to do so: "If *you choose*, you can make me clean" (emphasis added). And we hear Jesus' compassionate answer to him and to us: "I do choose." Jesus wills our wholeness and well-being.

Thank Jesus for being a healer as well as a teacher. And, even though Jesus told the leper to keep quiet, I'm glad that the leper told the world and inspired others.

Dear Jesus, thank you for healing me of many illnesses and diseases across the years. Thank you for calling nurses and doctors into your healing ministry. Amen.

Transfiguring

FEBRUARY 13–19, 2012 • W. PAUL JONES

MONDAY, FEBRUARY 13 ~ *Read 2 Kings 2:1-9*

This week we will be climbing, step by step, the mountain that ascends to Jesus' own Transfiguration. Transfiguring means being changed so as to glorify. We begin with Elijah who lives each day faithfully. So may we, for each day could well be our last.

We accompany Elijah on his pilgrimage to Bethel, Jericho, and the Jordan River, gathering up in himself places and people of Israel's rich past to take with him as a chariot offering. Three times his faithful companion, Elisha, insists, "I will not leave you." At each place, persons know of Elijah's imminent leave-taking and accept Elisha's pastoral advice to "keep silent"—recalling when Job's friends remained with him a week and "no one spoke a word" (2:13). Like Moses and Joshua before him, Elijah parts the waters. And as God asked Solomon, Elijah asks Elisha, as we too should ask others, "What may [I] do for you, before I am taken from you?" What richness Elijah is gathering up as an offering to God in death.

God gives life only one day at a time, so like Elijah, each day we live on the forward edge of the past. Each evening we die into God, offering up the gift of our daily chariot into the whirlwind of God's transfiguring fire. And if God so wills, the next morning will be a fresh resurrection, calling us again to a day of transfiguring by dying to self. In this calling, may Moses, Joshua, Elijah, and Elisha be our models as we "strike the water" that blocks the way, in order to provide a dry exodus path from slavery toward the promised transfiguration of all things.

Lord, may I die my life into you. Amen.

Author, professor, activist; monk, Hermitage Spiritual Retreat Center; Lake Pomme de Terre, Missouri

Today we see Elisha transfigured by receiving the mantle of inheritance. By wearing it patiently, we too may see the whirlwind. Moses had to wear it for forty years in Pharaoh's court and another forty years as a fugitive sheepherder before seeing the flaming bush; then there were forty days on flaming Sinai before receiving the law and forty years more in the flaming desert before seeing the Promised Land. Noah endured the flood for forty days before receiving the green twig of a new earth. Elijah fled Jezebel for forty days before hearing in the whirlwind God's still small voice. Jonah proclaimed God's destructive whirlwind for Nineveh in forty days, before God saved it in a whirlwind of forgiveness. Jesus endured a whirlwind of temptations for forty desert days before he emerged for mission. The distraught disciples waited with the resurrected Christ for forty days before receiving their call in the Pentecostal whirlwind. And soon we will enter forty days of Lent, watching patiently in hope of our own double blessing.

The firstborn of each family in Israel could ask as an inheritance a double blessing. Of whose spirit do you crave a double share? The courage of a Martin Luther King Jr., the popularity of a Michael Jackson, the compassion of a Mother Teresa, the wealth of a Bill Gates? The choice determines our whole life. In his receiving, Elisha tore away his old clothing, as each of us must discard what hinders our transfiguring. Then he took up the inheritance of Elijah's mantle as the vestment of his calling. Our choice provides a mantle of inheritance, evoking the hope that when we too are seen no more, others might recognize it as worth picking up, wearing it into the future. Mockingbirds are terribly misnamed. They do not mock; they honor the sounds they inherit from others by incorporating them into a transfigured song.

Lord, teach me to sing. Amen.

Today the transfiguring of Israel's two great prophets expands into Israel's transfiguring through covenant. In this psalm, God gathers "my faithful ones, who made a covenant with me by sacrifice!" A covenant is not a contract in the sense of a mutually beneficial agreement between two parties, in which unfaithfulness by one will invalidate the arrangement. A covenant is unbreakable, even by gross unfaithfulness. Covenant is the nature of Israel's relationship with God, made through Abraham and reaffirmed with others such as Noah and Moses.

While a contract is self-serving, Israel's covenant calls her not to special privilege but to special sacrifice—dying of self to live for others. God calls Israel to transfigure all nations. Through her "perfection of beauty, God shines forth" and "summons the earth from the rising of the sun to its setting" that all "shall glorify me" (Ps. 50:15). Although a covenant is unbreakable, each party must honor the partnership or be subject to judgment. "God himself is judge," and Israel is found terribly wanting, "for you hate disciplines" (Ps. 50:17).

The good news for Christians is that God has expanded this covenant to include the whole of creation. Yet why should we want to be bound by an unbreakable covenant? Because, as a gift of unconditional love, it transfigures us. We all crave an unbreakable love, not a conditional one that renders us fearful of never measuring up. God's covenantal love in Jesus will not allow anything to "separate us from the love of God in Christ Jesus our Lord" (Rom. 8:39). In thankfulness we become "a sacrifice of thanksgiving" (Ps. 50:14). "Just as I am, without one plea," says the old hymn, in which, as Isaiah prophesied, God writes each of our names on the palm of God's hand—with a cross as pen and blood as ink.

God, I am unworthy, but may your palm be large. Amen.

Today our ascent climbs from two great Old Testament prophets to the greatest New Testament one. Paul's transfiguring comes through experiencing God's trinitarian fullness. Until Paul's awakening on the Damascus road, this God had been veiled by "the god of this world." We, Paul, and Jesus in the desert, find ourselves bombarded by society's idolatrous promises—do this, buy that, join this, try that. The lure of such "gods" remains the same—the three *P*s of prestige, possession, and power. Their expression for Paul came through his religion. Seduced by the power, praise, and reward resulting from persecuting Christians, he refused to be open to their expanded understanding of the God that he as a Jew also worshiped.

This expanded God we call the Trinity. Although not well understood by many Christians, one verse from today's reading illuminates the Trinity better than any other approach I know. Drawing from his own transfiguring experience, Paul begins with "the God who said, 'Let light shine out of darkness.'" This God is the one "who has shone in our hearts." Here God functions as the Holy Spirit, taking up residency in the temple of our souls, closer to us than life itself. This God is even more expansive, for the Spirit allows us to see "the light of the knowledge of the glory of God in the face of Christ." Thus the Creator of the universe is also the Inspirer within, who awakens us to recognize Christ as our Redeemer. Creator, Inspirer, and Redeemer reveals the triune God of Father, Son, and Holy Spirit.

Many people worship a god who is too small, but Paul offers a transfigured God—not just an inner presence or just the Mystery that sustains and impulses every living thing or the redemptive Lover who will not let us go. God is all of these.

Lord, flood my imagination. Amen.

The Trinity is Christian shorthand for the triune work of our God—the wholesale Creator painting with huge brush the expanding galaxies of creation; the retail Redeemer painting lovingly with delicate brush each hair on our heads; the Inspirer God who signs a lease on the apartment of our souls. Ours is the God in whom we live and move and have our being—the God who is in us and we in God. But how do we know this? Because the supreme "glory of Christ" is that he "is the image of God." Jesus is the definitive disclosure of the character of God.

This triune God involves not only an expanded understanding but an experience that transfigures our motives, lifestyle, character, and goals. In the case of every Christian I know, someone has lived so transparently as to become Christ for him or her. Thus, the world's transfiguring depends on our living for others the good news, using words only when necessary. True witnesses are those who become "slaves for Jesus' sake," so emptying themselves that they become transparent vehicles for experiencing the One who "emptied himself, taking the form of a slave" (Phil. 2:7).

Paul never met Jesus in the flesh; he only heard a voice that said, "I am Jesus, whom you are persecuting" (Acts 9:5). So how does he know Jesus? I believe that the scales fell from his eyes when, in his memory, the stoning of Stephen became a transparency through which the love of the crucified Jesus shone. Both Stephen and Jesus died forgiving their persecutors, and each surrendered to God with the same words. (See Acts 7:59-60.) The face of Stephen became transfigured for Paul, as did Moses for Israel and Elijah for Elisha. Paul explains this as "carrying in the body the death of Jesus, so that the life of Jesus may also be made visible in our bodies" (2 Cor. 4:10). Dying to self makes for a transparency through which Christ transfigures the world.

Lord, let me be empty that you may be full. Amen.

Given eyes to see, we can experience Jesus transfigured through vision. Some scholars fail to see the Transfiguration as adding anything new, concluding that it is a leftover Resurrection story inserted here as an anticipation.

I believe it plays a far more important role. In Christ's transfiguration converge the two strands of God's workings, previously seen as competing, now transfigured through vision as the goal toward which all of history is being called. Significantly, Moses and Elijah speak with Jesus—they represent the priestly and prophetic traditions respectively. As transfigured by their convergence in Jesus, worship becomes the dazzling foretaste of the prophetic kingdom—the vision of a new heaven and earth in which God shall wipe away every tear from our eyes, and death shall be no more. In Isaiah's vision the wolf and the lamb shall feed together, nations shall learn war no more, and a little child shall lead the childlike into a kingdom of peace.

This event occurs "six days later," meaning the seventh day, recalling the day God rested, transfixed by the intended beauty of Creation. On this day the church gathers weekly to rehearse this vision. And on this day the author of Revelation saw the vision of Christ's transfiguration of the cosmos and its history as promise.

The Mount of Transfiguration is a convergence of mountains: Mount Sinai where Moses encountered the transcendent God of Creation; Mount Horeb where Elijah encountered the immanent God of the "still small voice"; and the Mount of the Beatitudes where Jesus taught us what it is like to live the vision of such a God.

Lord, may I have a double portion of your vision? Amen.

Today we stand with Jesus and his three disciples on the mountaintop. On them, and thus us, will soon fall the mantle of crucifixion and resurrection. As preparation, we receive a foretaste of the transfiguring that will brand them and us for a lifetime.

Mountaintops are to be visited, not lived on. We climb to the top in order to renew a perspective capable of sustaining us in the valley. In coming down, the disciples find, as do we, persons who need healing and healers arguing among themselves how to do it. This is why we return to a transfiguring mountain for foretaste, without which we are unlikely to remain faithful.

At my monastery, a hermit lives on the hill and prays for my community and the world. From time to time, each of us climbs to sit with him on his porch, for without this vista we tend to forget why we are baking fruitcakes in the valley. Jesus descended so that we can ascend; we descend so that others may see him ascending.

Jesus instructs the three disciples that no one speak of the vision they have seen, until the Resurrection—presumably because only then can they and we tell it by being it. Yet, like Peter, we are tempted instead to make something—like a booth or a family-life center. The transfiguring foretastes always pass, leaving us, like the three disciples, with "Jesus only." And much of the time a cloud overshadows the disciples and us, leaving us only with *words about* Jesus. Faith, as foretaste, sustains us between those transfiguring moments as "the assurance of things hoped for, the conviction of things not seen" (Heb. 11:1). It is all about transfiguration.

God, sustain me by letting me "taste and see that the LORD is good." Amen.

Remember and Be Thankful

FEBRUARY 20–26, 2012 • BLAIR GILMER MEEKS

MONDAY, FEBRUARY 20 ~ *Read Genesis 9:8-17*

The assigned passages for the first Sunday in Lent include the ending of Noah's flood, and we may well wonder what this flood has to do with Lent. Where will these images take us on our spiritual journey, led by the scriptures? Do they speak to our individual experience and to our faith community? Such a journey requires setting aside time for reflection and prayer, asking the Holy Spirit to guide us.

In last week's Gospel story of the Transfiguration, we read of Jesus' glorification by God on the mountaintop, providing a gateway to Lent as Jesus descends the mountain and begins his journey to the cross. Today's reading also takes place on a mountaintop where Noah sees God's glory and hears God's amazing promise to all creation. He experiences God's covenant, sealed by a bow in the sky, only after forty days of flood.

Floods and drowning were strong images for early Christians when they thought about baptism and redemption. (See Isaiah 43:1-2; Romans 6:3-5.) Drowning may not be our greatest fear, but we all have fears. God announces our redemption with the words: "Do not fear . . . you are mine." This week we will also read about Jesus' baptism and begin Lent as a time to remember our own baptism and be thankful.

Noah's story ends with a great burst of hope based on God's promises. In baptism we begin a new life, responding to God's promises. Lent, far from being a "downer" of a season, is filled with hope and thankfulness.

Saving God, bring us safely through the troubled waters, and fill us with hope and peace that we may serve life. Amen.

Author, leader, and seminar teacher; living in Brentwood, Tennessee

TUESDAY, FEBRUARY 21 ~ *Read Joel 2:1-2, 12-17*

Tomorrow is Ash Wednesday, and we listen to the startling phrases from Joel: "Blow the trumpet . . . tremble . . . the day of the LORD is coming . . . rend your hearts and not your clothing." The problem is we don't remember the rest of the verses, and our idea of Lent may stop there. It feels as if a "great and powerful army" is heading straight for us.

But the prophet then announces that this God of ours is, in fact, willing to relent. Is it possible that we can change God's mind? Like a good parent or teacher, God sees the fear in our eyes, hears our prayers for change, and offers us the chance to return.

We say that God never changes, and that's a comforting thought; but we misunderstand if we think of God as intractable or unaffected by what we do. The Bible says that God is steadfast in love, and God's steadfastness includes a willingness to change course, to respond to our longing for a new relationship, to forget our sins and remember them no more. This forgetting seems almost impossible for humans. We may still remember who said what hurtful thing to us on the playground in third grade. We may forgive our family and friends when they apologize, but we almost never forget, not even trivial transgressions.

Praying the Lord's Prayer includes the expectation that God will forgive us as we forgive others. One step on our journey requires that we learn to forgive the way God forgives. We can't do this alone, but God goes with us. God's never-wavering love offers to forget our failings and limitations. God wants to change us and make us new and alive with hope. God is "gracious and merciful, slow to anger, and abounding in steadfast love." Lent begins with hope because we can stand on this sweet promise from God.

Give us a holy Lent, O God, and encourage us with your promise to remember our sins no more. Give us thankful hearts for the freedom your forgiveness brings. Amen.

WEDNESDAY, FEBRUARY 22 ~ *Read Matthew 6:1-6, 16-21*

ASH WEDNESDAY

"Darling, where is your heart?" Years ago Percy Faith's version of this song played endlessly on the radio, full of violins and sentimentality. I remembered this song today because of the words in Matthew's Gospel: "Where your treasure is, there your heart will be also." The song belongs more to Valentine's Day than to the beginning of Lent, but the question is similar: What do we treasure? If we know the answer, we know where our heart is.

Matthew 6 gives the context. We can denounce the hypocrisy of those who make a show of praying. We can praise the humility of those who pray for mercy before God alone. But where are our hearts? If praise is what we treasure, we can live admirably and do good works but still keep the focus on us and our actions. Do we give ostentatiously only to boost our self-image? Those who pray and fast in secret, asking God's forgiveness, treasure their relationship with God more than the praise of others. They respond to God's grace with almsgiving and acts of mercy, scarcely aware of their own good works. They focus on God's grace-filled act of redemption.

Lent invites us to engage in prayer and scripture study, to increase giving and acts of mercy; and we do these things because we treasure what God has already done for us—not to call attention to ourselves. In worship this day we receive a mark on our forehead, a visible sign of where our heart is. The mark is the sign of the cross, the same sign we received in water at our baptism. It points not to ourselves but to Jesus' redeeming love. "Remember your baptism and be thankful."

Bring us to our knees, Lord, to receive the ashes and remember your love. Keep in our hearts the poor, the lonely, the broken-hearted, that our hearts may be closer to you. Amen.

Lift up your hearts," begins the ancient Communion liturgy, still in use around the world today. Worshipers respond, "We lift them up to the Lord." Sharing the bread and cup at the Eucharist is a sign of where our hearts are and what we treasure.

Psalm 25 begins with similar words: "To you, O Lord, I lift up my soul." When we lift up heart and soul to God, we offer God our life. It's easy to stray from God's path and lose touch with God. Only laying the burdens of the soul at God's mercy seat can restore this relationship.

The psalmist asks God to lead him, teach him, make him to know God's ways. Then he gets creative: "Don't forget about your mercy and your steadfast love, O Lord; they've been your trademarks forever" (AP). "Do not remember the sins of my youth or my transgressions." Surprisingly, it's all right to tell God what to remember and what to forget.

"All the paths of the Lord are steadfast love and faithfulness." If we walk with God, we know that God's steadfast love leads to forgiveness and also to God's "selective memory loss" of our sins. It's nearly impossible for humans to forget the wrongs others have done them, but it is even less likely that we can forget our own wrongdoings and times of broken relationship with God. Yet that is what God's grace encourages us to do.

In baptism we're given new memories, and we come alive to Christ's resurrected life. In the Eucharist we join the forgiven and freed community of Christ's body. The sacraments are healing, not only for individuals who are sick with the memory of past sins but for a community that is broken, out of relationship with God and one another.

"Prone to wander, Lord, I feel it, prone to leave the God I love; here's my heart, O take and seal it, seal it for thy courts above." Amen.

All of us lose our way now and then. The good news of Lent comes in God's desire that we hold on and not look back. God will help us find our way again. Lent encourages us to hold on to the life we were baptized into and get back on the track of Jesus' path.

But Jesus was not just a good role model: "Christ also suffered for sins once for all, the righteous for the unrighteous." Jesus' dying for us is his journey alone; we neither need to die for our sins nor are we able to follow Jesus in this unique act. We are, however, asked to take up our cross, and we are likely to find that followers of Jesus will suffer at the hands of opponents to God's way of life. By working for God's justice and mercy, we may work counter to prevailing interests that put the accumulation of wealth and power above the survival needs of earth's inhabitants.

The writer of First Peter reminds us that Christ made a proclamation also to the "spirits in prison," those imprisoned by their own greed and willful obstruction of God's intentions for creation. God's grace is not for us alone, but God waits patiently to offer redemption even to those whose pride blinds them. God waits on Noah's naysayers and on the people who get in the way of our discipleship today.

Noah came through the water unharmed, thanks be to God; early Christians saw this event as an image for salvation through water. But baptism is more than a good bath; it is an invitation to participate in Christ's resurrection life. God lifted up the One who was lifted up on the cross and placed him at God's right hand to reign over authorities and powers; even the angels are subject to him. The reign of the crucified and risen Christ is at hand, and we are called to hold on.

Merciful God, give us grace to live in your household of life now and keep us looking forward to Christ's gracious reign. Amen.

Noah spent forty days passing through a wilderness of water into life under God's covenant. He was not alone on this journey but may have wished he were, what with a boat full of noisy animals and bored kinfolk. More to the point, Jesus' wilderness sojourn echoes the forty years Moses spent leading the Hebrews through the wilderness, leaving slavery behind. Elijah spent forty days in the wilderness, fleeing Ahab's wrath. Elijah and Moses were Jesus' companions at his transfiguration, and all three hear God's will revealed to them in God's own voice.

The wilderness in Mark's brief Gospel is an unfriendly place. With Satan as the tempter, Jesus is in grave danger. This wilderness is not a place we would go by choice.

We have perhaps had wilderness experiences or watched a loved one bear a long trial. Unemployment is a wilderness common to many. Illness or grief can be a long and difficult road in a harsh land. Alienation from family or friends, loneliness, struggling with dependency, all have in common the wild beasts of fear and doubt. Are we able to endure? The temptation is to doubt ourselves and God's presence with us.

The Gospels tell of Jesus' ordeals: the forty days after his baptism and his time of agony before the crucifixion. In the wilderness angels wait on him; in the garden he asks the disciples to pray with him. Can we pray with Jesus? We do pray with him in the Lord's Prayer, "Do not bring us to the time of trial, but rescue us from the evil one" (Matt. 6:13).

Leaving the wilderness behind, we can emerge with new strength and courage. The issues don't disappear, but we have come close to death and learned to lean on God's promise of new life: "The kingdom of God has come near."

Merciful God, guide us in our troubled times. Give your angels charge over us and show us the springs of living water even in the wilderness. Amen.

First Sunday in Lent

Ruby, born six weeks early, weighed three pounds, ten ounces. She was tiny but feisty and after ten days in intensive care came home to a loving family. Four months later on Epiphany, grandparents, uncles, aunts, and cousins gathered for her baptism. Her grandfather scooped water onto her head "in the name of the Father, and of the Son, and of the Holy Spirit," asking the congregation to love and support her. Ruby was joyfully welcomed into God's household.

Jesus' baptism in the Jordan seems to have little in common with infant baptism today, but there are crucial likenesses: the symbolism of the water, the coming of the Holy Spirit, and the recognition by the community that the person baptized is God's child. As Ruby's grandmother, I am thankful that God knows her name and loves her beyond measure.

Churches are finding ways to reintroduce practices that more closely resemble Jesus' baptism. His baptism was unique, however, because his ministry was unique. Mark announces it this way: Jesus preaches good news that goes beyond words. By his life, death, and resurrection, he proclaims the nearness of God's reign. Paul connects us to Jesus through baptism: "we have been united with him in a death like his" and "will certainly be united with him in a resurrection like his" (Rom. 6:5).

We, like Jesus' first disciples, struggle to grasp the full meaning of Jesus' call and to see God at work in a troubled world. Celebrating the sacraments, observing Lent and Easter, are ways the church practices living a life under God's glorious reign. We also recall—with every baptism—the words spoken about Jesus at his baptism: "You are my Son, the Beloved; with you I am well pleased," and God's good pleasure with us all.

God, help us to remember our baptism, believe the good news, and walk in newness of life. Amen.

Movement toward Covenant

FEBRUARY 27–MARCH 4, 2012 • JOHN INDERMARK

MONDAY, FEBRUARY 27 ~ *Read Genesis 17:1-7*

I distinctly remember kneeling before another in the midst of community three times: my confirmation day, my wedding day, and my ordination day. All three times, kneeling embodied a gesture of awe at a solemn moment of giving and receiving promises. All three times, kneeling postured my reception of some grace coupled with vocation. Welcomed by the gospel, I now live as a full member in Christ's church. Joined with this other, I now live in love and fidelity as husband and wife. Empowered by God's Spirit and church, I now live in ordained service to the ministry of Word and sacrament.

An older word defines such inseparable couplings of grace and vocation in relationship: *covenant.* In biblical terms, as in today's verses from Genesis 17, covenant describes the relationship between God and human partners. Here God takes initiative in enacting covenant with Israel—and thus, with us. Such grace is the first movement of covenant. But covenant is more than God announcing gracious intentions of relationship. Covenant invokes our response. "Walk before me" is the covenant asked of Abram, and still asked of us. Abram will get around to walking but notice his first response: "Abram fell on his face"— not exactly kneeling but reflective of the same movement of worshipful awe in response to God's gifts of grace and vocation.

May we open ourselves in this season of Lent to what it means to walk in faithfulness and kneel in awe before the God who beckons us into covenant.

What gracious experiences of covenant with God have moved you to kneel in awe, figuratively or literally?

United Church of Christ minister, author; living in Naselle, Washington

Movers *and shakers.* Whom does that phrase bring to mind? Someone with extraordinary political power who knows how to get things done? Someone with vast financial resources who can bankroll any endeavor, for good or ill?

While Paul does not employ that phrase per se in Romans 4, it does fit his description of Abraham. The movement comes in Abraham's trusting response to God's covenanting promises. Faith sets Abraham's and Sarah's feet on a lifelong movement toward those promises. The "shaker" part of Abraham manifests in his worldview, where "hoping against hope" opens him to the possibilities of a God who can bring something out of nothing—even life out of death. Abraham's God makes promises that unleash the news that creation is a work in progress, the future is wide open, and individuals and communities of faith need walking shoes more than pew cushions.

So if God truly calls into existence things that don't exist, what does that say about the way you conduct your life and, in particular, the things you have given up on as hopeless? "It will never be." "It's as good as dead." Some regretted aspects of our lives deserve that judgment. But what about dreams given up, hopes abandoned, promises buried deep? Covenant with God bears the hope of radical new beginnings. Just because it isn't now or never has been, doesn't mean it never will be—*if* you believe Paul's testimony about God calling into existence things that don't exist and giving life to the dead.

The film *Cool Hand Luke* ends with these final words spoken about the now-dead but ever-smiling Luke by his best friend: "He's a natural born world-shaker!" That eulogy fits Abraham's journey by faith; may it describe ours as well.

Ever-surprising God, bring life to deadened places in my spirit; move me to such hope that shakes the world with gospeled new beginnings. Amen.

Headstrong. My dictionary defines this as "inclined to insist on having one's own way; willful and obstinate." This dictionary provides no illustration. For such illustration, please turn to Mark 8:32: "Peter took [Jesus] aside and began to rebuke him." In the interval between verses 31-32, it seems clear that Peter will have nothing of the messianic path Jesus has just described. Suffering. Rejected. Killed. Even "after three days rise again" can't undo Peter's displeasure with Jesus' portrayal of where the story is leading—which is to say, where God is leading. That is not Peter's way for the Christ. So the disciple rebukes the teacher in words left unrecorded, though perhaps not far from "my way or the highway."

Jesus responds with what we might view as headstrong willfulness when he rebukes Peter. But the rebukes differ in one critical aspect: community. Peter takes Jesus aside, *mano a mano*. It's just you and me, Jesus, so let me set you straight on this Messiah thing. But notice what frames Jesus' response: he turns and looks at the disciples—and only then does he rebuke Peter. Covenant, discipleship, following: all are about community. Jesus speaks to Peter and to us for the sake of the whole community, so that we may travel together the way of God's Christ.

God's Christ forms the key qualifier. Peter likely wanted some form of national deliverer from Roman rule. And what of us? What kind of Christ do we try to make Jesus into today? A champion of our favored political philosophy? Our guarantor of a "name it and claim it" gospel of health and wealth? "But turning and looking at his disciples," Jesus reminds Peter and reminds us that God's Christ embodies more than our pet theologies and obstinate ways.

There is the way, the Christ—and the church—of the cross.

Pray for the community with whom you follow God's Christ.

THURSDAY, MARCH 1 ~ *Read Psalm 22:23-26*

How is it that the arguably bleakest of lament psalms pivots from its opening cry of God-forsakenness to this passage's invocation of praise within the "great congregation"?

For the answer, you may wish to ask Haitian earthquake survivors who found themselves pulled from the rubble not hours or days but a week or more after being buried alive.

For the answer, you may wish to ask addicts at rock bottom of their habit and its horrific consequences, who suddenly find themselves back in the land of the living, with hope.

For the answer, you may have to suspend your disbelief at the miraculous in life and stand in awe that at times and in ways exceeding our comprehension, life lost becomes life found.

For the answer, you may have to trust the word of a God who hears afflicted ones and satisfies poor and hungry ones— and in such trust, to go and do likewise as God's servant.

This psalm pivots on God's deliverance. How does its praise and undercurrent of deliverance for poor and afflicted ones connect with your experience; what informs this call to praise in your "great congregation"? One striking perspective in these verses comes in the intensely personal thrust and communal consequence of its summons to praise. "[God] did not hide his face from me, but heard when I cried to him. From you comes my praise in the great congregation." In other words, the psalmist's experience becomes the litany raised in the community. Where other psalms invoke praise based on celebrated actions in the past, these verses solicit worship from the gathered folk. We are not here because of what God used to do. We are here because of what God continues to do: for the likes of poor and afflicted ones . . . even for the likes of us.

What acts of personal deliverance form your praise and service of God?

The television sitcom *Seinfeld* had an episode where the eternally bungling character of George decides to do the opposite of what he would usually do. For a short time, "opposite George" turns his life around. Counterintuitive describes George's strategy: to go against what common sense or conventional wisdom would dictate.

But counterintuitive thinking runs deeper than fabricated characters who aim for a laugh. Consider the discipleship summoned by Jesus. If you would follow, deny yourself. If you would save your life, you will lose it. Such ways are not the usual prescriptions for life doled out in corporate climbs to success or financial strivings for the beautiful life.

The covenant of discipleship into which Jesus calls us as individuals and as communities of faith is inherently counterintuitive to ways of thinking, living, and being community that prize what we can grasp or produce for ourselves or claim as justifcation for our standing with God. In Christ, discipleship comes in the gift of letting go of such things as "saviors" of our lives, so that we may learn the grace of being held and loved by the One who covenants with us through the grace of unconditional acceptance.

The movement toward covenant with God does not always take us on the path we expect. So where might this counterintuitive discipleship invoked by Jesus intersect with your faith journey? In what ways and in what habits might your usual practices of thinking, believing, and serving need a refreshing brace of Jesus' contrarian call to save by losing? What might you need to lose, what might you need to set aside, for the sake of following?

God, open me to Christ's call, especially when it steers me against the grain of my assumptions. Amen.

Blessing" language may sound a bit, well, archaic. We still have some remnants in our vernacular. A person sneezes, and what do we say? "Bless you." *Blessing* has also become a synonym for table prayer, whose offerings at times may drift either into a state of rote habit or into a perfunctory act of civil religion prior to a service club meal.

We need to hear the biblical language of blessing—and God's blessing of Abram and Sarai now to be Abraham and Sarah—in something other than such current casual attitudes about blessings. For in this act of blessing, God offers a new identity, and with it a new horizon, to these two. Their blessing is to be ancestors to nations and kings. God thus moves in blessing ways toward them in covenant.

Does God still move in such ways of covenant blessing toward us as well? That is to say, do we also find ourselves on the receiving end of renewed identities and expanded "families" in Christ? Or do we nonchalantly reduce God's blessings to how much is on our table or in our bank account? Those too become ways we reduce the understanding and experience of God's blessing to something we can taste or control or spend.

The movement of God's blessing toward Abraham and Sarah and you and me aims to connect us in hopeful and restorative ways to the world around us. God blesses, us like them, with a gift and call to be new persons. God blesses us, like them, with a gift and a call to community that stretches across generations for the sake of a gracious covenant on an ever-expanding arc.

God bless you.

Prayerfully reflect on times, experiences, and relationships that have conveyed to you the "blessings" of God. In what ways have these blessings renewed your sense of identity and call?

SECOND SUNDAY IN LENT

Covenant movement has been the common thread binding this week's meditations together. Covenant beckoned Abraham and Sarah to follow and trust words of blessing. Covenant moved Paul to confess a God who brings into existence things that never existed. Covenant summoned would-be followers to take up their cross and follow God's Christ. Where does covenant now transport us? Worship.

Does that surprise you? Ought covenant not sound its final crescendo with a forte rendering of missional sending or servanthood practices? Actually, covenant does just that. But worship is the source from whence all discipling movement flows, for good or for ill. The possibility of "ill" traces to the uneasy recognition of worship that leaves us cringing at God's invocation for all manner of privileged agendas and maintaining of status quos. The potential of "good" arises out of the hopeful realization that worship can transform us in the most intimate yet universal of ways.

Hear these verses of Psalm 22. Listen for worship's intended participants: "all the ends of the earth, . . . all the families of the nations, . . . all who sleep"—before God *all* shall bow. Worship is not a closed circle defined by our likes and dislikes. To worship this God is to worship the Holy One of all creation and to have our worship thus transformed by the scope of its God-intended circle of "all." To worship this God means we also worship the Holy One to whom "dominion belongs" and to have our worship (and discipleship) stamped with lines of authority that no earthly powers can usurp or claim for their own. Worship has consequences, and those consequences lead us to covenant faithfulness to the God whose movement toward us binds love and grace, justice and compassion, in a seamless whole. Come, let us worship.

Move me, O God, into deeper relationship with you, and more gracious connection with all. Amen.

Liberating Laws

MARCH 5–11, 2012 • CAROLYN STAHL BOHLER

MONDAY, MARCH 5 ~ *Read Exodus 20:1-11*

Oftentimes, being given rules or laws provides simplicity for us, even freedom. Think of the teenager's relief when the parent names a curfew. Though the teen seldom thanks the parent, now she will not have to wrestle within herself to decide when to be home. In many ways, the Ten Commandments function like that for the Israelites; now they have some clarity.

What we call the first commandment is the Divine naming God's self: "I am Yahweh." Though the Israelites live in a culture with many gods, now they need not weigh the pluses and minuses of the various gods. They can mobilize their energies with focused, undistracted attention to Yahweh.

At the time, the people believed Yahweh to be a "jealous God." Most of us today seldom think of God as jealous, let alone jealous of other gods! We believe—or not—in God and rarely ask, "What God?" though we wisely ask, "What is God like?"

The fourth commandment comes as a gift. We are to stop working! God, our wise role model, rests after six days of Creation. If it's good enough for this God around whom we are to orient our lives, then it is good enough for us—as a community. This rule comes as a gift for all. The entire day of rest is not just a special gift to the male head-of-household; everyone, including family members and slaves, is required to rest from work.

Creative God, thank you for a community of humans with whom to sort out how to live faithfully and peacefully. Help me to rest, to spend time taking deep breaths, and to enjoy creation. Amen.

Lead Pastor of Redlands First United Methodist Church and author of *Opening to God* (Upper Room Books) and several more recent books; living in California

Most of the laws of Judaism, and even Christianity, relate to either ancient property notions or purity boundaries. This is true of the final five commandments. The sixth commandment tenderly encourages us to heed the generations—past and future.

As my sister and I grew up, our mother told us the same poetic story every Thanksgiving Eve. We loved the story and memorized it so we could teach it to our children. Now we gently remind our grown children to tell that story to the next generation. We resist the temptation to write down the story, as it is special when *remembered.*

The "command" to honor one's father and mother reminds the Israelites that their forebears had gone through a lot—the Exodus! They had gained wisdom through their experience of liberation. This commandment says, "Don't let that wisdom go!" Far from requiring a generation to obey every request of the elders, this commandment, for a community whose religion was entirely oral, expressed a yearning to retain wisdom and to stay connected.

To fully appreciate the other commandments, we need to recollect that the male head-of-household was thought to "possess" his wife, children, and slaves. Therefore, the command against adultery was to ensure that one head-of-household would not "steal" another man's wife. Likewise, in ancient times refraining from murder was a prohibition against "stealing" a life. Not coveting fostered an acceptance of one's own possessions in relation to those of another.

Through the centuries, these commandments have taken on significance for human relationships, as their original intent to govern property has receded.

God, thank you for the wisdom handed down to us. May we be wise in what we lovingly teach the next generation. Amen.

Liberating Laws

"Where is the one who is wise?" Paul asks the people of Corinth as he seeks to persuade them to accept what he admits at first sounds foolish. This "foolish wisdom" is that Jesus the rabbi who taught, healed, loved, and saw God in all people, though crucified, lives in those who are "in Christ," that is, those who experience the transforming power of God. Jesus was humiliated and rejected, even by those who thought they had understood him. Yet, attesting to Jesus' broken life becomes a way of breaking open the tenacious power of God's creative love in our lives.

This sounds silly. Those who follow the "loser" have won? Those who remain in relationship to the rejected are radically accepted by others in the new community?

A woman on a church committee that was interviewing potential youth directors at church spoke up, saying she hoped the church youth group was a place where everyone was accepted. She recalled a time when her family had moved to a new town when she was twelve. She had approached a few girls at lunchtime and asked if she could join them. The girls gathered in a huddle, then one reported, "Unanimously, no." This woman survived that rejection and became "strong in her broken place" as she sought to create safe places where acceptance of all would be the group's wisdom.

Paul names here what for him is the core of Christian belief. He identifies Christ as both the power of God and the wisdom of God. We are made stronger when we accept those who think they are weak and those who have been treated as weak. We live more fully, and we might say that Christ lives more fully in us.

Divine Friend, help all who feel rejected or humiliated to find you in the depths of their being. May you transform us by your love. Amen.

We might appreciate the poetic phrase "The heavens are telling the glory of God" without realizing the potency of Psalm 19's first line. Creation itself is instructing us about God! This may sound like more "foolishness," but virtually all of us can testify to creation's ability to convey the power of the Creator. We recall a sunset that "taught" us to let go of worry. We remember coming upon an oasis amidst a desert hike that gave us deep assurance that people can live in peace.

It is not difficult for us to empathize with those of the ancient Near East who worshiped the sun, as well as other astral objects, for the sun is so obviously powerful. This psalm seeks to *oppose* the worship of the sun, yet it does so cleverly by naming how the universe, including the sun, instructs humanity about God. The sun is described as a created object, not a god. Yet, we can learn from it. The sun constantly energizes, and through photosynthesis makes life possible. In a similar way, argues the psalmist, God's instruction makes life possible. When we Christians search for a metaphor to help us consider a "Trinity," thinking of the sun instructs us, for it is one source that at the same time offers "life," "light," and "warmth."

This psalm returns us to the Exodus theme: instruction and law can provide wisdom that leads to liberation. The psalmist argues that life depends upon Torah and instruction, just as life depends upon the daily rising of the sun.

Light and Love of the Universe, may we be guided by your wisdom. May we cooperate with earth so that as we breathe in we receive the gifts of interdependence and our exhales offer humility and cooperation. May we walk lightly upon earth and learn from creation. Amen.

The first commandment in Exodus presents God as saying, "I am Yahweh." Here, in Psalm 19, the psalmist experiences God, still Yahweh, as Rock and Redeemer. I have written in my book *God the What? What Our Metaphors for God Reveal about Our Beliefs in God* that "monotheism is a belief in one God, not a belief in one metaphor." It takes dozens of metaphors to describe all the ways we experience God.

Rock and Redeemer point to strikingly different experiences of God. Addressing God as "My Rock" suggests a trust in God's strength and dependability. When the psalmist calls God "My Redeemer," the psalmist claims God's intimacy. We need to understand the context of the reference to redeemer to grasp the closeness this name implies. Family members in ancient days could buy back, or "redeem," relatives who had fallen into slavery. God as redeemer suggests God is family. When we acknowledge God as strong and dependable (Rock) as well as intimate and caring (Redeemer), we wisely seek to align our heart and mouth, thoughts and actions, with the Divine.

The psalmist yearns to speak and think in ways that are "acceptable" to God. In other contexts "acceptable" refers to a worthy sacrifice. The psalmist seeks to live consciously dependent upon God. Though the language of the psalm suggests that this dependency is "sacrificial," the psalmist envisions depending upon the Rock and Redeemer as a blessing! Sacrifice and discipline reside in the mind of the perceiver. When people tell me I'm "disciplined" because I swim, I find the comment puzzling. Limiting my chocolate intake requires discipline; exercise is joyful. For the psalmist, depending upon God is a gift of joy.

Rock and Redeemer, Womb of Life, Choreographer of Chaos, Dance Partner, thank you for being there, here, now, dependable and personal. May I be open to you as I discern and follow your guidance. Amen.

*C*ontext matters. To have a clue about this "cleansing of the Temple" passage (included in all four Gospels), we must pay attention to historical context. Jews were required to present burnt offerings of cattle, sheep, and doves in the Temple. However, many traveled long distances to participate in this Passover pilgrimage feast, and they were unable to bring their animals. So, animals were available for purchase in Jerusalem to allow worshipers to fulfill their religious obligation.

Context matters. The taxes due at the Temple, according to the regulations, had to be paid in the local currency. The "money changers" were performing a service for devoted pilgrims.

Context matters. We need to be careful about rushing to judgment about what Jesus was judging. Jesus as presented seems appalled at the whole system, not just at some particular salespersons or coin exchangers. This scene provides us with a humbling Rorschach upon which to meditate. Religious laws change over time. Frequently we make assumptions about "right" or "wrong" using our own culture as the norm. Paying attention to context liberates us to see more clearly the intended purpose of laws.

The Ten Commandments and other religious laws liberated the Israelites from ambiguity, enabling them to cohere as a community. Temple tax and animal sacrifice were part of the system of religious "laws." Here Jesus challenges those practices of both the Temple and the people in need of the services rendered. He liberates early Christians from attachment to those very laws.

Transforming God, may I see others within their context, with their histories, from their points of view. May I be less attached to "how things should be" and more open to your liberating love. Amen.

THIRD SUNDAY IN LENT

When the Jews demand a sign from Jesus, they are trying to discern his authority. In a time of transition, the early church is in the process of granting to Jesus' word the authority tradition had previously granted to scripture.

For the Jews, the Temple served as the locus of God's presence on earth and the Torah helped them understand how to follow God. Jesus' reference to rebuilding the Temple in three days jars them. This shift in authority requires both detachment from the familiar and openness to the Spirit.

Only a deep immersion in a culture based on law fosters appreciation of the message of liberation from the law. The teenager who valued her dad's midnight curfew might also appreciate her dad saying, "I think you are wise enough now to decide for yourself when you need to come home. You know where you are, what you're doing, and what you need to do the next day." She appreciates liberation from the curfew in a way that her friend, who never had a curfew, could never understand. However, her newfound freedom may also be jarring. Now she will have to make known to her friends *her own* choices.

Jesus was not against maintaining the religious laws. Yet, he wanted more. His desire for "more than" the law meant that at times an idealized vision for humanity superseded the religious laws. When devout followers of religious laws are told that they have a higher vision (to love their neighbor, for example, even if that means they do not obey all dietary laws), they often experience both freedom and a sense of burden. It is good to be free of some detailed laws, but how can they ever love enough?

God of love, help me to discern the Spirit's yearning in my soul. Amen.

Are We There Yet?

MARCH 12–18, 2012 • BILL DOCKERY

MONDAY, MARCH 12 ~ *Read Numbers 21:4-5*

As someone who used to report stories for newspapers, I continue to follow the global flow of news and information. Too often the news is about political disruptions and natural disasters. We watch disasters as they unfold as tens of thousands of innocents die, hundreds of thousands are endangered, and whole societies uproot their lives and flee persecution.

Though there was no Cable News Network correspondent or Facebook friends to provide moment-by-moment details, the same dynamics that drive modern refugees are evident in the Old Testament story of the Israelites' flight from Egypt. We can sense the fear and confusion of a people following Moses into the desert, fleeing slavery but with no clear sense of who they are or where they are going. And, yes, despite the chaotic journey toward safety and salvation, we sense that the Israelites were, in a word, *human.*

Like kids in the backseat on a lo-o-ong car trip whimpering, "Are we there yet," the Israelites were prone to whine at God and their wilderness leaders. As Numbers tells it, while the tribes try to avoid unfriendly locals, they lose their patience and speak against God and Moses: "Why did you bring us out of Egypt to die in this desert, where there is no food or water? We can't stand any more of this miserable food!" (GNT)

Whether we are Israelites escaping Egypt or contemporary refugees seeking safety, sometimes our sense of entitlement overwhelms our gratitude, even when salvation is the end goal.

God of disruptions and upheavals, touch me now as I flee; comfort me now as I fear; still me now as I complain. Amen.

Writer and research communicator, University of Tennessee; Knoxville

We can almost imagine God responding like a frustrated parent to the moanings of the Israelites: "Don't make me come back there!" and "If you think the food is bad, just wait till you see the snakes!" It doesn't take much to envision a divine forefinger punctuating each word emphatically, pointing at the immature, impatient travelers in the backseat.

God was not kidding about the snakes—poisonous ones that bit people, who then died. The Israelites did not take long to reconsider their complaints. Deadly serpents have a way of putting unpopular menus into perspective.

Soon the Israelites beg Moses to intercede with God. Moses does, and God responds. At God's direction, Moses fabricates a serpent of metal and puts it on a pole. "Anyone who had been bitten would look at the bronze snake and be healed" (GNT). The metallic serpent stayed a part of the Israelites' religious observance through the reign of King Hezekiah. (See 2 Kings 18:4.)

It seems strange that a serpent would become the icon for healing and salvation for an errant people. After all, the creature's first appearance in Genesis is as the embodiment of Satan, the tempter, whose betrayal costs Adam and Eve their place in the Garden.

Yet that is the testimony of scripture. Jewish scholars attribute the healing not to the bronze idol but to the Israelites' willingness to submit to God's will, while Christian scholars see a foreshadowing of Jesus' redemptive death on the cross in the raising of the pole.

What comes clear is that God can turn a profane symbol into a way for the faithful to experience the healing that comes from an encounter with the Holy.

O Creator, amid troubles and afflictions, sweep aside my immaturity and let me gaze on what is holy and find healing. Amen.

Ionce worked on an asphalt crew paving a highway near the Great Smoky Mountains National Park. The weather was July-hot; the paving material sizzled at more than 270 degrees when spread on the road surface; and the passing traffic hardly stirred the parched air.

That summer I learned what respite is—a minute of shade from a nearby sapling, a seat on the bumper of a work truck as I swilled ice water. Scant as those moments were, it was a Jonah-like refreshment that made harder parts of the day bearable.

We experience as miraculous the rescues God gives us. Like a splinter removed or an abscess drained, a painful condition eases. Fear of injury and death recedes. Anxieties soften and melt away. We feel ebullient, filled with wonder that the danger has passed, the suffering is over.

Too often when threat and discomfort evaporate, the memory of the wonder fades too. We adjust to the coming of miracles; and, when miracles are past, we readjust to the mundane. Against just such a memory loss, the psalmist calls us to mindfulness:

Give thanks to the LORD, because he is good;
    his love is eternal.
Repeat these words in praise to the LORD,
    all you whom he has saved. (GNT)

Shoveling blacktop, I also learned the transitory nature of respite. Sun moves; shade disappears. The work moves down the road. Sweat again drips from eyebrows and soaks shirts.

But God's rescue is not short-lived. Divine refreshment transcends our days of sweat and dust. It comes for all who labor and find themselves burdened with care. All we must do is recognize and claim it.

O Source of rescue, thank you for moments of respite in my day and for the liberation your love affords me, now and forever. Amen.

Though the brass serpents raised high on staffs disappeared from Jewish religious practice long before Jesus' birth, when Nicodemus comes to him with questions, Jesus turns to that passage in the Torah to help explain his role as savior of all.

"As Moses lifted up the bronze snake on a pole in the desert," Jesus tells Nicodemus, "in the same way the Son of Man must be lifted up, so that everyone who believes in him may have eternal life" (GNT). The statement at once ties Jesus to the redemptive action of God to save the afflicted Israelites in the desert and at the same time presages the approaching time when Jesus will be raised on a different kind of pole, performing the same redemption for all human beings.

Jesus next speaks the key scripture that defines a Christian's commitment to Christ as savior: "For God so loved the world, that he gave his only begotten Son, that whosoever believeth in him shall not perish, but have everlasting life" (KJV). All the essential elements are there. In one simple sentence, the verse describes God's motivation for sacrifice (love), the condition necessary for humans to claim the promised salvation (belief in Jesus), and the result of that claim (eternal life). Two thousand years of Christian history, myriad religious practices, uncountable acts of goodness have flowed from that straightforward verse that defines what it means to be Christian.

Lest we misunderstand the nature of that salvation, Jesus proclaims that the purpose is not judgment or condemnation but salvation for the world. Yet clearly the basic impulse that drives God is love for God's people, a love that prompts compassionate redemption for all of us.

God, let me not use your light to judge others but to illuminate my own life so that your salvation shines forth in me. Amen.

FRIDAY, MARCH 16 ~ *Read Ephesians 2:1-7*

As we say in the Baptist church where I grew up, I walked the aisle when I was eleven years old, some five decades ago. Vacation Bible school was in session. Our church building was a sanctuary in more ways than one. The massive brick structure offered not just a place to teach kids about Jesus; at a time when home air-conditioning was the exception, the ground-level classrooms were the coolest refuge in town.

Going forward was not hard. For a preteen, it felt momentous, something that would change my life forever. I walked forward at the invitation and confided my decision to the preacher.

Salvation is a word we may associate with spiritual revivals, and it shows up in all four scripture passages this week. Ephesians addresses God's saving activity in Christ. The first three verses state what we're saved from: death through sin, following the ways of the world, and being children of wrath. The writer is not chastising so much as reminding us of the past so that we can more readily value being included in God's life-giving story of salvation in the present!

At eleven, my life-changing commitment didn't hinge on turning from my past "sins"; but in the coming years it raised weighty questions about how to be a Christian. Many times I wanted to abandon that statement of faith, but the commitment I made then has ended up making me. It has never turned me loose, though my understanding of what it means has changed as I have matured.

I have come to appreciate the richness of God's mercy and kindness. I value God's willingness to take the initiative for my benefit and salvation. I am "alive together with Christ." With that promise, I try to meet each moment with hope.

O God, hear me, strengthen me; let me hear you. Amen.

Are We There Yet?

Some time ago I visited a historic Baptist church in rural southwest Virginia. Point Truth, a Primitive Baptist church, was a far cry from the big congregations I have attended through the years. It met monthly, and energetic exhortations of four preachers marked its worship over the two-hour service. Its members were given to ecstatic displays of joy and tears.

The service embodied a captivating informality. The children played in the nearby cemetery while the adults worshiped, but they would pop into the sanctuary at will to drink from the water pitchers at the front of the room. I left with a sense of an unpretentious, warm, and accepting group of believers.

The Baptists at Point Truth share the common Calvinist roots of other Primitive Baptists: the notion that God knew from the beginning who would be saved. But on one major point the Point Truth believers differ: When they say that Jesus died for all, they mean *all*—even people who have not yet acknowledged it. Hell, for this church, is failing to understand that you are already saved and living as if you are not.

The insight at the center of this unorthodox faith has left me much to ponder. Now I do not worry about heaven or hell. It is not given me to separate the sheep from the goats. If we treat everyone we meet as if they are saved, then we recognize our shared bonds: the need for redemption and the hope that redemption has taken place.

The writer of Ephesians seems to hint at this: "It is by God's grace that you have been saved through faith. It is not the result of your own efforts, but God's gift, so that no one can boast about it. God has made us what we are" (GNT).

God, may I feel your salvation in my heart, and may I seek and find it in others. Amen.

FOURTH SUNDAY IN LENT

"Are we there yet?" Yes, we are there. We have found a way through the wilderness. We have arrived at the destination. God did have to come back here, but our encounter with the Holy was not a spanking or a time-out or even a finger-wagging. It was an embrace.

For all our foolishness, our petulance, our bickering, our mistreatment of ourselves and our fellow humans, the source of all that is holy offers us rescue—a way to recognize the Divine in ourselves and find and honor it in others.

Awareness of that holy kinship lets us find healing without resorting to brass serpents, leads us to turn in praise to God and reach out to others of God's children who are on this trip with us.

In John 3:16 Jesus did not give us an abstract statement about belief, a yes-or-no check-box answer to qualify us for discipleship. In Matthew he lays out the only commandments we need: "Love the Lord your God. . . . Love your neighbor as you love yourself" (22:37, 39; GNT)—a simple, practical, oh-so-difficult standard. In Luke he ties eternal life to how well we follow those commandments: "Do this and you will live" (10:28, GNT).

Disasters and displacements will come again. We will find ourselves in the wilderness again, beset by serpents, anxious about our future, fearful of pain and death. We will quarrel with our fellow refugees and question the wisdom of our leaders. We will need respite again, but this time there is a difference.

We are there, but we are not there by ourselves.

O God, may I respond in humility and hope to the rescue you have provided. May confidence in my deliverance color my life as I interact with all of your children. Amen.

A New Covenant and a New Heart

MARCH 19–25, 2012 • JOHN M. DRESCHER

MONDAY, MARCH 19 ~ *Read Jeremiah 31:31-34*

As we near the end of Lent, notice particularly God's words to Jeremiah regarding the new covenant God will make with the people. This covenant will differ from a list of laws written on tablets of stone; God promises to put God's law within them, written on their hearts. Then they will have the desire from within to do God's will. And God adds, "I . . . will remember their sin no more."

I recall the story of two women who came to their pastor and said, "Pastor, God has spoken to us. We have a word from the Lord." The pastor, skeptical of such statements responded, "The next time the Lord speaks to you, I want you to ask him what sins your pastor confessed to him last night."

After several days the two women returned and stated again, "The Lord has spoken to us." And the pastor inquired, "Did you ask God what sins your pastor confessed to him last night?" The women replied, "Yes, we did. God said he didn't remember." The pastor responded, "The Lord has truly spoken to you." God, in the new covenant, will forgive and forget.

At times it seems that the greatest distance in the world is the seventeen inches between the head and the heart. We may know God's will in our heads, but our lives remain unchanged. We may believe in God without loving or obeying God. But, when God's will becomes our heart's desire, all of life changes. We love and serve God, knowing our sins are forgiven.

O God, give us the confidence, trust, and joy of knowing our sins are forgiven and forgotten. Amen.

Campus pastor, Quakertown Christian School; member of Finland Mennonite Church; living in Quakertown, Pennsylvania

Many believe this psalm reflects David's contrition after his grave sin with Bathsheba and Uriah. The psalmist cries out to God, confessing his sin and asking for God's forgiveness. God forgave David, who knew again the joy of salvation.

A woman came weeping to my study. She spoke about an act of unfaithfulness she had committed against her husband years earlier. She had carried this painful guilt for many years. She wanted to know what to do. I said, "Let me ask you several questions. First, do you believe that what you did was sin?" "Oh, yes," she replied, "I know it was sin." "That," I said, "is conviction. Second, were you ever sorry for this sin?" She answered, "Every time I think of it I am sorry." I said, "That is contrition. Third, are you still committing that sin?" "Oh, no, it was that one time." I responded, "That is repentance, the turning from the sin. A final question I want to ask you: Did you ever ask God to forgive you for this sin?" "Yes," she answered. "I suppose thousands of times." "Now let me give you God's word of forgiveness. God says, 'If we confess our sins, he who is faithful and just will forgive us our sins and cleanse us from all unrighteousness'" (1 John 1:9). As I shared these words, it became evident that a great joy and peace came into her life.

Psalm 51 begins by asking for mercy. What is the mercy that you need today from God? Such mercy comes from God's steadfast love, which we meet in the many promises of the covenant God made with Israel's patriarchs and with King David. Years after the Davidic monarchy, Jeremiah prophesied a new covenant. Still later, Jesus proclaimed a new covenant of water and the Spirit. Throughout these covenants come constant reminders of God's steadfast love and mercy.

Faithful and forgiving God, give me the ability to confess, repent, and receive your forgiveness and cleansing. Amen.

Years ago I visited a bishop who lived in a retirement home. He asked me, "Do you think that many persons carry their guilt because they have never really repented? They are convicted by their sin and have asked forgiveness and yet they do not turn from their sin."

I have come to agree with the bishop. We deal with guilt by confessing our sin, and God gives the guilty conscience peace as we not only confess our sin and ask forgiveness but as we turn from the sin. Psalm 51 offers insights into sin and guilt and also the path to forgiveness and freedom from guilt, which often follows our sense of sin.

What elements are involved in finding forgiveness and freedom from a guilty conscience? In these five verses, I notice four elements of repentance. I need to recognize that sin has obtained control over my life. I need to understand that sin is directed not against self or others but against God. I need to have the willingness to assume full responsibility for my sin. Finally, I must abandon all efforts to claim to merit God's love or to think that I can earn God's love.

Do these elements speak to my daily need for forgiveness? My sin is not on the order of that of King David. I do not commit adultery, nor do I arrange the deaths of others; however, as I go through an inventory of my day, these elements of repentance help me recognize what robs me of my joy and gladness. Are they sufficient for me to find a sense of forgiveness and freedom from guilt? What other essential elements does this psalm teach? As you read Psalm 51 in its wholeness, note that which delights God.

Faithful and forgiving God, May I be conscious of what robs me of joy and gladness. I wil heartily repent, and you will heartily forgive. Amen.

Who has not, at one time or another, felt this way: "No one understands, cares, or knows what I am going through"? Feeling that *someone* cares makes a difference in our lives. Yet, some people in our world worship gods, who in their deity, look down on the poor and needy and hold disdain for the weak and helpless. These gods know nothing of grace and mercy. In contrast, how different is our God!

In earlier portions of the book of Hebrews, the writer refers to the saving work of Christ under the figure of priestly service. The priest was to represent God to us and us to God. The priest must be completely human and chosen by God but must also have sympathy for the erring, the ignorant, and the wayward. Israel looked for and longed for such a savior over the centuries. And Jesus fulfilled the Old Testament prophecies concerning the messiah.

In this scripture the writer relates how Jesus satisfies these qualifications. He is divinely appointed; we see Jesus in his essential deity, full humanity, and infinite compassion.

The opening sentence of Hebrews refers to Christ as having "made purification for sin" by the sacrifice of himself. He urges us to come with boldness to the throne of grace to find help from one who is "touched with the feelings of our infirmities." Jesus was tempted in all points as we are. Because he experienced what we experience, he is able to help us.

Now the writer also invites us to see all that Christ went through and how through suffering, submission, and resurrection he is the "source of eternal salvation to all who obey him."

O God, I thank you for a Savior who sympathizes with me and is able to help me in all my need. Amen.

FRIDAY, MARCH 23 ~ *Read John 12:20-26*

Many times in my prayers, I have prayed to see Jesus more clearly. My heart's desire is to see Christ in greater and greater fullness each day, until that day when I see him face-to-face. After the triumphant entry into Jerusalem prior to the Passover, some Greeks come to Philip and Andrew, disciples with Greek names, and ask to see Jesus. These Greeks become representatives of untold millions of Gentiles who come to see Jesus and hear the message of the gospel.

The quest for Jesus triggers an opportunity for glorification. Four times the Gospel of John tells us quite explicitly that Jesus' time or hour "has not yet come" (John 2:4; 7:6, 30; 8:20). Now Jesus says, "The hour has come for the Son of Man to be glorified." At first it seems that Jesus ignores their request. He does not seem to respond directly to these seekers. Looking deeper into the Gospel, we realize that Jesus is teaching his visitors that day and continues to teach each of us some important lessons. The question for daily reflection is simple: How well am I paying attention?

Only as we are ready to die to ourselves, like the seed in the fertile soil that dies in order to be fruitful, do we really see Jesus. When we lose our lives for Christ and the kingdom of God, leaving behind the self-centered, self-serving, and worldly life, then we will know the fullness of life eternal. As we follow and serve Christ, we see our gifts and vocational calling in Christ's mission. Only when these things happen do we see Jesus as he is and bring glory to him. In our love and witness, God will continue to bring glory and honor to the one we serve.

O God, we want to see Jesus. Then enable us to introduce him to others. Amen.

In John 12, Jesus is coming to the close of his public ministry. From now on he reveals himself more in secret to his disciples. His ministry and teaching revolves around three dominating truths: that he is Christ, the Son of God; the faith and unfaith that follows; and the kind of life from which faith issues.

We know Jesus as fully human and fully divine. In the most traditional language, God took on human flesh. And when we understand this, we can see how his soul was troubled as he faced the cross. He could have asked for ten thousand angels to deliver him or he could have turned from the cross. To choose the angel option, Jesus would have to deny his humanity. To go to the cross without struggle would mean denying the cost of our redemption and God's grace.

But Jesus acknowledges that he has come for this very hour and that through his suffering and death God will be glorified. A voice from heaven affirms this statement; to the crowd around Jesus, the voice sounds like thunder. Jesus does not need the affirmation; the affirmation comes for those who were present then, and it is needed now. Everyone will realize the importance of Jesus' death, "the judgment of this world." The moral character of the world will be revealed and its sin condemned. "The ruler of this world" who sought to destroy Christ and his mission will be "driven out" and defeated.

The Cross remains the supreme moral magnet of the world. As Jesus is lifted up, his cross has attracted multitudes, making them willing, as devoted followers, to take up their cross and to follow him.

O God, my redeemer, teach me daily the meaning of the cross as I walk with Jesus. Amen.

SUNDAY, MARCH 25 ～ *Read Jeremiah 31:31-34*

FIFTH SUNDAY IN LENT

When I read this passage from Jeremiah, I think of my dear friend John. By his own confession he lived for money and for sports. He had his mansion, his luxury car, and a successful business. Yes, he was religious, but it was not a matter of the heart.

Then John experienced a spiritual rebirth. His life changed to one of love for God and for others. I took great joy in seeing John work and worship to the glory of God. The old life was gone, and a new life was begun. In the words of Jeremiah, my friend received a new heart and an overwhelming sense of God's forgiveness.

We began this week's meditation with Jeremiah's prophecy and now we conclude with the same scripture. We began by noticing what is most essential. God will put a new covenant of love within our hearts. With God's new covenant, we will do what is right because of inner conviction and desire. With the new covenant comes new power, new promises, and new persons.

Jeremiah also speaks to the heart of the gospel when he speaks of forgiveness. Here we have one of the clearest statements of God's desire for each of us. God promises forgiveness of all our iniquity. God will "remember our sin no more." Praise God for this twofold restoration and new life.

Our texts this week remind us of the cleansing and healing power of God's love, a power to create new hearts and clean hearts, a power to transform lives. Thanks be to God for this marvelous love!

Teach us, O God, to live with your law written on our hearts. Grace us with a sense of your abiding presence and your transforming power. Amen.

Compelled to Shout "Hosanna!"

MARCH 26–APRIL 1, 2012 • DON SALIERS

MONDAY, MARCH 26 ~ *Read Mark 11:8-11*

The storm is gathering as Jesus moves steadfastly toward Jerusalem. The crowds greet his entrance to the city: "Hosanna." As a child I thought the word meant something like "hurray!" It took a number of years before I learned it was also the cry "Save us!"

Christians think of Palm Sunday as the "triumphal entry." We recall Sunday school pictures showing the palm-strewn pathway and the crowds all welcoming Jesus with shouts of jubilation. Few of us then thought of Jerusalem as a troubled political center of ancient Israel's hope and expectation. When Jesus appears, the city is in an uproar, fervently hoping that this donkey-riding figure will fulfill the divine promise by overthrowing Roman political oppression.

But my childhood images of triumph and happy "hosannas" did not adequately encompass the results of Jesus' coming. How could I understand a "king" who was to be executed as a common criminal? How could I understand a ruler who faced humiliation and abandonment by his closest followers? How can current notions of "triumph" grasp what took place once the parade had ended? What compelled them to shout, "Hosanna"?

If we listen carefully we can hear beneath the enthusiasm of the crowd a deep cry for help. "Hosanna" in light of oppression; "Hosanna" by the poor and hungry; "Hosanna" for mercy and redemption. So we will follow Jesus toward Jerusalem, along with his bewildered disciples, crying, "Save us from death-dealing!"

Most Holy God, save us from easy thoughts about Jesus; lead us into the mystery of suffering, death, and resurrection. Amen.

William R. Cannon Professor of Worship and Theology, Emeritus, Emory University; church musician, pastor, and author

Sometimes our lives can seem very unsteady. When the world around us loses its bearings and chaos rules, our personal lives can feel like they are coming apart. When sudden change in family or among friends comes with deep hurt or unexpected loss, we feel all at sea. When a friend of mine lost his mother in an accident, he told me, "Everything seems strange and empty, and everything I think or do is in a fog—I feel like I'm losing my way." Such disorientation easily calls faith into question.

When I have these experiences, I find myself being drawn back to the psalms. Perhaps *compelled* might be more accurate. So many of the psalms sing lament and praise, desperation and doxology. In the midst of finding words to express grief and anger and sorrow, we also find a phrase like "steadfast love." Our psalm opens with the powerful refrain, "[God's] steadfast love endures forever!" We find this refrain in many other psalms, most especially in Psalm 136 where it forms a perfect litany of life before God. To hear once again that God's steadfast love endures forever, even against the evidence of our lives at the moment, is to be reminded of the very nature of the Holy One, Holy Three. The Eternal God takes on the human story from the inside out.

In times of uncertainty, disorientation, and loss, we can cry out, "Let your steadfast love come to me, O LORD, / your salvation according to your promise" (Ps. 119:41).

How do we come to know this? We know this by following the way of Jesus. He knew about the unsteadiness of the world. He faced head-on the struggle with the chaos of sin and death. He entered into our world of turmoil and strife and remained steadfast in love.

Reflect on where and when you have known the steadfast love of God.

It would be foolish for someone who wished to build a strong fortress to select the weakest or a flawed stone to set the corner of the foundation. Such a choice would weaken the whole structure. That is plain good sense. Yet our day's psalm presents the startling image that the very stone the builders rejected has now become the cornerstone of a new building, a new house, a "mighty fortress" as Martin Luther's hymn has it. What a strange matter this is.

Psalm 118 has been part of Christian worship from the earliest days of the church. Is it any wonder, then, that this image of the rejected cornerstone is applied to Jesus Christ? Indeed, the world rejected him, and his followers who shouted, "Hosanna!" were soon hearing, "Crucify!" Even the disciples turned away. But God's love calls out: "Come to him, a living stone . . . chosen and precious in God's sight." That love compels us to be "like living stones, [to] let [our]selves be built into a spiritual house" (1 Pet. 2:4-5).

The psalmist pleads for the gates of righteousness to open that he might enter and give thanks. The cry for salvation has been answered. Indeed, the church still sings, "This is the day the Lord has made; let us rejoice and be glad in it." We still cry out, "Save us, we beseech you, O Lord!" Jesus draws us into crying out on behalf of the whole world and ourselves. When he enters our world and comes into our lives, we are built up in praise because he has opened the gates of righteousness and has become the foundation of all human hopes.

As the great seventh-century hymn sings, "Christ is made the sure foundation, Christ the head and cornerstone."

Lord Jesus, build us into a house of living stones with your righteousness and love as our steadfast foundation. Amen.

THURSDAY, MARCH 29 ~ *Read Mark 11:11, 15-18*

I am struck afresh by the sentence just after all the "Hosannas" and the "Blesseds." Jesus enters the Temple after the ecstatic reception and "looked around at everything." No other act in Jesus' whole life and ministry quite equals his anger at the commercialization of the holy place. A "den of robbers," a place where vendors exploited honest, faithful folk. This Jesus, whom his parents found at an early age in the Temple, even then searching scripture with the teachers and praising the God of Israel, now confronts the money changers. A dramatic scene indeed, coming as it does in the last week of his life.

We are not exempt from the issues in our day. We can easily point fingers at some churches that resemble big business more than "houses of prayer for all nations." Getting rich in the name of God is not new.

It becomes more difficult to raise questions about our own ways of exploiting the power of "religion." Instead of pointing the finger, let us examine the difference between faithful giving of our time, gifts, and money for ministry and the competitive race to outdo other churches.

In a society completely saturated by preoccupation with money, we need to remember what makes the church faithful. We pray and work for justice, mercy, and compassion for all, and the church is the community of intercession for the world.

This scene reminds me of Fred Pratt Green's powerful hymn "When the Church of Jesus Shuts Its Outer Door." The last verse sings, "Lest the gifts we offer, money, talents, time, serve to salve our conscience. . . . Teach us, dying Savior, how true Christians live." Jesus and the disciples then leave the city, only to return for the holiest week.

From cynicism and exploitation of the poor, save us, good Lord. Amen.

This is the source of the song we sing on Palm/Passion Sunday. The ending of Psalm 118 opens a great window onto themes in Hebrew scripture. Some scholars propose that this psalm of thanksgiving originally celebrated a great military victory in the history of ancient Israel. Others think of it as a sung or recited acclamation of praise in a thanksgiving festival. In either case, it carries the unmistakable note of jubilation. No wonder the Gospel writers of the New Testament would find these words appropriate to the triumph of Jesus Christ over the forces of evil and death.

The psalm ends as it began with that wonderful refrain: giving thanks that God's "steadfast love endures forever." Reading over the whole psalm once again, we may find that it is a kind of sung parable about the coming Holy Week itself. On Palm/Passion Sunday we greet Jesus' entry into Jerusalem, perhaps not quite understanding all that will take place. The difficult words of verses 17-18 now resonate: Jesus Christ was put to suffering for the world's sake, but death did not have the last word. "I shall not die, but I shall live." He did undergo death, but it cannot hold him. Even though the world may ignore or oppose his way of love and justice, that lavish love for all God has created will not cease.

Empires will rise and fall, our lives will experience limitations, difficulty. Death will come to us all, but the steadfast love of God still enters Jerusalem and still calls out to us. The divine love, as Charles Wesley wrote, excels all human loves. This is the love we must learn to receive again and again because the struggles of life will always be part of our mortal days.

Pray or sing: "Blessed is the one who comes in the name of the LORD!"

Many years ago I worked with a modest-sized congregation that expressed an interest in a more meaningful approach to Lent and Holy Week. "We've never done a Palm Sunday procession—we're not high church." After discussing how the children could be involved, the members decided to go ahead. Some still worried that the younger children would end up sword fighting with the palms! Nevertheless, preparations began with various Sunday school classes.

Palm Sunday came, cool but clear and sunny. The children gathered outside the front doors of the church and received palms and last-minute instructions to come down the aisle waving branches as the congregation sang "All Glory, Laud, and Honor."

A large rough-hewn wooden cross for Holy Week was standing just inside the altar rail. Of course, a few palm-branch sword fights did break out just as the procession began up the front steps. But then a strange thing happened. As the younger children moved inside the sanctuary, they spotted the unexpected cross at the end of the aisle. They spontaneously became quite focused. Each child quietly placed his or her palm branch at the foot of the cross and moved to join the parents. The entire procession—from the little ones to the senior highs—all followed. The congregation never forgot the opening of that Holy Week.

Palm Sunday came alive that morning. So too, in joining the procession that follows Jesus into Jerusalem, may we be led to awe and wonder at the cross. Holy Week will unfold the mystery of why we now call this day "Palm/Passion" Sunday. Follow him toward his passion for us and the whole world. Our "Hosannas" ("Save us, Lord!") will be turned by his passion to "Hallelujahs"!

Let the children teach us how to move with Jesus again. But, O merciful God, focus our attention on the cross that is the triumph of your lavish love for the world. Amen.

SUNDAY, APRIL 1 ~ *Read John 12:12-19*

PALM/PASSION SUNDAY

John's Gospel tells the story of the triumphal entry into Jerusalem with great economy yet with a twist—the name of Lazarus appears. Following the crowd's shouts of "Hosanna," the writer cites a prophetic passage that predicts a king riding on a donkey's colt. In typical Johannine fashion the story of that parade turns into a great testimony. Only *after* the Resurrection do the disciples come to understand what the entrance into Jerusalem on that day meant. Only *after* the Resurrection does the crowd that had witnessed Jesus calling Lazarus out from death come to understand the significance of that event.

Often we do not understand significant events in our lives until later. Something happens or is said to us; then years afterward, it suddenly dawns on us: "Oh, that's what happened!" or "That's what he meant!" God sees the truth but waits for us.

And don't forget the Pharisees' witness: "Look, the world has gone after him!" All of this is told "only after." The deeply moving Farewell Discourse that follows in John's Gospel (chapters 14–17) are written "only after." Just so, we cannot fully understand what Palm/Passion Sunday means as an isolated event, however "triumphal" it may have been at the time. It becomes the triumph of life over death and a sign of the "world going after him" only because it leads to his passion, death, and resurrected Spirit-giving.

On this day we make our processions too, waving palm branches in joyful imitation of that day nearly two thousand years ago. But let our palms find their place at the foot of the cross. There Jesus' compassion compels us to shout "Hosanna! Save your people!" Blessed be God who will yet bring life out of death.

Blessed are you, Incarnate One of God, for raising up witnesses to your Passion in every generation. Amen.

Destination: Known

APRIL 2–8, 2012 • TOM STEAGALD

MONDAY, APRIL 2 ~ *Read John 12:1-11*

What do you do when someone you love is going to die? Go to the kitchen, as Martha does? Or make an extreme gesture of affection, as Mary did? Maybe, like Judas, you get fussy. This is no ordinary dinner party: a shroud hangs over it. Why?

After Jesus raised Lazarus, friends of Mary and Martha who witnessed the miracle told the religious authorities that Jesus had performed yet another sign. "If we let him go on like this," the leaders worry, "everyone will believe in him" (John 11:48).

Perhaps word has gotten back to Bethany that the family had best be careful because both Jesus and Lazarus are on the high priest's "enemies list." You can feel the stress as you read. Add to that this awkward moment of reprimand, which is no less awkward because of the setting's familiarity.

A deeper awkwardness than we realize may exist. Judas does fuss at Mary for her scandalous generosity—and it is a scandal, her letting her hair down in public, taking a family treasure, and spilling it so freely onto Jesus' feet. We have been taught to hear Judas's rebuke with a biased ear, but perhaps Judas also wanted to honor Jesus by reminding everyone in the room of Jesus' teaching. Didn't Jesus say to that young man to "sell what you have and give it to the poor"? If we really love Jesus, Judas may be barking, the best way we can show that is to obey him. Maybe both Mary and Judas offer gifts to Jesus, each of which turns out, in its own way, to be something of a scandal.

O God, let me give myself and my gifts to Jesus in a way that honors him. Amen.

Pastor of Lafayette Street United Methodist Church, Shelby, North Carolina; author of *Shadows, Darkness, and Dawn: A Lenten Journey with Jesus* (Upper Room Books)

What do these Greeks, Gentile God-fearers in Jerusalem for the Passover, really want when they approach Philip and say, "Sir, we wish to see Jesus"? People wished to see Jesus for various reasons. Do the Greeks want, out of curiosity, to see Jesus the miracle worker?

Some people wanted to see Jesus because they desired something from him. Crowds had followed Jesus throughout Galilee not because they chose to follow him or be his disciples but because they desired food or healing, even an exorcism for themselves or a loved one. There were so many of these folks, in fact, and some of them so insistent, that time and again Jesus would hide himself from them. Did the Greeks want something?

Some people, of course, only wanted to see Jesus dead. Seeing him, those particular persons did not see him at all.

Conversely, what did Jesus see when he looked upon the curious, the merely desirous, or even the sinister and dangerous? Perhaps he saw sheep without a shepherd; poor and oppressed who had no other resource; sinners who needed prayer and forgiveness.

What did Jesus see coming when he heard that these Greeks had come in search of him? That "hour" had come, the time when he would be "glorified"—a deeply theological and ironic description of his crucifixion. In John's Gospel, Jesus seems to know that the shame of his impending public execution will, by the grace and power of God, be transformed into the wonder of universalizing atonement: that when Jesus is "lifted up" on the cross, all will be drawn to him. All will be able to see the love of God, whether Jew or Greek, man or woman, slave or free. Whoever wished to really look would really see.

Lord Christ, help us to see the fullness of your love for your children. Amen.

Sometimes in our familiarity and haste we bypass verses of scripture. Because we already know the story of who "betrayed" Jesus, our attention in this passage jumps quickly ahead to the conversation between Jesus and Simon Peter, the piece of bread, and Judas's leaving the meal to meet with the religious officials. But what of verse 22: "The disciples looked at one another, uncertain of whom he was speaking"?

There seem to be several options for interpretation—and for devotional consideration. One is that the disciples look at one another with suspicion, each of them so sure of his own allegiance to Jesus that Jesus' pronouncement sounds an alarm, a call to arms against the potential betrayer. Could be.

Or could it be that each of the disciples is humble enough, uncertain enough, to know that given the right set of circumstances or stressors, any one of them has it within him to do what Judas would in fact do? Interestingly, in Mark's account of Jesus' Last Supper prediction, Mark tells us that each of them says to Jesus in turn, "Lord, is it I?" Could well be.

For only those who love Jesus can betray him. His enemies might hate him; others might disregard or ignore him; but only those who sit at the table can get up and leave, and only those close enough to kiss him can give the kiss of death. That Judas is the one who guided the soldiers to Gethsemane on fresh-washed feet, his breath smelling of sacrament, is a particular instance of what is possible for all disciples.

It is unfortunate that we so quickly rush to blame Judas, so quickly leave him and this verse of scripture behind; for indeed, this Holy Week calls all of us to examine ourselves, to hear Jesus' prediction, uncertain of whom else he might be speaking.

Forgive me, Lord, when I turn away from you and your purposes. Amen.

MAUNDY THURSDAY

Ever since God called Abram and Sarai to leave kindred and home and work and go to a land God would show them, tired and calloused feet have been a sign and symbol of the faith, outward and visible expressions of hope, trust, and grace.

When Jesus calls his disciples, they step away from home, family, and work to follow him. They traipse around Galilee, then south into Judah, and finally into Jerusalem. Later, Jesus says that with the Spirit's help their feet will take them back to all the places they have already been and more besides, and this time not just as followers but as guides, teachers, and witnesses. Their worn soles, much as Jesus' ruined hands, will be beautiful on account of the lengths they go to spread good news.

Now, Jesus takes into his hands the feet of his disciples, to bathe them with cool water and perhaps his own tears. The Gospel does not mention tears, but it is not hard to imagine. Having loved them, he loves them to the end. Having known them, he knows what is coming for them—and for himself too; how his own unwashed feet will soon be pierced, bathed in blood; how soon these feet that had walked in close formation behind him will scatter in all directions for fear and self-protection. The feet that left seashore and tax booth, walked away from convention and routine, will run, newly washed, into the imagined safety and cover of darkness.

The scene takes our breath: Jesus, the Word of God and Voice of Creation, the Rabbi of rabbis, all but naked as he will be on a Roman cross, kneeling before his students, giving his bare back to them before he gives it to his tormentors. His back, his hands and feet and side, their washed feet—all of them scandalous signs of unfailing love.

O Lord, let my devotion to you be seen in my hands and feet. Amen.

GOOD FRIDAY

There but for the grace of God, go I." We hear that particular benediction with great frequency, and I want to believe that sometimes the phrase articulates a deep and genuine, even spiritual, form of humility. That said, I suspect that often it strikes me as a matter of pride and even relief, more than humility: that somehow the misfortune of that one or those over "there" proves that "I" am especially graced—that God loves me more than God loves that one, protects me and us more than God protects "them."

Health, safety, prosperity, "protection" from tragedy—many consider each a sign of God's favor. Conversely, sickness, poverty, misfortune signal God's disfavor. Even Jesus' disciples ask, "Who sinned, this man or his parents, that he was born blind?" (John 9:2) In another case, Jesus responded curtly to the crowd's satisfaction that the Jews who were killed by Pilate at the Temple were "worse sinners than all other Galileans" because "they suffered in this way" (Luke 13:2).

The prophet Isaiah, whose poetry may reference Israel, a king, or some other "suffering servant," suggests a radically different way of viewing the servant's suffering: that the suffering endured is vicarious, for others—that the servant's suffering somehow protects others. The irony of the text is that those protected deem the suffering one deserving of it, when in fact it is for their benefit.

Christians quickly seized upon this text as a description of Jesus' passion and death and of our own developing awareness that he suffered for us, each and all. As we look at the Cross we exclaim, "There but for the grace of God, go I"—but not at all as we usually mean it.

Thank you, Lord Jesus, for your willingness to care for me even when I don't see it. Amen.

Low in the grave he lay . . . " Meanwhile, did Jesus' followers go to synagogue or Temple, any of them? My guess is no, they did not, whether for fear or fatigue or catatonia. Only occasionally do mourners of the recently dead attend worship so soon after a loved one's passing, though they might benefit if they did. To gather among the faithful, to hear again the promises of scripture, to sing the songs that proclaim God's certain triumph—what better way to rail against the darkness, to remove the sting of death, to gain the first measure of victory over death?

If Jesus' disciples had attended sabbath or Passover services—it was a "high day" that year as Passover fell on the sabbath proper—those most crushed by his death might well have heard this text from Exodus: the victory of God over Pharaoh at the Red Sea. And it might have given them the kind of deep comfort only the stories of the faith community can afford.

All seemed lost for the Israelites. Yes, they had left Egypt, but Pharaoh's army had come after them in "bold" pursuit and was about to overtake them. Moses still had the staff of wood that had worked miracles in the sight of Pharaoh, but what was that against Egypt's best chariots and troops? The Israelites had nowhere to run, no retreat, no option—except the sea. The Israelites were panicked, despairing; but Moses summoned them to trust that, despite appearances, they would experience victory. And, by grace, they did.

On that first, interminable Holy Saturday, were Jesus' first followers able to see past the pain? Could they sense or begin to sense that Jesus' death was not the final word or the only word? that despite all appearances and expectation, God would turn their hopelessness and despair into unimaginable victory?

Remind me of your surprising and irresistible victory, O God. Amen.

EASTER SUNDAY

The women start for the garden tomb "very early on the first day of the week, when the sun had risen." Mark is telling us more than the time. The "first day of the week" recalls Genesis 1, when against the swirling darkness and primordial chaos God's voice rang out: "Let there be light," and there was light.

Mark is not telling us just that the sun has risen, but that light has been spoken into the darkness of the previous days. These women are the first to enter the garden of God's new creation that the recreating God has begun by Jesus' resurrection.

The women cannot see all that yet, of course; too bright a light blinds as surely as too deep a darkness. Soon, however, everything will appear different, will be seen in a different light: the light of Resurrection. Soon, and very soon, their every sentence will end in an exclamation point.

For the moment, however, they have only question marks— "Who will roll the stone away for us?"—and amazement. When the young man in the white robe tells them to "Go, tell his disciples and Peter that he is going ahead of you into Galilee; . . . just as he told you," they go surely enough, but they "said nothing to anyone, for they were afraid."

Fear closes their mouths, as it sometimes closes ours— whether the fear is that it might not be true, this gospel we proclaim; or the fear that it might indeed be really true, but we do not have the heart to live out the Resurrection.

Is that Mark's intent? To force us into a crisis of recognition? To see our fearful selves in these women, we who are often reticent to speak of what we have seen and heard? If so, Mark also intends us to repent, in the knowledge that if the truth be told, we of all people must tell it.

Give me grace over all my fears, Resurrected One, and let me proclaim your truth with joy! Amen.

Because Jesus Rose

APRIL 9–15, 2012 • MARK A. PEARSON

MONDAY, APRIL 9 ~ *Read John 20:19-23*

Today's reading describes one of Jesus' post-Resurrection appearances that took place the evening of that first Easter. Jesus spent forty days on earth after his resurrection and before his ascension back to heaven to demonstrate he had truly risen.

Jesus speaks peace to these terrified disciples, and he speaks peace to us today. Moreover, he doesn't just describe peace; he bestows it. Yes, they face and we face real problems. We are not to deny them. But Jesus says, "Trust me." Sometimes Jesus takes our problems away in an incredible fashion. Other times he gives us wisdom and strength to deal with those problems. On still other occasions he does neither but walks with us as we go through a tough time.

Jesus demonstrates that his Resurrection body is both similar and dissimilar to his pre-Resurrection body: similar in that Jesus has hands and can speak, eat, and breathe; similar in that he is an individual person, not one absorbed into some "world soul." But this body is dissimilar in that he can pass through locked doors and suddenly vanish and reappear elsewhere. (See Luke 24:31, 36.)

After death and resurrection, believers do not become disembodied spirits or indistinguishable parts of a great collective spirit, nor are they reincarnated back to earth; but, rather, believers possess new bodies, as individuals now made perfect for life in heaven.

Lord Jesus, thank you that believing in your resurrection is not wishful thinking. In your precious name. Amen.

President of New Creation Healing Center and president of the Institute for Christian Renewal; Kingston, New Hampshire

Jesus commissions each of us to extend his work in the world today. We need not, out of false humility, believe we can do nothing great as he did. We must not, out of arrogance, go off message and remake him, his teaching, and his work to our own agenda. "As the Father has sent me, even so I send you," he told them and tells us.

First: the mission. Matthew describes Jesus' mission as teaching, preaching, and healing (4:23; 9:35). *Teaching* tells us that the Christian faith has specific theological and ethical content. *Preaching* describes exhortation and encouragement to apply faith content to our walk with Christ and our work for Christ. *Healing* is the one we most likely fear. In part, we pay too much attention to the flamboyant "faith healers" and not enough to the balanced, sane, and effective ministers of healing. Only when we pray for people will we see God work through us.

As Jesus sends us as he was sent, our work for Christ involves teaching the faith as he taught it, urging and encouraging people to walk with and work for Christ as outlined, and healing as we pray with others to be made whole.

Second: the method. Jesus does not begin his adult ministry until he becomes Spirit-empowered at the River Jordan (Luke 3:21-22). Similarly, he told the first disciples to wait in Jerusalem for the coming of the Holy Spirit (Acts 1:3-5). We received the Holy Spirit at our baptism, but we need regular refilling. When the writer of Ephesians tells the believers at Ephesus, "Be filled with the Spirit" (5:18), he uses the present continuous tense. A better translation would be, "Keep on being filled with the Spirit."

Lord Jesus, help us teach your truth, exhort and encourage one another, and be instruments of healing. Remind us to pray regularly for Holy Spirit empowering. In your name. Amen.

After Jesus' ascension, the disciples wait for the Holy Spirit (Acts 1:4). This is not a time of idleness but an active time of community building. We can safely surmise the disciples had various issues with one another. It will take time for love, humility, and reconciliation to manifest in this aggregate of individuals and for them to become a real community.

The psalmist celebrates this. How good for brothers and sisters to live in unity! Unity, of course, does not mean uniformity, nor does it mean affirming unscriptural belief or conduct. But within the boundaries of Christian doctrine and moral practice, there is room for diversity of personality, style, gifting, and expression. What creates unity and helps it thrive is an eager desire to maintain it; an understanding of Christianity as "body life" not just "me and Jesus"; and mutual forbearance, forgiveness, and love.

The believers "were of one heart and soul," which may have been the premise on which they willingly pooled their resources. Throughout the centuries of the church, few have taken the event described in Acts 4 (all had their goods in common) as a commandment binding on all Christians. What is binding, however, are the attitudes and actions of generosity to those in need. "There was not a needy person among them." What an astounding statement and experience! In community, we will feel the precious oil of unity running down over us, overflowing to all around. Thus, there is a mutuality that befits a fellowship in unity.

Lord God, deliver us from a me-centered discipleship. May we desire unity and do our part to bring it about. Help us never to be too proud to receive help from the community or too selfish to offer help to the community. In Jesus' name. Amen.

Christian disciples can go to one of two extremes when it comes to sin. We will either deny our sin or we will wallow in guilt. Sometimes our self-centeredness makes us deny our sin because we think anything wrong must be someone else's fault. Sometimes our denial hinges on a mistaken understanding of what constitutes sin. Still other times we deny our sin, because somewhere in our past we learned that to admit a sin brought mean-spirited punishment, not tough-love encouragement that led us toward maturity. Whatever the reason, denial of sin keeps us stuck. As observant participants in Alcoholics Anonymous or other Twelve Step programs know, you cannot reap the benefits of the program without first admitting you have a problem.

Scripture is the chief place where God tells us what sin is. We all are tempted to selective reading—embracing those passages that describe the sins of others while ignoring those that describe our sins. Jesus warns us against this, calling it specks and logs. (See Luke 6:41-42.) We must also be on guard against filtering scripture through personal philosophy or political ideology because the Bible cuts across such distinctions. That's why it helps to study the Bible with people whose viewpoints differ from ours. We in the church can help one another recognize and overcome our specks and logs.

When we sin, God doesn't stop loving us; but we may sense that something blocks both God's blessings and our conscious sense of God's presence. Admitting our sins and naming them is the first step to removing that block.

Lord God, I confess that I am a sinner. I have sinned in thought, word, and deed and in what I've left undone. I come to you in my darkness, asking you to make me whole. Help me submit to all of what you teach. In Jesus' name. Amen.

Yesterday we considered how Christian disciples may deny their sin. Today we will address how sometimes we can go to the other extreme and wallow in guilt.

Some feelings of guilt signal our sense of being out of relationship with God. God, through our conscience, will remind us of what we thought, said, or did contrary to God's will. Our guilt then may encourage us to turn to God, confess the sin, receive divine forgiveness, make amends, and move on to new life.

Once we confess our sin, God is quick to forgive. The Holy One has put our transgressions "as far as the east is from the west" (Ps. 103:12). God promises, "I will not remember your sins" (Isa. 43:25). If we've truly confessed our sins to God, if we've promised to work on our spiritual growth and act on that promise, and if we're planning to apologize and make restitution to others we've harmed, then our guilt is gone! Gone!

This is possible because Jesus paid the penalty for our sin. The epistle writer describes this (depending on your Bible translation) as "propitiation" (KJV) or "expiation" (RSV) or "perfect offering" (JB) for our sins. Paul put it this way: "In Christ God was reconciling the world to himself, not counting their trespasses against them, and entrusting the message of reconciliation to us" (2 Cor. 5:19).

The church is neither to be a gathering of mutually enabling deniers of sin nor a community of self-righteous judges but a fellowship of people encouraging and exhorting one another toward greater holiness of life.

Thank you, God, that Jesus paid the penalty for my sins. I do not have to keep punishing myself for what I do wrong. Help my church to be a fellowship of forgiven and forgiving sinners seeking to grow into maturity in Christ. In his name. Amen.

I think Thomas gets misjudged. We don't call Peter "Denying Peter," though three times he denied knowing his Lord. We don't call David "Adulterous David," though he had that affair with Bathsheba. But we do call Thomas "Doubting Thomas." Rather than deriding him, we should be grateful to him for at least three reasons.

First, Thomas raises the questions others might have been thinking but were not expressing. In the upper room, Jesus told his closest followers that they knew where he was going. Thomas spoke up and said no, they didn't (John 14:1-6). May God give us the courage to be that brave soul, saying or asking what needs to be said.

Second, Thomas wants proof that Jesus has been raised from the dead. His is honest doubt seeking a real answer. When Jesus appears to Thomas, he does not rebuke him for wanting solid reasons to believe but accommodates him. Like Thomas, we might be wary about claims people make—whether political, religious, or otherwise. But we need to come with honest doubt—asking questions with an open mind to what the answers might be.

Finally, when Thomas receives sufficient evidence to believe, he commits. Jesus' resurrection vindicates him and his teachings. Jesus proves himself much more than a mere teacher, and Thomas commits at the level of which Christ is worthy. Christian commitment demands obedience ("My Lord") and worship ("My God"). Jesus receives both Thomas's promise of obedience and his act of worship because they are rightly given.

Lord God, help me, like Thomas, not to be shy in asking the questions on my mind and heart, not to be afraid of expressing honest doubt, not to be lax in searching for answers, and not to withhold my commitment to your son as Lord and God. In Jesus' name. Amen.

John's Gospel tells us that the incredible things written—Jesus' wise words taught and powerful signs and wonders done—are just a sampling. When the Gospel writer uses the word *sign,* what does he mean? Think of a road sign that gives information and points in a direction. Jesus' miracles helped the recipients and pointed the way to God. What do Jesus' signs tell us about God?

First, God is powerful. The God who made the universe is omnipotent. The Creator can change water into wine, heal the sick, multiply food, raise the dead, and much more. Therefore, we need never doubt God's ability to help us at our places of greatest need.

Second, God is loving. Jesus' signs are not stunts to dazzle or show off. He helps people in need. Therefore, we need never doubt God's willingness to love in practical ways those who come in faith.

Third, God is contemporary. I'm sure that in Jesus' time many people celebrated the mighty deeds of love that God had done "long ago" but thought, *That doesn't happen now.* Many today wonder if God is still at work. For that very reason we need to tell others about God's activity in our lives and in the world. They desperately need to know that God's loving power and powerful love are available to them today.

The writer closes by telling us he wrote his Gospel so that we would believe. This doesn't mean we understand every aspect of the faith. It means we trust God, who is revealed in the pages of scripture. It's not just Bible facts—it's a life-changing, eternal relationship with the Lord of the universe.

Lord, I confess my skepticism about stories of answered prayer. Help me know that your love is powerful, and your power is loving. It's for today and it's for me. I thank you for being real and personal and for loving me. In Jesus' name. Amen.

Because Jesus Rose

Life-changing Joy

APRIL 16–22, 2012 • MICHELE CUSHATT

MONDAY, APRIL 16 ～ *Read Acts 3:12-16*

Mere weeks after the greatest failure of his life, a transformed Simon Peter assumes the stage in the middle of a bewildered Jerusalem crowd. Moments before, a man crippled from birth had leapt to his feet at a word from Peter: "In the name of Jesus Christ of Nazareth, walk" (Acts 3:6, NIV). A few simple words and a beggar turns dancer. No wonder the crowd responds with amazement bordering on reverence toward Peter.

Peter wastes no time in setting the record straight. He knows the healing had nothing to do with human words or abilities and everything to do with a crucified and resurrected Savior. Peter too had been crippled—with fear, pride, and ignorance, three flaws that led to three denials when Jesus needed him most.

But God is a God of miracles, for beggars crippled from birth and for prideful disciples. Peter's Savior, raised from the grave, offered Peter forgiveness, restoration, and a second chance either to deny or proclaim the good news. In that moment, Peter's prior failure becomes a platform for triumph as he testifies boldly to the truth of the one true healer—Jesus Christ.

What is your greatest failure? What still holds you captive to regret and weighs you down with shame? Have you allowed Christ to heal the past with forgiveness and restoration? A crowd of seekers awaits you to point them toward healing. Allow your defeat to sprout legs and begin to dance at the word of Jesus Christ. And then discover the miraculous joy of a crowd captivated by a Savior.

God, thank you for healing me and giving me reason to rejoice. Use my life as a platform for your purposes. Amen.

Author and speaker, speaking coach for Dynamic Communicators Workshops; Highlands Ranch, Colorado

Searching for a fun after-school activity, my son signed up for cross-country. Several of his friends planned to do the same, and he looked forward to hanging out together after school—until his first run. He discovered it isn't easy or fun for a beginner. One mile in and he wanted to find a different sport or at least find a way to be on the team without actually running.

When it comes to our spiritual journey, we often want the perks without the process. We want a relationship without investment, redemption without the bloody cost, and spiritual refreshment without the journey through repentance.

In the years before Jesus began his earthly ministry, John the Baptist came to prepare the hearts of people, delivering a message of repentance: "Repent, for the kingdom of heaven is near" (Matt. 3:2, NIV). Only a repentant heart is ready for a relationship with the Savior.

Years later, Peter carries this same message of repentance to a Jerusalem crowd, a crowd who had "handed over and rejected" Jesus weeks before. In his speech, Peter raises three opposites to make his point with the crowd: you/God; killed/raised; life/dead. God's action has turned the death-dealing action of the people on its head. The people's own ignorance of scripture makes them unable to see the very signs that point to Jesus as Messiah. This ignorance is not only that of the people but their leaders as well. Peter knows firsthand the importance of repentance; his own sin and shame have been wiped out! Now, repentant and refreshed, Peter urges others to follow his example, to turn to God and know the miracle of a clean heart.

Knowing and being known by God require repentance. It's the first step toward being right before God and experiencing the joy of a refreshed soul.

God, make me aware of anything that is interrupting my relationship with you. Teach me the joy of a repentant heart. Amen.

We don't know the circumstances the psalmist faced: family discord, a season of drought, or some other disaster. We do know this for certain: the psalmist turns to God for rescue and relief.

The Psalms record authentic struggles and cries for deliverance. Those of us who experience our own hardships find camaraderie through their transparency. We find that we're not alone in our anguish; and by studying the psalmist's response to pain, we hope to unearth the secret to enduring our own.

The opening words of the psalm are straightforward. The situation is so dire there's no time to waste in calling upon God for assistance: "Answer me when I call, O God." In the second half of verse 1 he recalls God's previous gracious action, which serves as a mainstay in his current time of trouble.

In verse 2 the psalmist addresses his attackers, those who have shamed him. And in verse 3 he asserts his claim to God's intervention as one of those "set apart." Despite his troubles, he calls to God fully expecting God to act. The psalmist's confidence in God runs through this lament as a constant thread. His imposing circumstances can't keep him from believing that God can both see and hear him: "The LORD hears when I call to him." Herein lies the psalmist's secret for security in insecure times. He not only believes in the constancy of God's presence but reminds himself of this bedrock of truth.

Difficulties are as certain as the rising and setting of the sun. Yet God's presence is a greater certainty than our troubles. The psalmist knew this and hung on to it as if his life depended on it. We would do well to do the same.

Father, you are an ever-present help in times of trouble! When difficulties threaten to overtake us, may we cling to the certainty of your presence. Amen.

After two decades of working for the same company, my husband gave up the security of a regular paycheck to start his own business. Reassured by his work ethic and passion, I supported his decision and felt a rush of enthusiasm about this new adventure—until that first Friday without a paycheck and the two months of Fridays that followed. Too quickly I went from a woman ready to tackle an adventure to a woman ready to crack under the weight of worry. What if we had to take out a second mortgage on our home? What if we ran out of food?

I'd long believed my joy came from my relationship with God—nothing more, nothing less. When our temporary financial drought sapped my enthusiasm and parched my spirit, I realized my joy had been secure only as long as my circumstances remained controlled and manageable.

The psalmist understands the difference between a fleeting happiness sourced in the reassurance of stuff versus a true, unwavering joy sourced in assurance of God's presence. "Let the light of your face shine upon us, O LORD. You have filled my heart with greater joy than when their grain and new wine abound" (NIV). Joy predicated on worldly belongings can change in a moment with an unexpected phone call, a bill in the mail, or a doctor's appointment. Confidence in God's presence and love weathers any circumstance, standing true through this lifetime and into eternity.

We can lose many nights' sleep over misplaced joy. When we turn our eyes to the true Provider, we experience a peace that overcomes panic. Then *true* joy can infuse our lives again. The psalmist rightly affirms, "I will lie down and sleep in peace, for you alone, O LORD, make me dwell in safety."

Thank you, Father, for the constancy of your presence. Forgive our attempts to find security in anything or anyone else but you. Amen.

There is something marvelous about a little boy's fascination with his daddy's shoes. A cherub face lights up with joy as too-small feet slip into giant-sized shoes, anxious to follow in his daddy's footsteps. During the early years of mothering, I caught all three of my children clomping through our home in an oversized pair of my husband's work boots. In spite of my good-natured protests, each persisted with a grin: "Look, Mom! I'm just like Daddy!" I beamed in response, knowing they couldn't have chosen a better man to follow.

As they grew into adults, I watched them slowly ease out of their daddy's shoes and consider "shoes" I didn't want them to wear, friends and influences that tempted them down paths of compromise. How I missed those toddler days and wished they'd go back to daddy's shoes! Often all I could do was pray, warn them of the danger, and remind them of both my love and the love of their father.

The letter of First John evidences the same tender concern toward spiritual children. After warning against loving the world and being led astray by false christs, the writer urges us to remember our heritage: "How great is the love the Father has lavished on us, that we should be called children of God!" (NIV). He reminds us to be on guard, to wear only the Father's shoes, and to hang on for a glorious reappearance, for "when he is revealed, we will be like him, for we will see him as he is."

No matter how old we are, may we marvel at being the children of such a Father, and may we wear our Father's shoes well.

Wonderful Father, how blessed we are to be your children! Guard us against anyone or anything that would lead us astray, and teach us to walk daily in your footsteps. Amen.

The disciples never expected to see Jesus again. After all, they'd heard about the beatings, the horrors of crucifixion. They grieved his loss as deeply as if he had been family.

But there Jesus stands, appearing unexpectedly and behind closed doors, like a ghost. I imagine these grown men and women rubbed eyes and pinched skin, hesitant to believe the miraculous. Although a few had claimed to see him, it seems too good to be true. How can the dead come back alive? How can a broken body be made whole? Even as this apparent apparition stands in their midst, they struggle to allow the stirrings of joy to take hold. They've lost too much already.

Jesus senses their doubt and fear and hurries to reassure them of his reality. "See that it is I myself. Touch me and see," he challenges. They need to realize they have not misplaced their hope; their belief has, in fact, been rooted in the right person. And so he reaches out scarred hands and asks for food, inviting them to celebrate the miraculous joy of his presence.

As I study this familiar scene, I return to a single thought: Though my heart breaks over dear friends who remain closed to faith in Jesus and situations that seem beyond the reach and rescue of God, my Savior is not bound by closed doors. There is no room beyond his ability to penetrate, no person who cannot experience his touch, and no circumstance beyond the reach of his presence.

"See that it is I myself. Touch me and see." Jesus pleads with us not only to believe him but to experience his resurrection power. Our Jesus lives. Joy!

Savior God, you are not a ghost, not an apparition unable to infuse my life with presence. You are alive! Fill me with joy in your presence. Amen.

There's nothing like a good story. But at times the events of my life appear random, like disjointed characters and messy scenes that don't add up to a story at all, let alone a good one. I search for a thread of purpose, something that will make sense of the unexplainable circumstances of my life. Often I feel only confusion.

In the days following Jesus' death, I believe the disciples faced a similar frustration. Before Golgotha, the story of their lives made sense and followed a path of purpose—they were disciples of Jesus, the Holy One of God who came to redeem Israel. But an angry mob arrested him, convicted him, and crucified him on a forsaken hill. Their prior purpose disappeared in a fog of confusion and grief.

Then Jesus reappears with a reassuring word: "Everything must be fulfilled that is written about me in the Law of Moses, the Prophets and the Psalms" (NIV). It was as if Jesus says, "Everything you've studied and learned up until now has been pointing to me. I *am* what you're looking for!" The miracle resides less in Jesus' presence with them and more in his presence opening the door to the fruition of God's plans.

Still the disciples don't quite grasp the situation. So Jesus "opened their minds to understand the scriptures." It is a full-circle moment, a moment when confusion lifts and the disjointed pieces of the story come together in the Story of all stories.

We can't always make sense of the seemingly random events of life; but when Jesus stands among us, he sheds the light of insight on even the darkest moments. With his help, we might see the makings of a good story and God authoring and bringing it to fruition.

Author of Life, open our minds to understand your word, and give us courage to testify! Amen.

Because You Asked

APRIL 23–29, 2012 • PAT EDMONDS

MONDAY, APRIL 23 ~ *Read Acts 4:5-12*

Things have been a little crazy. Two strangers are preaching and teaching their way around Jerusalem. The religious elite are not happy with the crowd's response. They thought they had dealt with the "Jesus" problem, the resurrection from the dead issue, but it was not to be so. People are listening in huge numbers to Peter and John's message on the matter and choosing to believe. Problem identified, solution proposed: arrest them! Squelch the messenger, and the message will die.

But the message is Jesus, the resurrected one. Peter and John make clear that it isn't about them, their thoughts, their ideas, their message, but rather it is from Jesus: "by the name of Jesus Christ of Nazareth." Everything they do and say comes from the power of that name—a name the leaders of their day have tried to eliminate, snuff out, discount. Not much has changed in two thousand years.

Many in our world continue to reject the "stone," to discount his importance, to credit everything and everyone but him for the good things in this world. What about us? Are we a voice through which Christ's spirit is revealed? Do we proclaim his continued involvement in all that is and that will be?

If the voices of those who call Christ their own when they're together go silent when they're not—when they're confronted or challenged—what happens next? God's message for this world will go forth, but will we miss the blessing that comes with being a messenger?

Jesus, make me a messenger of your message, today, tomorrow, and every day you give me. Amen.

Jesus follower, contractor, business owner; living in Portland, Oregon

Psalm 23 is one of the most familiar passages of scripture in all of Christendom. Children recite it; soldiers going into battle recite it; cowboys in old Westerns recite it when they bury their friends—as well as their enemies. But familiarity can breed complacency.

The psalmist reminds us of all that God does for him, for us, for all who love God. A shepherd provides an apt understanding of God's protection, provision, passion, and constant presence. Sheep, by nature, are not self-preservationists. They wander in their wonder, put themselves in harm's way, blindly follow one another without asking where they're going or why. Generally, they're not even soft and cuddly but smelly and oblivious.

Given that information, a shepherd is a good thing, both for sheep *and* people. This shepherd knows the location of the best pastures. He's aware of the pitfalls that would deter the sheep from safe arrival. He sees the predators who stalk nearby, waiting for the sheep to wander off, to lust after what they think the shepherd is denying them.

We might remember that "greener grass" is often the by-product of more manure. This comparison made perfect sense to the psalmist and the people of his day.

What analogy makes sense for me? Do I have a context to understand all that God does for me? Will I choose to spend another day living in the complacency of my familiarity, or will I choose to place myself in the care and keeping of the Shepherd?

God, at the end of my day I want to know you more, trust you more, love you more. Amen.

WEDNESDAY, APRIL 25 ~ *Read Psalm 23:1*

I shall not want." How inhuman is that statement? We all want something. We want good things; we also want escape from and forgiveness for the things we wanted that weren't so good after all.

What would it be like to live without want? Scripture doesn't instruct us to live without passion, desire, motivation, urgency, effort, or even want—but want of what? Want of a closer relationship with the Shepherd? Want of a deeper trust in the One who promises to take care of our *every* need—not our every *want*, our every need? Want of a faith that says everything has a refining purpose in life? Want of a greater understanding of God's book of instruction?

"I shall not want." Is God not living up to the promise of scripture when we find ourselves wanting? Whenever that thought crosses my mind, I usually receive a visual reminder of God's care: the refrigerator box house under the freeway overpass; the guy who's eating alone and looking like he's lost something important; the phone numbers in my cell phone that belong to people who actually want to talk to me. It's not that God doesn't care for the guy in the box or the one alone at the table. It's my upside-down perspective that if I don't have all I want, then God's asleep on the job! When I say it out loud it's so convicting I can hardly admit that I thought it in the first place.

The hope, the promise, when we want what God wants us to want comes in verses 5 and 6: an overflowing cup, goodness and mercy all the days of our lives. What more could we want?

Lord, teach me to want you and only you—all the days of my life. Amen.

Knowledge is good; understanding is better; and action is the best of all, when you're talking about the love of God. "We know love by this, that he laid down his life for us." That action, in and of itself, teaches us about love. The gospel's strong assertion of the close association believers have with Jesus surfaces in the following statement: "We ought to lay down our lives for one another." For the writer of First John, we know love not simply through words "but in truth and action." Being a Christian means you act on what you know. When you see something that's wrong, you move to make it right. When you see someone in need, you move to meet that need or solicit help from someone who can. When you see despair, you offer hope and a helping hand.

Few of us will ever face the challenge of giving our physical life for someone else. But all of us may find ourselves in a place that demands we give up our comfort, our stuff, our agenda, our preference, our time, our pride for the betterment of someone else. Oddly enough, we are the persons who usually gain the most from such an exchange.

When we respond to God's prompting to be about God's business in this world, we live without condemnation, and "we have boldness before God." Ignoring God's prompting is a mighty dangerous way to live—especially when we consider the promise in verse 22: "we receive from him whatever we ask, because we obey his commandments and do what pleases him."

Lord, I want to do what you want me to do because nothing else will do. Amen.

When we take what we know and show it, our hearts don't condemn us. We don't live with regrets. Coulda', shoulda', woulda' isn't in our vocabulary. We can approach God in confidence, not because of what we've done but because we know we've done what God desired.

I wonder why we so often take what God intended as a simple way to live in harmony and distort it into something complex, burdensome, and condemning? "Do more, be more, give more" becomes our mental mantra; when we don't live up to our own expectations, we assume that we're not living up to God's either. In the words of the writer of First John, God issues the following two commandments: (1) "believe in the name of his Son Jesus Christ" and (2) "love one another." Not a huge agenda—but somehow we keep attaching more and more to it until it's a burden that no one could possibly live up to. We can easily find ourselves becoming self-righteous and judgmental of those who don't measure up to a standard they were never commanded to measure up to!

Keeping these simple commands comes with great reward: We get to "abide," to live, commune, fellowship, chill "in him," and God reciprocates. How amazing is that? Plus, we "receive from him whatever we ask, because we obey his commandments and do what pleases him." One translation says this allows us "to set our hearts at rest in His presence." I can hardly recall the last time I felt my heart was "at rest" in divine presence. I still tend to live most of my relationship with Jesus in that "fear and trembling" stage. Maybe it's time for a radical change.

Jesus, let me get past myself and live with you the way you intended for us to live together. Amen.

The Good Shepherd (Jesus) lays down his life for his sheep, which doesn't seem like a fair exchange in any world. I think I would be a pretty good shepherd, but I can't see myself giving up my life for a sheep.

That would probably put me in the "hired hand" category mentioned in verse 12. I would watch out for the sheep, steer them clear of danger, reign them back in if they start wandering off, keep a sharp eye out for predators. But at the end of the day, the sheep belong to someone else; I just want a paycheck and to go home at night. I'm taking care of me first.

But what if we talk in terms of the flock I'm helping to shepherd, the flock known as my family? They don't always follow where I lead. They can be selfish, sneaky, and downright cantankerous. But let the "wolf" come after them and that wolf has got to get through me first. I'm not turning tail and running. I have a stake in those sheep, and there will be none left behind if the wolves show up at our door.

As a Christian, what other flock(s) am I responsible for? Does Jesus expect me to lay down my life for "all" of his sheep? Or just the ones I care about? If Jesus has my back when the wolves of this world show up—because they have, they do, and they will—should I be more vigilant in defending his sheep when they can't protect themselves? It's good to know that Jesus counts me as one of his flock, and I'm just as important to him as all the rest. I need to remember that more passionately and intensely the next time I'm tempted to run when the wolves come after one of his flock.

Jesus, you're the Good Shepherd. I call down the power of your Holy Spirit to make me a better member of your flock today. Amen.

Sometimes scripture confuses me. I read it over and over; and the more I read, the less I understand. When I think I'm getting a handle on a concept, Jesus delivers the punch line and I'm lost all over again. I thought I was getting this "good shepherd" thing under control and then *BAM*, the other shoe drops.

Shepherd: sheep know me; I know the sheep; simple enough. Father knows me; I know the Father—now we're clicking. But wait, hovering around the edges is a new group of sheep, and it doesn't sound like they're welcome, at least not by the sheep that already live in the pen.

But Jesus has a plan to create a megaflock, to mix and match and be the good shepherd for all. He will lay his life down for all of them, because he can and then he can take his life up again. No other shepherd has ever been able to pull that one off.

Who are these "other sheep"? Are they other Jewish Christian communities? Gentiles? Those who will come to believe? Jesus is talking to his Jewish flock, but his intention is unclear. Bringing in Gentile sheep would certainly preclude winning "Good Shepherd of the Year" if your Jewish sheep are voting. And one verse beyond today's reading tells us: "the Jews were divided because of these words." They didn't like it, plain and simple. They thought he was a raving lunatic. They certainly didn't want to hear that someone else might be invited into their exclusive club.

The lessons here for all of Jesus' followers are substantial. The shepherd, not the sheep, decides who is a part of the flock. If you're a part of the flock, you don't keep the Good Shepherd all to yourself. The best thing that can happen is that your flock becomes larger, more eclectic, more diverse, more interesting.

Jesus, open my eyes and let me see; open my heart and let me be you to my world. Amen.

A Growing Season

APRIL 30–MAY 6, 2012 • DAVID MEDLIN

MONDAY, APRIL 30 ~ *Read Acts 8:26-40*

Philip is a good and faithful servant of the Lord. An angel of the Lord commands Philip and, without question, Philip obeys. I wonder how I would respond in a similar situation if told to drop what I was doing and go.

Philip's journey involves more than simply going along a wilderness road. In verse 29, the Spirit tells Philip to go over and join the chariot of an Ethiopian eunuch. So Philip goes, and thus opens up the opportunity to witness to a person very different from himself who has the potential to carry the message to far-off lands.

This story offers two lessons. The first comes in Philip's openness to hear the call and take action. The second is the attitude of the eunuch and his willingness to ask for help. When he requests aid in understanding the scripture, he opens the space for witness to take place. The eunuch also begins asking Philip some basic questions of faith that lead to his baptism.

Stories like this encourage us to be prepared to respond to a call to action. Like Philip, we may not know why the call has come to us or where it will take us, but it is the getting up and going that is truly important. In doing so, we open ourselves to miraculous possibilities. That response further opens us to God's action in us.

Holy Spirit, open my heart to hear your call. Grant me the courage and faith to follow where you lead me. Amen.

Full-time businessman and part-time Army officer; living in Saint Charles, Illinois

An angel of the Lord prompts Philip to "get up and go." The Holy Spirit, always at work in the book of Acts, nudges Philip to make contact with the eunuch, certainly a somewhat uncomfortable encounter. The Spirit's prompting of contact with the eunuch signifies a paradigm shift in itself and reinforces the truth that God's message of love is open to all people from all walks of life. No doubt Isaiah's message resonated with the eunuch, who surely saw parallels between his own situation and that of the "sheep led to the slaughter." Philip guides the man's understanding of the reading.

All of us at one time or another reach the limits of our own understanding and need mentorship. We must, like the eunuch, be big enough to admit our inadequacy and ask for help. And, like Philip, we always stand ready to minister to another whether we planned to or not. The Bible contains many stories of ministry that result from chance encounters. Bringing the light of the good news to others is a key tenet of our calling as Christians.

As a society we also tend to gather with those with whom we feel most comfortable. In this case, Philip opens himself up to an encounter with someone different from himself. The eunuch, after hearing Philip's explanation of the scripture, sees water and asks what prevents him from being baptized. That is the faith in the moment that we all should seek! Not a Why? but a Why not? Why not now?

God of all seeking hearts, help us minister to one another, guiding one another in understanding and love. Amen.

Beloved, let us love one another," states the epistle writer. Why? Because love is from God and in showing love to one another, we honor God and reflect the love God has for us. Through love, God lives in us, and by loving others we strengthen our relationship with God.

This concept isn't easy to master. History is littered with horrific examples of humans unable to love one another, often based on an outward physical difference. The human genome project reports that human DNA is greater than ninety-nine percent alike, with only a few letters out of three billion in our DNA code changing our physical appearance. We are essentially far more alike than we are different.

Desmond Tutu, in his nonviolent battle against apartheid in South Africa, rallied around the concept of *ubuntu*, "I am what I am because of who we all are," which affirms the fundamental humanness of us all and asserts the need for support of and reliance on all people. Ultimately his work and those around him who demonstrated tremendous Christian love despite adversity turned the tide in South African apartheid.

The challenge of First John in verses 20-21 is a valid one: "Those who say, 'I love God,' and hate their brothers or sisters, are liars; for those who do not love a brother or sister whom they have seen, cannot love God whom they have not seen. . . . Those who love God must love their brothers and sisters also." God's love of us engenders our love for others. We do not claim credit for loving others, nor do we love only those who seem lovable. Because of our experience of God's love, we love both God and neighbor.

God of all peoples, soften our hearts and help us to look past our differences to love one another. Amen.

THURSDAY, MAY 3 ~ *Read 1 John 4:7-21*

Little on the evening news reminds us of God's love for us or for the world in which we live. Where then should we look to find light in dark times? How can we break free from the chains of anxiety and fear? Today's epistle both challenges and encourages us to conquer these obstacles through the redeeming and relational powers of love.

The epistle begins with the word *beloved*, affirming that we are both loved by God and by other Christians. This already present identity of "beloved"—not a love that awaits our merit to secure it—also says to us that we are worthy to give and to receive love as we are now. John then challenges us to share the gifts of love with one another as God did for us through the atoning sacrifice of Jesus Christ. I find in the statement "God is love" a needed focus on the physical embodiment of God in Jesus, a demonstration of love in action.

We often set out to meet the world where we are, only to discover that where we are makes us feel ill-equipped and underarmored to take on the world. Just "being" seems too hard. Perhaps we have been hurt in the past, and opening ourselves up to love or to be loved makes us too vulnerable. We may flee from love and intimacy with others and with God because we lack the courage to take relational risks. Then the fear of not being loved and the ultimate fear of death confront us. Yet, First John reminds us that we have the power through "the confidence of perfected love" to break these chains that bind us.

As Christians, we know that God loves us, that we are called to love one another, and that Jesus has triumphed over the power of death on the cross. What shall we fear? God's "perfect love" casts out all fear, and love will reign.

Renew in my soul, O God, the courage to be. Help me meet the world where I am with a heart full of love. Amen.

A Growing Season

The first verse of Psalm 22: "My God, my God, why have you forsaken me?" sounds familiar. Most of us recall these words from the crucifixion narrative in the Gospel of Mark. As Jesus hangs on the cross, he utters these words of the psalmist. I always thought this a strange thing for Jesus to say. Didn't he know what was going to happen? Why would he believe that God had abandoned him? Then I started to look at this question in a different light. Certainly Jesus was in agony as he suffered on the cross. How interesting that he would not curse God or deny God but affirm God's existence and their relationship through this question.

Psalm 22 thus begins as a lament for all that is wrong in the world and the psalmist's sense of God's being so far away. This absence is quite personal. But as the psalm progresses, the psalmist affirms a trust in God's presence and ability to help in a time of suffering. He recalls God's saving actions on behalf of his ancestors and how God gave him life.

How often have we, like the psalmist, reached a low point in life and had to look back to see the blessings all around us—if only we will look!

Verses 25-31 indicate the psalmist's renewed trust in a God capable of rescuing humankind from every danger and snare. He moves from feeling beaten down and broken to standing in the assembly of the faithful and proclaiming the goodness of the Lord. Despite times of fear and doubt that will come, the psalmist reassures us that God reaches all the nations of the world and that generation upon generation will praise his name.

Lord, renew a right spirit within me when I doubt your presence. Let your past and present deeds comfort my troubled mind and bring me peace. Amen.

SATURDAY, MAY 5 ~ *Read John 15:1-4*

Any serious gardener knows that a number of variables affect crop production: the quality of the soil, fertilizer, water, sunlight, pests, pruning, and weeds are just a few. These verses from John present God as the gardener and us as the potential crop. Jesus reminds us that he is the true vine, the source of all nourishment and growth.

My grandfather used to grow muscadines, which are a type of grape. As a child I was amazed that the puny looking vines could produce such great bunches of grapes later in the season. Like any good farmer, my grandfather ensured that his grapes had the right nutrients, the right amount of sun, and were pruned. He taught me that just because a vine had many offshoots, not all those offshoots would bear fruit. In fact, the farther the shoots were from the main vine, the less likely they were to produce fruit.

We must constantly ask ourselves if we are still connected to Jesus, the true vine. If we are not, it is unlikely we will bear fruit. We must be sure that we are getting the right nourishment as well. This includes regular giving and receiving of love and the fertilizer of God's word that promotes our growth. Finally, we must also acknowledge that there may be seasons when we feel barren and unproductive. Let us remember Jesus' words: "He removes every branch in me that bears no fruit. Every branch that bears fruit he prunes to make it bear more fruit." We may need to go through a pruning of our lives in order to free up space for growth.

Perhaps some areas of our life are crowding out the potential for growth. By abiding in God and continuing to connect to Jesus as the true vine, we will be sustained.

O Lord, giver of life, nourish our souls by your word, that we may continue to grow and bear fruit. Amen.

Often when I step up to the Table to receive Communion I remember the many saints who have gone before me, the friends and family members who taught me lessons of love and life. For me, taking Communion offers a time to reconnect and reflect on our relationships as a priesthood of believers.

Communion becomes one way to connect with Jesus as the true vine. Though our spiritual tree may have many branches, Communion brings us back to Jesus as the central vine that sustains the growth of so many others. Like a branch that cannot survive when separated from the trunk, we cannot survive when separated from Jesus. "Apart from [Jesus] you can do nothing."

Our vitality and usefulness stems from our "abiding" in Christ—both as individuals and as a community of faith. Part of our calling as Christians is to bear much fruit. But remember, Jesus does not specify what this fruit should look like.

Sometimes people look too simply at this exhortation to fruitfulness and think that they must have lots of children or become a minister or evangelize around the world. I am reminded of the passage in First Corinthians where Paul speaks of the variety of Christian gifts. We are called to acknowledge the gifts we have and share them with others. It is interesting to note that many people don't believe they have gifts at all. But most of them are not looking inward and are too focused on comparing themselves to others. Let the disciples serve as an example to us of the motley bunch of gifts that can serve God in magnificent ways. Some of them healed, some questioned, some evangelized, some fished, some washed, some sacrificed; but all found something to give. When we abide in Christ, the true vine, our ever-resourceful God will ensure our fruitfulness.

Gracious God, grant us today the insight to know what gifts we have. May we be fruitful in their use. Amen.

The Growth of Love in Our Lives

MAY 7–13, 2012 • SCOTT WAGONER

MONDAY, MAY 7 ~ *Read John 15:9-11*

Growing up as a missionary's kid and a pastor's kid, I called many places home. Each of these homes provided a place where I could dwell and abide, a place of refuge, a place to return after being away. When people ask where we are from, we refer to our home.

Jesus invites us to abide in his love for us. This deep love naturally flows from God's love for Jesus. In other words, the love God has for his son, Jesus, is the same love Jesus has for us. This love sustains, nourishes, strengthens, accepts, and affirms. This same love caused God to say at Jesus' baptism: "This is my Son, the Beloved, with whom I am well pleased" (Matt. 3:17). And this love says to you and me, "You are my son, my daughter, the Beloved. With you I am well pleased."

Often we don't choose to abide in Jesus' love. That is not where we decide to live. Our "abiding" places might be people's approval or our achievements. Sometimes we "abide" in activities or habits that simply serve to distract us from the spiritual journey. Sometimes we "abide" in a languishing soul. When we live this way, we may feel unrooted or unanchored; perhaps we just drift.

Jesus gives us a place to abide, to dwell, to live. Jesus offers a reference point for our spiritual journey. His love for you and me is that reference point. May all of our identities find a home in the love of Jesus, and may it be our dwelling place for years to come.

O God, may we abide and rest in your love and discover our true identity in you. Amen.

Quaker pastor, Deep River Friends Meeting; High Point, North Carolina

It begins with God. God's love flows into and through the heart of Jesus. Jesus, full of the love of the Father, then loves us in response to the Father's love. We are the recipients of the divine progression. But this progression of love doesn't end with Jesus. It continues on through us and toward those around us.

This love is not just a sentimental kind of love. It is a love that involves a willingness to sacrifice. Jesus reminds us that "no one has greater love than this, to lay down one's life for one's friends." We know this kind of love as exemplified in the life of Jesus. Jesus laid down his life for the world—for you and me. He sacrificed all his rights and privileges to place God's will and purposes first. God's purpose was and is redeeming love. Jesus' willingness to lay down his life opened the way for that redeeming love.

Jesus invites us to love in such a way that we also lay down our lives for our friends and for those with whom we interact. This might require sacrifice on our part; we might have to give something up. I might have to sacrifice some time or give up my need always to be in control. I might need to let go of my own agenda or lay down a meticulously planned schedule to be present in love to those around me. Our greatest acts of love don't come with great achievements but with simple acts of sacrifice and surrender.

Will we sacrifice and lay down important matters so that those around us can experience God's redemptive and restoring love? What do you need to lay down so that others are lifted up?

O God, show me today how I can lay my life down for someone close to me . . . for someone who needs my presence. Amen.

In a recent church finance meeting, I heard a statement I have heard many times: "The church is a business, and we need to run it that way." Even a church needs good organizational management and administration with healthy accountability. But, take that statement to its extreme and what you have is a functional mind-set that relies on human power and efficiency. It offers no room for relationship and a mystical sense of God's presence and leadership.

Jesus offers a different perspective. Jesus lacks interest in operating as management or the CEO. He does not look to maintain executive distance from us. Jesus calls us friends and invites us into a living relationship with him in which he lets us in on his feelings and thoughts. Jesus also lets us in on the mind and heart of God. He hides nothing from us. As his friends, we are let in on everything, and Jesus shares freely with us that which God has shared freely with him.

The key to this relationship is obedience. Not a "should-and-ought" kind of spirituality but one in which we seek to be faithful to Jesus' leading and guidance. As we obey the commands of scripture and the leading of Christ, we discover that a relationship is being formed and sustained. Jesus lets us know everything we need to know to flourish. What I need to be about is living in faithfulness to all that Jesus has shared with me.

I have to ask myself at times, *Is my spiritual life a business deal or a relationship?* A business deal simply requires transactions, but a relationship offers a sense of mutuality and intimacy. Jesus invites you and me into a relationship—a relationship that flourishes and bears fruit. In this way we grow in love, and it shows in our love for others.

O God, may I grow in my intimacy with you and may I discover the joy of living in relationship with you. Amen.

As we grow to love God, we truly desire to live faithfully in the ways of God and to obey God's commands. When some people hear the term *obey*, they immediately think of negative connotations. It feels so restrictive. It feels like a huge burden. But our scripture text informs us otherwise: "The love of God is this, that we obey his commandments. And his commandments are not burdensome." God's grace is not just about forgiveness and acceptance but also about offering us freedom through faithful living and obedience to God's ways.

Folks sometimes talk about receiving victory in their spiritual journey, but I often get a sense that it's something they think they have to achieve on their own. The wonderful promise this scripture offers is that as we obey God's commands and live faithfully in the way of God, we experience a victorious Christian life. God's ways are the way to victory and triumph in a world that is often languishing. They are the way to a flourishing life.

The word *flourishing* best describes for me God's intent for our lives and our spiritual journeys. God desires that we flourish in life and in all we do. The opposite of *flourish* is the word *languish*. When we languish we lack energy, vitality, and hope. We live but are not alive. Others might prefer to talk about living "defeated" lives. It is pretty much one and the same. An obedient life is a flourishing life. As we grow in our love for God, we realize that God's ways are *the* way.

O God, I want my life to flourish and my spiritual journey to flourish. May I be obedient to you in all ways. Amen.

FRIDAY, MAY 11 ～ *Read Acts 10:44-46*

I've seen some pretty astounding things in my lifetime. I've seen a sunset in New Mexico. I have watched in astonishment as a butterfly emerged from its cocoon and made its appearance as a colorful, beautiful creature. My experiences of being "astounded" draw me to the part of our text where it states that the circumcised believers and Peter "were astounded that the gift of the Holy Spirit had been poured out even on the Gentiles." Peter and the other believers were witnessing something they had never seen before—nor had they expected to.

Peter and the circumcised believers knew that God loved everyone, but they just couldn't bring themselves to accept the fact that those who were uncircumcised could experience the living Christ in this way. For Peter and his friends, circumcision came first. How astounding it must have been to witness the Holy Spirit at work—even in the Gentiles.

We too may find it hard to see the Holy Spirit at work in groups that differ from us. We sometimes fall into the trap of thinking that while God loves everyone, *our* particular group is exclusively anointed by the Holy Spirit. How astounding it must be when we experience the Holy Spirit being poured out even on the Baptists . . . or the Quakers . . . or the Presbyterians . . . or the Episcopalians . . . or the Catholics . . . or the nondenominational church down the street. It's then that our narrow vision of God's kingdom stands convicted.

Our growth in love challenges our narrow and exclusive understanding of the Spirit's work; we see God's presence moving powerfully among many groups. At that point we acknowledge the church as much bigger than our narrow understanding, and true fellowship can begin.

O God, expand my understanding of your Spirit's work in the lives of others. Expand my vision of your presence. Amen.

The Growth of Love in Our Lives

Counselors will often point out that one way people choose to hurt one another is by withholding. We withhold attention or affirmation, recognition and acknowledgment. In some relationships, couples withhold physical affection. Withholding signals a serious problem that requires attention; the pain has degenerated into a power struggle. Withholding is a passive-aggressive way to get the upper hand.

Peter acknowledges that the Holy Spirit has been poured out on the Gentiles. He realizes that neither he nor the other circumcised believers have the right to *withhold* from the Gentiles the public act of confession that would symbolize their transformation as well as their participation in the fellowship. "Then Peter said, 'Can anyone withhold the water for baptizing these people who have received the Holy Spirit just as we have?'" Peter orders the Gentiles baptized in the name of Jesus and then he accepts their invitation to stay for several days.

Love grows and matures when we can recognize God at work in others rather than withhold recognition and affirmation. The "other" doesn't have to be another denomination. This can be other churches within our own conference. When we compete, we withhold. When we want to get the upper hand, we withhold. When we want to be in control, we discredit and invalidate the other. God's love grows and God's reign flourishes when we recognize God's presence at work in other Christians and other churches.

Once we do that, God transforms our hearts and lives into places of hospitality. Rather than exclude people, we, like Peter, can invite them in.

O God, help me not to withhold when I have the power and opportunity to offer recognition, validation, and affirmation. Amen.

Ayoung girl sang on a talent show. Her amazing voice made her an overnight sensation. The song became a hit on You-Tube, and everyone posted it on Facebook. It was hard to imagine that such a powerful and beautiful voice came from such a young child—ten years old to be exact. For that reason she faced detractors who believed that she was just mouthing the words while someone else's voice played in the background.

Sometimes I realize that when I worship, often I'm just lip-synching. I mouth the words, but they are not really my words or my voice. They do not come from my heart. I just go through the motions or sing an old song. Nothing new has happened to me or touched my heart.

Psalm 98 is a psalm of worship. The first verse invites us to sing a new song to the Lord. Singing reminds me of moments of worship and tender moments of experiencing God's presence. We sing and worship because of the marvelous things God has done for us. God rules all of creation! So the earth sings! The trumpets and horns sound. The sea joins in; the hills sing, and the floods provide the rhythm section! Creation's worship is a response to God's coming judgment. No fear of God's righteous judgment here.

When I am conscious of my pretense, I pray for a new heart and a new song. As I begin to contemplate the marvelous gifts God has given me and God's marvelous grace and mercy in my life, a new song comes forth. Then I welcome—with all of creation—God's coming to judge in righteousness and equity. I join the hills, the floods; I toot my horn! I am no longer lip-synching; I am worshiping in spirit and in truth.

O God, may the song of my heart be a new song and not an old song played over and over again. May I worship with a renewed heart and a joyful soul. Amen.

"Now Choose"

MAY 14–20, 2012 • JENNIE CHURCHMAN

MONDAY, MAY 14 ~ *Read Psalm 1*

Psalm 1 serves to introduce both the Psalter and the spiritual life. It presents us with two options: we can follow the advice of the wicked or we can choose the path of God. Clearly this does not constitute much of a choice. Who would choose the advice of the wicked? That way is one of darkness and evil, cruelty and revenge. The path of God is light and goodness, mercy and grace. Of course we'll choose door number two; we're not stupid. Ah, but we are human, and that is the problem.

We hit our stumbling block in the very first verse: "Happy are those who do not . . . take the path that sinners tread." But what other path is available? We cannot take even one step in this life and not be on that well-worn trail because we are all sinners. We sin daily. We sin spectacularly and quietly. We sin intentionally and thoughtlessly. We cannot avoid the path that sinners tread because it is life—real, human life. So has this psalm—and God—set us up for failure?

By no means! All of us travel on Sin Boulevard, but another meets us there as well. Who might that be? This psalm points the way. "Happy are those [whose] . . . delight is in the law of the LORD." In other words, happy are those who delight in the Word of God. This Word gives our lives direction, accompanies us day and night, and transforms our wallowing into flourishing by the ever-flowing streams. This Word is a grace-filled gift to everyone on the very human path of life.

God of clarity, empower us through your Word to choose the path of life. Amen.

Pastor, The Way at Northway Christian Church; Dallas, Texas

The possessive pronouns in this passage are striking: *yours, mine.* "All mine are yours, and yours are mine," Jesus prays. Yours. Mine. Whom is Jesus talking about? The disciples. This prayer comes at the Last Supper after Jesus has washed his disciples' feet, foretold Judas's betrayal, given the new commandment, and preached a passionate final sermon. Now Jesus prays for his beloved ones.

That alone is heart-stopping. I have often envied the disciples for the time they had with Jesus; this scene is no exception. What must it be like to have Jesus pray for you? How overwhelming. I bet they couldn't even breathe. I bet their hearts were racing and their eyes were wide with bewildered wonder. I bet they were just starting to settle in to a spirit of prayer when Jesus' words began to sink in: "I have made your name known to those whom you gave me from the world."

The disciples surely knew from the first day they met Jesus that he was a gift from God. His wisdom, his manner, his spirit left no room for doubt. But with these words, Jesus makes the stunning statement that the disciples are gifts to him! In the face of such a proclamation, there is really nothing to do but fall on your face and cry out, "My Lord and my God, I am not worthy."

"Oh, but you are," Jesus says to his disciples then and now. You are. You are fearfully and wonderfully made. You are called and empowered. And you are mine. I need you to carry on my work. I need you to pass on to others the wisdom I have shared with you. I need you to love one another as I have loved you. I need you to be the gift to the world that you are meant to be.

God of grace, awaken our hearts to your reality: we are worthy. Amen.

Our culture highly values belonging. From the youngest ages, we feel pressure to fit in. No child wants to be the odd one out or the last one picked. Adolescents are the fiercest advocates of conformity, but even adults are not immune. Be honest. Haven't you occasionally worried about being left out? Some of this worry comes instinctively. Being social animals, we find that the "pack" gives us a measure of security. Belonging to the world is the way of the world.

But it is not the Jesus way. He makes that clear here: "They do not belong to the world, just as I do not belong to the world." As Christ's disciples, we are not supposed to fit in or belong. Jesus expects that our Godward orientation will make us outsiders, outcasts, strangers in a foreign land. We receive protection by and orientation to a name not certified by the world. Great. Our gut says, "Conform," but our Christ says, "Don't." What are we supposed to do with that?

Choose Jesus. The alternative is the path Judas chose. Now I realize the text says Judas was "destined to be lost," but let's debate this Gospel's theology another day. Clearly Judas chose the way of the world. He chose to conform, to succumb to fear, to kowtow to power, to lust after money. I feel for Judas. He seemingly never understood what Jesus could offer him. In the face of danger, Judas ran to the pack when he should have turned to the Good Shepherd.

Jesus makes no secret about the reality of evil. Some of that evil is obvious; much is insidious. When we choose the cares of the world over the call of the Good Shepherd, we lose our way and find ourselves in the dangerous places. Christ longs to protect us, but we must willingly cling to him. Will that make us outsiders? Indeed. But we will be safe in the fold.

God of the safe places, remind us to cling to you. Amen.

THURSDAY, MAY 17 ~ *Read Acts 1:1-11*

ASCENSION DAY

The disciples still don't quite get it. Throughout Jesus' ministry, many fell into the popular thinking that the messiah would be a warrior sent to overthrow mighty Rome and thus save his people. While Jesus' crucifixion no doubt puts a damper on the messianic hopes, his resurrection surely fanned the flames of their zeal. "He conquered death? Now he'll vanquish our enemies!"

Even after forty days of intense instruction about the kingdom of God, the disciples still misunderstand: "Lord, is this the time when you will restore the kingdom to Israel?" Did you catch that? They want to know if Israel will now be independent again. Jesus had said "kingdom of God," but all they heard was politics. The disciples want justice and freedom for the people, but their vision is too limited. God's kingdom stretches far beyond the confines of Judea. It reaches into Samaria and to the ends of the earth. In other words, God's kingdom is not only for them; it is also for Samaritans and Gentiles. God's kingdom is for all.

While the disciples process this information, Jesus is lifted up and carried away from them. They stare after him with mouths gaping and heads spinning. "What do we do now? He was the one. Now he's gone again, and we're not any closer to the kingdom God promised. We can't do it alone."

Here is good news: they are not alone, and neither are we. The power of the Holy Spirit urges Christ's disciples on. It keeps our focus on the things of God rather than the things of this world. It gives us the courage to seek justice and the strength to work for freedom. It leads us out of our comfort zones and into the places Christ calls us to go.

God of power, expand our vision and move our feet to do your will. Amen.

"Now Choose"

For me the standout word in this passage is *testimony*. The epistle writer repeats that word or some derivative seven times here. The Greek word is *martyria*, literally meaning "witness." Of course, this conjures up images of *Law and Order* and John Grisham, but biblical testimony is much more than a courtroom scene. Even if you've never studied Greek, you will recognize the word *martyr* in this ancient root. Biblical testimony—biblical witness—means taking a stand with your life.

The first apostles regularly put their lives on the line for their faith. They boldly proclaimed Christ to the indifferent, the skeptical, and even the hostile. They left their families, sidelined livelihoods, offered resources, and sacrificed physical well-being to testify to their faith in Christ. What gave them the courage to do it?

The answer lies in their hearts. "Those who believe in the Son of God have the testimony in their hearts," First John promises. This witness—this Word—lived in them as part of them It pulsed through their veins, becoming the lifeblood of their conviction. I believe this heartfelt conviction gave them the strength and stamina to be bold evangelists for Christ.

We have it too. The testimony of God lives in our hearts. But the question is this: are we willing to share it? It seems to me that we twenty-first-century Christians have become a little lethargic. Our pulse has slowed; our blood has thickened. Perhaps it's the absence of danger. In this time and place, we can testify to our faith without much threat of bodily harm. But instead of invigorating us, that safety has sedated us.

It is time to wake up, get out there, and make a difference. All around us are lonely and longing people who could use the life we know. But first we must share it.

God of courage, awaken in us the passion for your life. Amen.

W hat a turnaround for Peter. Just a little more than a month earlier, scripture presented him in a different light. He lurked in the shadows, following the arrested Jesus at a distance. Then he vehemently denied that he knew Jesus. Even at the empty tomb, Peter did not fully understand. He ran to the tomb—you have to give him credit for that—he looked in, he was amazed. But then he went home. Home? How could he possibly have gone home after that?

But now Peter stands up among the believers. He finds his voice and accepts his call. He claims his identity as "the Rock," and now he acts like the sure foundation Jesus expected him to be. Peter has finally put his gifts for ministry into action. He has emerged as a leader within the fledgling Christian movement.

Now recall Judas's story. Jesus called him too. We don't know anything about Judas's call experience. We don't know if Jesus had a special name for him. But we can know this: Jesus saw something in Judas. He invited him to be one of the Twelve. What was his gift? We'll never know because Judas forfeited his gift.

It is tragically ironic that Peter, himself a guide for this group of believers, identifies Judas as the one "who became a guide for those who arrested Jesus." Both men are leaders. Peter's path has led to life; Judas's to death. What a sad end for a once-promising disciple of Jesus Christ.

What about our gifts? Obviously we have them because Jesus has called us to be his disciples. Will we stand up, find our voices, and embrace our gifts—or will we forfeit them? The choice is ours.

God of patience, forgive us for being slow to embrace our gifts;
give us courage to stand up and claim them. Amen.

Y ou could call Matthias the forgotten disciple. His name is not one we ask our children to memorize, and his story is not one we often tell. Jesus himself did not call Matthias, but that doesn't make him any less a disciple. He still chose to follow Jesus, leaving home and work behind. He experienced Jesus' entire ministry, from baptism to Ascension. He was just as much a witness to the Christ-event as the eleven remaining disciples.

That makes him a fitting model for us. As those born late in time, we find ourselves at a disadvantage. We were not there for Jesus to call us in person. We were not there to experience the Gospel events firsthand. But like Matthias, we have still chosen to follow Jesus, leaving our own agendas behind.

But Matthias is more than a role model; he is a trailblazer, the first in a long line of ordinary, largely nameless disciples who chose to accept the call. Matthias didn't have to accept this responsibility. He could have said no and returned to the safety of his ordinary life. But he did not. The Jesus story so moved him that he wanted to ensure that others heard it too.

Because of his faithfulness, we also have become witnesses to the Christ-event. While we weren't there in person, we know Jesus because men and women like Matthias introduced him to us. Christianity has spread by one person telling another person about Jesus. Our movement could have died out with the last of the Twelve, but it did not because of Matthias and countless others who followed him.

The name Matthias means "Gift of Yahweh." His gift to us is nothing less than our identity as disciples of Jesus Christ.

God of good news, empower us to be Matthias for the next generation. Amen.

Come, Holy Spirit

MAY 21–27, 2012 • SUSAN MUTO

MONDAY, MAY 21 ~ *Read Acts 2:1-13*

The day that will mark the birthday of the church had come, but no one knew what to expect. It would not begin with a gentle breeze but with a violent wind. What happened next would transform the lives of the apostles and send them where they would not have chosen to go. Tongues of fire settle on their heads and redirect their powers of speech so that all who hear them understand. The crowd responds not with belief but bewilderment. How can these relatively uneducated Galileans address people from many lands and be understood? Their words of power can change lives. Should the people bow in awe or sneer?

Let us imagine ourselves in that crowd of people torn between devotion and disbelief. What would it be like to hear for the first time of Jesus Christ, who died, is risen, and will come again? Would we accept this awesome revelation or demand logical answers to our incredulous questions? Would our response to the coming of the Holy Spirit have been doubtful or full of delight?

This event reminds us of how great the leap of faith really is. The revelation we are inclined to take for granted ought to evoke both fear and trembling. Faith is a gift that defied understanding on the part of these first Christians and that still takes us beyond what eyes can see or ears hear. The message conveyed at Pentecost penetrated the barriers erected by doubt and from that moment on changed the world.

Come, Holy Spirit, illumine our minds with the light of faith. Draw us past perplexity that we may ponder our personal calling and be enkindled by your love. Amen.

Dean, Epiphany Academy of Formative Spirituality; Pittsburgh, Pennsylvania

Peter, the betrayer of Jesus, who became the rock on which Jesus would build his church, speaks with authority. Flanked by the apostles, he addresses the crowd's concern. No one among them is drunk. They have never been more sober. He reports that at nine o'clock that morning the Spirit hovered over them with tongues of fire, reformed them from within, and made them messengers of the Most High. Not with his own words but with those of the prophet Joel, Peter explains what happened. Let us listen to this prophecy as if for the first time, personalizing its declarations, each according to his or her gifts.

We may be young or old, male or female, slave or free, Gentile or Jew and yet be designated by the Divine as prophets who refuse to be satisfied with the status quo. Life as we know it takes another turn. Nature itself records the end of one era and the beginning of another. This transformation will take us with Jesus from the agony in the garden, through the scandal of the cross, to the glory of Easter morn. Blood, sweat, fire, smoke, and mist—these and other symbols of turmoil point to the change that earth and its inhabitants are about to undergo. With the coming of the Spirit, our salvation is at hand.

As the apostles were given a new start by the Holy Spirit, so too must we become Pentecost people, shunning all projects of self-salvation and letting God be God in our lives. Our posture becomes one of abject humility, for only when we bow down before the Most High and call upon God's name can we detach ourselves from all forms of idolatry and make a radical commitment to charity.

Come, Holy Spirit, pour upon bare heads and bruised hands the balm of salvation. Anoint us with the oil of gladness that we may have the courage to proclaim that Jesus Christ is Lord. Amen.

This psalm ebbs and flows between observations of nature, God's first revelation, and our response to them with childlike wonder. From the most minute grain of sand to the magnificence of the stars, God's handiwork defies description. No human mind can fathom the beauty and order found in the universe. Only the wisdom of God could have calibrated the mysterious movements of the heavens and the earth, their violent upheavals and subsequent restorations.

Stand at the edge of the ocean and try to imagine the creatures inhabiting it and every crevice of creation. Look at the sand crabs crawling swiftly to safety as seagulls swoop to have their fill. From killer whales weighing tons to bait fish light as a feather—all that God has made, great and small, gives praise to the Almighty and looks on high for sustenance and protection.

So generous is the Divine, so loving and reliable, that it hurts us when God seems to turn away. This apparent absence, though usually a sign of God's deeper presence, leaves us feeling as if this bout of aridity will never end. Our hands and hearts are empty. When will the Holy fill them?

We respond to this divine-human game of hide-and-seek with heartfelt prayer. We beseech God to renew the face of the earth; to let us plant seeds of faith, hope, and love in family life, church, and society; to gather us around the Communion table to share the bread and wine that nourishes us in body and soul. With every breath we pray that God will send the Spirit to grace us anew. Only then can we integrate sanctity and service, worship and work, presence and participation in fidelity to our calling in Christ.

Come, Holy Spirit, and form us into the people of God we were meant to be. Discard our old, unfruitful selves. Let us not die and return to dust before we have been transformed by you. Amen.

This part of Psalm 104 contains three petitions, all signifying the meaning of mature faith. The first is at once simple and profound. With the psalmist we acknowledge our deepest intentionality: that the glory of the Lord will endure not for a while but forever; that the grace of God will not be here today and gone tomorrow like a reed blowing in the wind but that it will last from the beginning to the end of time. Praise the Lord!

In the second petition, we ask God, despite our sinfulness, not to forsake the works of God's hands that span the vastness of creation. Flawed though our vision may be, we cannot help but behold their beauty. Even in the face of natural wonders ranging from volcanic eruptions and violent storms to lush rain forests and flowing streams, we acknowledge with joy that God's providence prevails. Our main duty is not to lament our losses but to adore and praise the Lord.

We ask thirdly that this meditation on the wonders of creation, complemented by the admission of our own littleness, be found pleasing to God. We can choose to grumble about life's limits, but a better choice would be to rejoice in the Lord and trust that God's ways are not our own. Our place is to pray that the good may prevail and the evil perish while knowing full well that final judgment is God's alone to give. Our duty is not to label anyone as deserving of ultimate condemnation, for only God can read the secrets of a person's heart. Our role is to defer to Divine Wisdom and say, "Bless the LORD, O my soul."

Come, Holy Spirit, and teach us how to adopt the mind of God. Convert our hearts that we may turn from what is false and follow the path of truth. Put on our lips the words the psalmist uttered: Praise the Lord! Amen.

The readings so far have been pointers to the apostle Paul's declaration that the whole of creation—wind and rain, seas and mountains, fields ripe for picking and deserts plagued by drought—all that has been made and held in being by God, especially humankind, has groaned for the day of the Lord. The groan that arises, at times against our will, signifies that there is another transformation we must undergo—from the alienation of sin to the adoption by grace.

For Paul and for us the hope of salvation is what has kept us from despair. Fortified by this virtue, we wait for the coming of the Lord with patience and unshakable trust. Seeing our sincerity, God mercifully sent us an Advocate who assures us that though we are weak in power we are strong in faith. When no words of prayer rise to our lips, we can proclaim the truth that we are not alone. When we do not know how to pray, the Paraclete intervenes and prays in us "with sighs too deep for words."

All too often our minds become clouded with endless questions and confusing responses. Our attempts to reach self-perfection come to naught. Now is the time to descend from the distractions of a busy mind to the longings of a faithful heart. Here we ponder the unique communal call God intended for us from the beginning. Here the Spirit draws us to conform to Christ in obedience to the will of the Father. We make this intercession in abandonment to God's providential plan for our lives. Though we may not understand how it will unfold, knowing that the Spirit prays in us is enough to assure us that a Divine Light will be our guide.

Come, Holy Spirit, and remove whatever obstacles prevent us from hearing and heeding the call to be holy. Teach us to say with Jesus, "Yes, Father, your will, not mine, be done." Amen.

In these unforgettable words from the Farewell Discourse, Jesus announces that he will go to the Father. Sensing the fear in his friends, Jesus assures them that he will not leave them to fend on their own. The Spirit will be with them wherever they are and in whatever they do.

What they cannot know at this tender moment of having to say good-bye to Jesus is that on Pentecost the promise of the coming of the Advocate will be fulfilled. Then bickering among them will have to cease. They may suffer due to their commitment to discipleship, but many converts in and beyond the house of Israel will be baptized by them. Instead of being overwhelmed by the demands made on them by conformity to the cross, the disciples will embrace them. They will come to know the Father, the Son, and the Holy Spirit in the intimacy of the Trinity.

In these final declarations, Jesus proclaims the distinctive doctrine of Christianity—the revelation of one God in three persons—a truth no other faith (neither polytheistic nor monotheistic) teaches. Having been with Jesus from the beginning of his public life, his followers know the meaning of faith not merely from an informational but from a formational perspective. Because their faith was weak, Jesus performed miracles that amazed their minds and moved their hearts. They marveled at his explanations of the teachings of the prophets. They witnessed the futility of the attempts initiated by treacherous foes to trap him. Though his departure has been foretold, Jesus comforts them as he has always done. Because they are his friends, there is no need for them to worry. The Spirit will inspire the words and witness they need to draw their listeners to a new way of life, pleasing to the Lord.

Come, Holy Spirit, and lead us where Jesus Christ asks us to go. Let us find the courage to testify to the saving power of his word. Amen.

PENTECOST SUNDAY

At the end of his earthly life, Jesus unveils the truth that all shall be one in him. This underlying unity is the fruit of our intimacy with the Trinity. The love between the Son and the Father outpours itself in the Spirit whose presence Jesus communicates to us as his lasting legacy.

The Spirit, who will glorify him, will give us the strength to illumine minds, uplift hearts, and transform lives—all thanks to the grace of God. Diverse as this burgeoning faith community of ours may be, what we, its members, have in common is our belief in Jesus Christ as our Savior and our God. No alien power will prevail against the church he came to establish. Our love for one another will be its citadel of strength and its witness to unity in diversity.

The knowledge of redemption entrusted to us will be passed on from age to age by all who have ears to hear and eyes to see. As believers blessed by the Spirit of truth and encouraged to share with others all that Jesus taught us, we will continue to grow in faith through the power of his word.

Then and now it is the commission assigned to every Christian to glorify God and to declare in word and song, in silent witness and bold proclamation, the revelation for which Jesus gave his life for the good of the world. We are to humble ourselves as he did and practice the art and discipline of self-emptying love. Only then can we hear the call to follow the Master despite the cost of discipleship. To be an epiphany of God's presence wherever we are is not a duty but a privilege.

Come, Holy Spirit, and radiate through our finitude the infinite goodness and mercy of God. Teach us to see in every obstacle a formation opportunity. Lead us to eternal peace and joy in oneness with the Trinity. Amen.

Becoming "Anew"

MAY 28–JUNE 3, 2012 • R. SCOTT SULLENDER

MONDAY, MAY 28 ~ *Read Isaiah 6:1-8*

Isaiah's call to prophetic ministry begins with a vision, a vision of God's holiness and majesty, which prompts Isaiah to cry out, "I am ruined! For I am a man of unclean lips, and I live among a people of unclean lips" (NIV).

In his contrite state, Isaiah receives a vision in which he sees "a live coal" touching his mouth and the accompanying words: "your guilt is taken away and your sin atoned for" (NIV). God touches the heart of Isaiah's problem, his "lips." God's forgiveness is like a precision-focused laser. We tend to prefer to confess in generalized terms on Sunday mornings. Isaiah names his own sin specifically, and God directs divine grace like a laser.

Notice too the phrase "your guilt is taken away." His sin has been forgiven or "atoned for" (NIV). It does not say that Isaiah has been made sinless, only that his guilt has been erased. Isaiah might very well continue to have problems with his lips from time to time. He is not and will never be a perfect person or a perfect servant of the Lord. But God releases him from the burden of his obsession, from the compulsion to be clean. With this release comes the power of renewal and the promise of transformation.

We are all subject to the temptation to turn religion into an obsession to be pure or clean or whatever the modern equivalent might be. God in God's grace does not ask that we be perfect but that we acknowledge our sinfulness and receive forgiveness.

I surrender to you, O God, my desire to be perfect, and rely instead upon your grace in all things. Amen.

Professor of Pastoral Counseling at San Francisco Theological Seminary; author

"Here am I; send me!" reverberates through religious history as a model of a grateful, unconditional, voluntary desire to serve. This desire to serve is born of inner transformation—an outgrowth and result of the process of spiritual renewal described in verses 1-7.

Out of this experience of renewal, Isaiah's eyes are opened and he hears the voice of the Lord with fresh ears. "Whom shall I send, and who will go for us?" One of the first results of spiritual renewal is ears that now hear and eyes that now see what was perhaps there all along but now comes into focus.

Well, that's obvious, thinks Isaiah. *That's a no-brainer!* "Here am I; send me!" He wants to serve. He wants to go. He does not doubt that he can do it. He does not know what the assignment is, nor does he know the details of the logistics, compensation package, or employment status. He is . . . just . . . willing to go. "Send me!"

Forgiveness leads to service. Inner healing leads to outward ministry. Spiritual renewal leads to faithful action. Not only does spiritual renewal lead to service, but we might even dare to suggest that the process of transformation is incomplete without service. Inner transformation is incomplete without an outward manifestation.

Yet, the mystery of faith is this: faithful service will lead us back to spiritual renewal. The more we serve, the more we will again and again be drawn back to our inner life. Spiritual renewal and service mutually reinforce each other, making our journey in faith an ever-growing circle, an ever-enriching experience of grace.

Renew my heart, O Lord, so that I too might be your servant, might respond with a grateful heart to your grace. Amen.

Stand on a mountaintop and watch a passing summer storm. In a warm summer evening, hear the cracks of thunder as the night sky suddenly becomes as bright as daytime. Even on the prairie or on the Gulf coast, watch from a distance the destructive and frightening power of a tornado or hurricane. Primitive humans stood in terror when such storms approached. They feared the storms and yet were fascinated by them, knowing they brought life-giving rains.

The psalmist sees God's sovereign power on display in the storm. He does not so much fear the storm as he has transformed the storm into an experience of God's majesty and power. Fear has been transformed to awe, even reverence.

There is a close connection etymologically and theologically between fear and reverence. These complex emotions are interwoven and related: fear, holy, adoration, faith, and fascination. We are afraid of the storm and yet strangely attracted to it, fascinated by it, in awe of it.

We Christians, so enmeshed in the love of God as we are, get a bit uncomfortable with the phrase "fear of the LORD." Yet Proverbs says that the fear of the Lord is the beginning of wisdom. In what ways might we have a healthy fear of the Lord?

The Holy One of Israel is a God of both love and power; the blending of those dynamics gives our faith a sense of wonder and urgency, which is unique and rare in this technological and scientific age that wants to explain away the mysterious and the awe-ful.

May I find you, O God, in all of the storms of my life, by transforming my fear into awe. Amen.

S o who or what are we humans? Are we animals with unique self-consciousness? Are we material beings, fully rooted in nature, with a spiritual capstone? Or are we essentially spiritual beings, temporarily housed in a material frame? It is not just a philosophical question. How we understand ourselves informs our values, our sense of worth, and the meaning we assign to life. Is human life a collection of material things and material pleasures, or are meaning and joy in life found more in the intangibles of life, like love relationships, purposes, ideas, morality, and consciousness?

We who live in Western industrial nations are more comfortable, richer, and more secure than any other portion of humanity has ever been. Are we any happier, more content than our forebears or those who live with less in the world today? If not, is it so because we have bought the idea that we are primarily material beings?

Paul contrasts life in the flesh with life in the Spirit. He puts a moral spin on this age-old debate, but consider his dualism first as an identity question. What are you? Material or spiritual? He suggests that if we see ourselves primarily as material beings, we will die. Surely he means that literally, but he may also mean it spiritually. When we live for material values, we miss a good portion of life's loveliness. What do you identify as the "deeds of the body"? In your experience, how does living "according to the flesh" take over your commitment to living according to the Spirit? The process of becoming anew includes a clear understanding of our essential nature and what really matters in human existence. Our indebtedness to God demands a life of the Spirit.

Remind me daily, dear Jesus, of my essential nature as a child of God—in the world but not of this world. Amen.

FRIDAY, JUNE 1 ~ *Read Romans 8:14-17*

As I get older, I find that I am becoming more like my father. People say that I look more like my father. I find myself saying things that sound just like what my father said to me when I was a child. I find myself adopting some of the attitudes and values of my father. Like father, like son.

The power of family links to influence us in subtle and obvious ways is strong. The influence can be positive or negative. Some traits or genes we would prefer not to inherit, like a temper or a predisposition to diabetes. I might like to inherit my parent's patience or a gift for music.

Paul suggests that we have a spiritual father since becoming Christian. We have been adopted by God, grafted into a new family tree. When we cry out to God, using the intimate and familiar phrase "Abba," the same salutation Jesus used, it is as if our very souls know that we are God's children. That's the proof! Our souls know at the deepest levels to whom we belong.

As children of God, will we inherit many of the traits and assets of our spiritual parent? Paul counts on it. Paul hopes that just as we tend to inherit the traits of our earthly parents, so too we will inherit the traits of our spiritual parent and our brother, Jesus Christ. With age and spiritual maturity, we will gradually become more like God. We can slow or facilitate this process by our faith and its practice.

Jesus had no biological children, but he has millions of spiritual brothers and sisters. In this sense, we are all "heirs of God." The link is no longer biological but spiritual. Is there a family resemblance? What spiritual genes have you inherited through your adoption into the family of God?

Create your likeness in me, O God, so that I might truly bear the mark of your family. Amen.

We are all Nicodemuses! We are all seekers. We seek someone who can help us become anew. Perhaps we are tired of our lives, tired of our bad habits, tired of our negative thinking, tired of our chronic health issues, tired of our unfulfilling job, even tired of our family. We long for something new. We have tried various new gadgets, new clothes, new hairdo, new car, new vitamins, maybe even a new family, but at last nothing is really new. We realize that *we* are the problem. *We* are the ones who need to be born again, made anew.

Jesus tells all of the Nicodemuses of the world that we must be born anew. We must have a spiritual rebirth. It is not enough to try to change the wineskins; we need to change the wine. That requires an inner transformation.

The image of rebirth is a radical one. It suggests that we must start over again, start life over again, start counting our birthdays over again. It suggests that being a Christian or walking in Jesus' way is really countercultural. Most of the world is going that way . . . and you are going this way. You have taken the road less traveled. We have begun to become anew.

As familiar as we might be with verse 3, notice the second half, "Truly, truly I say to you, unless one is born anew, he [or she] cannot see the kingdom of God" (RSV). Being born anew has something to do with "seeing" things differently. Rebirth involves a matter of new eyes—new ways of perceiving, thinking, and understanding. New eyes allow us to see something we do not currently see or perhaps ignore something we focus on too much now. Same life, same body, same job, but a new way of seeing it all. I see now what I had been blind to before.

O Lord, as you opened the eyes of the blind, open my eyes that I might experience rebirth every day in countless ways. Amen.

Martin Luther called John 3:16 the "gospel in miniature." It does capture a brief and precise summary of the Christian claim, at least from the Johannine perspective. It is also an amazing promise.

Sometimes I reduce this summary verse even further, down to just two words: a noun and a verb. "God . . . gave." That says it all too! God, the creator and ruler of the universe, beyond most human experience and explanation, without compulsion, force, or guilt, *gave*. Why? We believe the nature of God is to give. The giving comes as an act of self-revelation, of opening up and becoming vulnerable. When we give, we take the initiative. When we give, we make ourselves vulnerable.

Giving and *loving*: similar words, spelled similarly and similar in meaning. We cannot love without giving. We cannot give without loving. When we give to others, it implies love, assuming that the giving is freely done. When we truly love someone, we cannot help but give to him or her. The more we give, the more we love. The more we receive love, the more we want to give back. A rising crescendo of loving and giving!

Clearly, inner transformation is a gift, something God does for us. We do not earn, accomplish, or even figure it out. Conscientiously performed religious practices cannot alone create the kind of inner transformation we seek. We receive it.

God wants us to be made anew, to be the people we were created to be. God is in the business of human transformation. The measure of an authentic faith is transformation, an inner transformation.

Help me, Lord, let down all of my defenses and barriers, receive your amazing gift of salvation, and begin anew the process of inner transformation. Amen.

Love of God in Worship and Life

JUNE 4–10, 2012 • R. CHARLES PERRY

MONDAY, JUNE 4 ~ *Read 1 Samuel 8:4-20*

As I write, South Africa has been preparing to host the Soccer World Cup. For weeks the media has been full of stories and comments about the World Cup and, to a certain extent, it has dominated the country.

Sometimes sports, money, success, and even family become our gods. We hear the word of the Lord coming to Samuel, "They have forsaken me and worshipped other gods" (REB). Samuel warns the people that they will lose their freedom if they persist in having a king. In the end he was proved right, for Saul ultimately failed as a king.

The warning of Samuel to the Israelites is a warning to us, not about kings and presidents but about the gods we worship other than the one true God. When we go off after other gods—which we can easily do because it is the way of the world—we lose touch with the God who has given us new life.

We can take several measures to avoid falling into the trap of worshiping other gods. The first is to worship God with the whole of our lives. The second is to remain within the fellowship of God's people, the church. Too often I have seen people drift away from the fellowship of the church and become slaves to the gods of the world. A third measure requires our active engagement for God in the world. By getting our hands dirty, we may keep our minds focused upon God.

God, I confess that at times I do not worship you as I ought to. Forgive me, and strengthen me inwardly and spiritually that I might faithfully serve and worship you. Amen.

Retired minister of the Methodist Church of Southern Africa

Hymns and songs of praise and thanksgiving are part of most Christian services of worship. Quotations and references to the Psalms feature prominently in many hymns and songs, and a psalm is often read during the time of worship.

In this psalm the psalmist bows down in humility and love before God, praising God for God's faithfulness and love. The psalmist acknowledges that God answered his call and has made him bold and strong.

We would do well to emulate this approach when we come to worship God. Our God is deserving of praise and thanksgiving. We might offer that praise and thanksgiving through singing, prayer, being quiet before God, and /or through our giving.

In congregational worship we come together to worship God and, in doing so, we take to heart the approach of the psalmist and bow down before God in humility. Likewise we acknowledge God's faithfulness and love.

We too cry out to God in our distress, and the Lord our God comes in power to embolden us and give us strength to carry on. Thus our worship takes on new meaning when we approach it in the same spirit as did the psalmist. We come, not in a spirit of what can we get out of it but what we can give to God in this time together with God's people. The ultimate praise and thanksgiving is to give ourselves to God.

Lord of life, I praise your holy name. Accept the praise and thanksgiving I offer to you and make me bold and strong to do your will. Amen.

Throughout most of my life, I lived in a country that was divided along racial lines. Each side perceived the other as the enemy. People on both sides of the divide took this understanding literally and did everything they could to destroy the other group.

The psalmist also had enemies. We don't know anything about the enemies he faced: they might have been personal enemies or even foreign countries. The thought of his enemies worries him. He seems to be encompassed about by trouble of one kind or another. Through all his troubles and the awareness of his enemies, the psalmist rests assured that God's love endures forever. He also knows that having been made by God, he will not be abandoned by the One who loves him.

We too encounter troubles of many kinds, and they sometimes rear their heads before us. Troubles come our way in the form of illness and accidents, broken relationships and tough decisions that have to be made that give us sleepless nights. Enemies come in the form of people who oppose us and people who cause unwarranted trouble for us.

In the midst of our troubles and the enmity that we sometimes feel directed toward us from others is when we need to realize God's great love for us. This love will hold onto us and sustain us through the troubles of the day.

Lord of life and love, give us strength in time of trouble. Amen.

Lay Witness Missions are built around the testimonies given by the missioners who usually come from different places and sometimes a variety of denominations. In coming to be part of a mission they give of their time and of themselves. Their prime function is to tell the local congregation what God has done in their lives and of the grace of God given to them in Christ Jesus.

This was the approach of the apostle Paul in his missionary work and in his letters to the churches. He shared his faith in Jesus, the risen Lord, with all who would listen to him. Paul had already visited the Corinthians and shared his faith with them, and now, in his letter, he urges them to do the same so that "the abounding grace of God is shared by more and more" (REB). The apostle spoke out about the resurrection of Jesus, and he assured his readers that the God "who raised the Lord Jesus to life will with Jesus raise us too" (REB).

As the apostle called upon the Corinthians to speak out about their faith, we are called to do the same. It is a faith in the risen Lord who gives new life to all who believe in him. We who follow Jesus have been given that new life. Our calling is to speak out about the risen Lord and to live as people who have been raised to life in Jesus. We do so not only to win the victory of eternal life but so that other people may hear and enjoy new life in Jesus.

Lord God, I thank you for the gift of new life in Jesus. Give me the love and courage to share that gift through my actions and words—that I may be raised to life with you. Amen.

The Soccer World Cup Final is almost upon us. Work started on South Africa's hosting the event years before the country was selected; six years of preparation have gone into making it a world-class event. As the time drew near, the momentum of excitement and expectation grew.

In this story we learn that the kingdom of God is gaining momentum because of Jesus' ministry. Crowds of people gather to hear him teach, which causes his family to hurry to save Jesus from doing anything foolish. They're ready to sponsor an "intervention." Then the scribes get in on the act and accuse him of conniving with the devil. Our Lord's ministry is indeed having an impact, as witnessed by the crowds of people and the reactions of his family and the scribes. The kingdom of God is gaining momentum.

The kingdom of God is among us; the rule or reign of God is present with us; and we long for the kingdom to gain momentum in a divided and troubled world. As followers of Jesus we have a role to play in assisting that momentum.

We begin by seeking the guidance of the Spirit of Christ and then obeying the Spirit. The kingdom is of God, not of our making. We are instruments in God's hands, and kingdom momentum requires obedient people.

We also need to live out our faith in Jesus in a world where our faith is often questioned and ignored. Yet, a "kingdom divided against itself . . . cannot stand." Kingdom living manifests itself when we bear the fruit of the Spirit of "love, joy, peace, patience, kindness, goodness, fidelity, gentleness, and self-control" (Gal. 5:22-23, REB).

God of love, may your kingdom come among us. Enrich my life with the fruit of the Spirit of Christ that I might better love you and serve you and work with you in the cause of your kingdom. Amen.

South Africa is a land of great beauty and wealth. It is a country of many peoples, most of whose ancestors came here hundreds of years ago. We also have a history of turning a blind eye to that which is sinful and wrong. Racial segregation was condoned by many for years, and acts of extreme violence were perpetrated against innocent victims in the name of freedom. Corruption and nepotism are still rife in certain quarters, and not much is done about it.

The sin against the Holy Spirit, of which Jesus speaks, is the opposite of what has happened and is happening here in my country. The sins of our past and present can be forgiven; indeed, that forgiveness is offered through our Lord's death upon the cross. The sin against the Holy Spirit, the sin that cannot be forgiven, comes when good is regarded as evil. This is Jesus' experience. The scribes consider Jesus to be possessed by the ruler of demons, which means his work is that of demons. In other words, it is evil. The scribes misperceive and label God's grace-in-action in Jesus. They not only reject it but attribute it to the devil. When the work of the Spirit is so seriously misunderstood and misperceived, then such an attitude is incapable of seeking forgiveness.

We learn to be constantly on guard in terms of our thoughts and our words. We can easily criticize or oppose that which is good because it does not suit us. The Holy Spirit reveals the truth, which serves as our touchstone.

Reflect on the truth as revealed in Jesus. Ask the Holy Spirit to reveal the truth to you and to make you aware of the good in the world around you.

SUNDAY, JUNE 10 ~ *Read Mark 3:31-35*

When my wife and I meet with family or friends, the conversation inevitably comes round to children and grandchildren. Family life is important to most people.

This passage gives the appearance that Jesus does not value his family. What might Jesus have meant when he speaks about his mother and brothers? Clearly some tension exists between his mother and brothers on the one hand, and Jesus on the other. He has left home and gone off to preach and teach. They worry about him. And yet notice that they are not "insiders." They wait outside and send in a message to Jesus. They seemingly have had no involvement in his ministry, but they worry about the rumors going round that Jesus is possessed. Jesus understands that a family can become selfish and exclusive. For him the family has expanded to include the wider fellowship of all God's servants.

My congregation hosted a Lay Witness Mission. After the final service the missioners and the local committee met for a brief farewell. The leader of the mission asked what was special about this particular congregation. The immediate reply was "Community"—a strong community of worship, fellowship, and service. It was a community of people who served God and welcomed any who came to share in that fellowship.

Doing the will of God creates that kind of family. We are all related to a wider family that cares and loves. The church can be just such a family.

Reflect upon how you can help build up the community of God's people so that all people will feel wanted and loved.

Journey to the Heart

JUNE 11–17, 2012 • YOSHIYA TAKAHASHI

MONDAY, JUNE 11 ～ Read 1 Samuel 15:34–16:1

Japan is my home country. Every now and then, I return. Whenever I go back, I enjoy seeing my family, eating Japanese food, and visiting my old teachers and friends. Going back allows me to reconnect with my roots and to remember that I had a life there. It gives me a strong sense of belonging.

Samuel goes back to his hometown of Ramah, but he feels no excitement about going home. Instead of finding a sense of belonging, he experiences what he has lost. He has stripped the blessing of kingship from Saul, and their relationship will never be the same. "Samuel grieved over Saul" as God regrets having made Saul king of Israel.

Grief is an emotional response to loss of life as it used to be and awareness that life will never be the same. Returning home Samuel experiences a sense of loss of relationship and loss of hope in the future. In the midst of his deep grief, the Lord calls Samuel, saying, "How long will you grieve over Saul?" Then the Lord tells him to leave Ramah and go to Bethlehem to anoint a new king in Bethlehem.

God does not deny our grief. But as with Samuel, God tells us that there is life beyond grief. "How long will you grieve?" We can experience hope out of grief. After hearing the word of the Lord, once again Samuel leaves home following God's call, trusting the Lord. God calls to us in the midst of grief and encourages us to see the new thing that God has in store for us.

Dear Lord, in the midst of grief, you hear our cry and call us to step out to follow you and discover your new plan for our lives. Amen.

United Methodist minister; Warren, Illinois

People call me by different names. Those who know me through my ministry call me Pastor Yoshi. My children call me Papa or Daddy. My wife calls me Yoshi or Yoshiya depending on her mood. People's relationship to me determines what name they use to address me. Just so, the people of Israel call God by various names in scripture.

Traditionally Psalm 20 is believed to have been sung in the Temple as the king prepared to go into battle. The worshipers prayed for God's protection of the king and his army. In this psalm, they invoke the name of "the God of Jacob" for protection. What relationship might this name imply between God and God's people?

When the people of Israel call upon "the God of Jacob," they remember God's revelation to Jacob, God's appearing in his dream at Bethel and promising to go with him and protect him. Jacob wrestled with God at the ford of the Jabbok, holding on until he wrested from God a blessing, a new name, and a new identity. When the people of Israel call upon the name of the God of Jacob, they claim their heritage as heirs of the covenant God made with Jacob, believing in eternal protection, identifying themselves as the people of God.

The psalmist and people beseech this God to fulfill all the king's plans, granting him his heart's desire. The worshipers affirm that God "will answer him from his holy heaven."

What names do you use to call upon God? What relationship does each name represent? What is your expectation of God related to that particular name? When have you prayed to God for "mighty victories"?

God of Jacob, hear us and respond to us when we call upon your name. Amen.

Amerian history has several rallying cries: "Remember the Alamo." "Remember Pearl Harbor." And now we remember 9/11. These words motivate and empower people to challenge the enemies who caused excruciating pain and humiliated the national pride.

The people of Israel discover their power and that of their nation not in locations but in the name of God. The psalmist sings before the battle, "Some take pride in chariots, and some in horses, but our pride is in the name of the LORD our God." The word translated as "take pride" may also be rendered as "to come to remember." The psalmist sings and calls the people of Israel to *remember* the name of the Lord God, rather than geography or military power or weapons and chariots and horses. When the people remember the name of the Lord, they remember not only what God has done in the past but look forward to a victorious future with hope.

However, many of us find it much easier to remember the negative experiences in our lives. With that remembering, we continue to ponder how to defeat those who caused us pain, humiliation, or embarrassment. But recalling the harm done to us in the past only leads to self-destruction. The psalmist calls us to remember the name of the Lord, the name of the God of Jacob. In so doing, we "come to remember," take pride in God's promise, power, identity, and character. We remember to whom we belong, and we rise and stand upright.

Dear Lord, help us remember your name, so that we can live in hope. We shall rise and stand upright in this world and the world to come. Amen.

Corn and soybean fields surround the town where I live. Here and there in daily conversation, I hear people talking about how the crops are doing in relation to the weather. They discuss how dry or wet the fields are. They talk about the moisture content in corn. Their conversations about the fields, the crops, and the weather usually end with, "Well, nothing we can do about it. We just need to wait and take what's coming."

In today's scripture passage, Jesus talks about the kingdom of God and parallels it to growing seed. The kingdom of God is like a farmer who scatters seed on the ground and forgets about them. The seeds grow without human notice or effort. The earth produces of itself. When there are full grains in the head, the farmer will come back to harvest the grain.

This parable emphasizes that the kingdom of God will come with little human effort and according to God's time. But it does not discourage human involvement. The planter *does* scatter the seed and then goes about his daily routine, trusting in God's providence. We may find it reassuring to note that the coming of God's kingdom to fruition does not depend on our efforts. We sow but do not determine the harvest. Jesus does encourage us to pay attention to the growth of the kingdom in our midst. We monitor the growth so we can participate in the harvest.

Farmers I know do not just sit and talk after planting seeds in their fields. They pay attention to their crops, checking soils, machinery, and weather regularly. When the crops are ready, they don't waste any time but go into the fields to harvest them. Are we ready for the work of the harvest? Surely God is watching and waiting to receive our help.

Lord Jesus Christ, help us pay attention to the growing kingdom of God in our midst, so that we can join in the harvest. Amen.

FRIDAY, JUNE 15 ~ *Read Mark 4:30-34*

In my denomination, many churches provide a house for the pastor who serves. In my current setting, our house, or parsonage, has over twenty trees in the yard. These trees provide shade during hot summer and protect our house from the cold and blistery wind, stopping drifts of snow in winter. A few years ago, we cut down some of the trees because they were dying. The trustees (those responsible for care of the property) planted hard maples, lilac bushes, and hydrangeas to replace those trees.

Selecting the kind of trees and flower bushes to plant and choosing locations to plant excited my family—even though we may not stay long enough to enjoy the trees and the plants fully grown. I can envision how a future pastor and family someday will enjoy the trees and plants we planted, hanging hammocks, picnicking under the shade of trees, enjoying the changing colors of leaves, smelling the scent of lilacs, and seeing the blooms of hydrangeas in the rain.

Today's reading produces in me the same excitement—and more. This parable provides a vision of the kingdom of God in the future. A mustard seed is very tiny, but it can grow into a plant about ten feet high. Using the mustard seed, Jesus describes the nature of the kingdom of God: small beginnings result in extraordinary presence, providing a shelter to all creations and creatures. The birds may safely nest. What a vision of the kingdom of God. The reign of God is in our midst and gives hope for the future. May we learn to see, taste, hear, touch, and smell the many experiences of God's reign that surround us!

God, thank you for giving us a vision of your reign that is both at hand and yet to come fully. Amen.

Paul uses the words *confident* and *confidence*. In these days, no one seems confident in anything. We don't know how long we can hold on to jobs. We don't know when our economy will come back. We have grave doubts about our political system. We are uncertain what the future will bring. Living in uncertainty makes it hard to be confident.

The Corinthian church suffered from divisions and problems. The church members openly challenged Paul's integrity and leadership. Yet in the midst of uncertainty in ministry, he felt ever confident about his faith and his call to leadership. This passage in his letter to the people of the Corinthian church reveals his unquenchable energy. He makes it very clear that differences exist between the way things *appear* and the way they *really are*. Nothing is the way it seems to be. Even though the Corinthians feel quite at home in their physical bodies and in the world, their true desire is to be "at home with the Lord." And what is the crux of Christians' ability to see and understand what is really real? Christ "died for all." Christians no longer view matters from a "human point of view." We look from the inside out. "Everything has become new!"

So what is the basis of Paul's confidence? He has experienced and understood that "the love of Christ urges us on." He chooses to "walk by faith, not by sight." Walking by faith gives him new life everyday. When the love of Christ is real in our lives, no matter how uncertain it looks from the outside, we feel confident because that love holds our heart firm and makes us new everyday.

Loving Jesus, while nothing in the world is certain apart from you, your love continues urging us to walk by faith. Amen.

After leaving Ramah, following God's direction, Samuel goes to Bethlehem. He does not know God's choice for kingship. This passage gave me the sense that Samuel, this seasoned man, is almost having to relearn how to be a prophet, the servant of God. God gives Samuel the actions and the words to say. Samuel looks for the wrong person as the new king of Israel. In the process of reorienting Samuel to be a prophet, God tells him the most important aspect to remember as the servant of the Lord, "Do not look on his appearance or on the height of his stature. . . . the LORD looks on the heart."

In Jewish-Christian tradition, the heart serves as the source not only of our emotions but also our thoughts. The heart represents not a small emotional part of us but a whole self, created in the image of God. We cannot attain the ability to look upon the heart of God and the heart of the people instantly, but it comes through a lifelong development of walking by faith.

When we walk by faith, we experience how God remembers our relationship with God as we remember and call upon the name of God. God waits for us to join the kingdom harvest as we pay attention. God acts according to God's timing, encouraging us to have hope in the future.

In the walk by faith, looking on the heart of God and the heart of all God's people, we will feel the love of God increase our confidence in God's faithfulness. God accompanies us in every step of our faith journey.

Dear Lord, may we acknowledge your presence with us; enable us to experience a new way of seeing. Amen.

God Is with Us

JUNE 18–24, 2012 • EMILY AKIN

MONDAY, JUNE 18 ~ *Read Psalm 9:9-14*

Standing in the cannon pit of a fifteenth-century fort, I could see for miles into the Atlantic. The Spanish fort towered over the harbor city. This was the stronghold for soldiers defending the city from invaders and for residents seeking safety from cannon fire. Stone walls offered protection. Stockpiled food, water, and ammunition meant that only the most overwhelming enemy could breach these defenses. But sometimes those taking refuge in such forts were defeated by disease and starvation instead of cannons and swords.

Today, few of us face the danger of invasion by a foreign army or navy. The dangers we must defend against are more spiritual than physical. Still, we erect our strongholds. We accumulate wealth to defend ourselves from poverty. Seeking higher and higher levels of education, we try to separate ourselves from the ignorant. The technology we rely on daily insulates us from discomfort and inconvenience. If we have a choice, we opt to live in secluded neighborhoods away from traffic and crime. We avoid contact with the poor and the sick. Our strongholds lead us to believe that we are safe from any danger.

But time and time again, people who have every resource to avoid danger are defeated by enemies from within: materialism, addictions, or ill health. We would fare better by looking beyond our temporal strongholds to real safety, the protection God offers all who ask for it. As the psalmist says, God does not forsake anyone who seeks God's protection. It is never too late to take refuge in God's stronghold.

Lord, give us the courage to seek your protection. Amen.

Freelance writer and church musician; living in Union City, Tennessee

Two armies prepare for battle, but they do not engage. Instead, the Philistines send their most ferocious warrior to challenge Saul's men to a one-on-one battle. Goliath is bigger, stronger, and better equipped than any of the Israelites. Saul and his men are "dismayed and greatly afraid" only because they allow themselves to be intimidated.

Actually, Saul has no reason to fear Goliath or the Philistines. Handicapped by fear and doubt, he ignores his most potent asset, the power of God. Has Saul forgotten his role as the leader of God's chosen people? Surely, he knew the heritage of Joshua, Gideon, and other generals who had led God's armies. Does he not remember God's intervention in the past?

God's help is available to Saul, but he does not seek it. He sees a giant of a man with a helmet of bronze, a coat of mail, a javelin and spear. He allows his fear to overwhelm him.

How often do we behave like Saul? Faced with our own "giant" challenges, we let fear outweigh our faith. We choose not to address our problems because we are afraid that we will not prevail. We worry about situations in our churches and communities, but we take no action to solve the problems. We convince ourselves that any action we might take would not be enough. So, we hide out in our camps, worry, and do nothing.

We can avoid making Saul's mistake. We can remember that we are God's people, and God promises help. The power of God is available to us as it was to Saul—for the asking.

Lord, we thank you for loving us enough to let us make our own decisions. Help us remember to look to you for guidance when we feel overwhelmed. May we face our challenges knowing that you are on our side. Amen.

David does not come to the battleground looking for a fight. He just comes to check on his brothers and bring them some provisions. When he hears Goliath's challenge, he has no idea this has been going on for forty days (1 Sam. 17:16). He cannot believe that this insult to Israel and God has not been answered by God's people.

Goliath seems confident that his superior size and equipment give him the advantage over any adversary. His imposing appearance and his swagger have so far intimidated a whole army. David's confidence arises from his faith that if he goes forth in God's name, God will protect him and give him the victory. He acknowledges his victories against lions and bears with help from "the living God." Saul hesitates to let David face Goliath at first, but then he clothes David in armor and straps his own sword on David. David refuses. Up to that moment, Saul has trusted in the ability and equipment of his army. But, the young shepherd boy reminds him of the army's greatest asset: God is on their side.

All of God's servants have crises of confidence at one time or another. Musicians suffer from stage fright, sometimes to the point that they are physically ill. Writers experience bouts of "writer's block," making them feel inadequate. Many pastors face an overwhelming array of duties and expectations but with scant resources. Faced with such problems, we sometimes give in to despair. We may attempt to "strap on" armor and swords to gain confidence. Yet, what we need at these times is someone like David who reminds us that our confidence is a function of our relationship with the triune God, not of our own abilities or possessions.

Lord, give us confidence in our abilities, but help us remember that our true strength is in you. Show us when and how to encourage others, and guide us as we do your work. Amen.

Both David and Goliath have confidence. But what about courage? In Goliath's case, how much courage does one need when he is much larger than any potential opponent? Or when he has impenetrable armor and the most lethal weapons at his disposal? Really, what is there to fear?

David is not even full-grown, nor is he equipped and trained for combat—but he has courage. The youngest male in his family, he is lowest on the status meter. Yet, God has designated him as the next king of Israel (1 Sam. 16:7). Chosen by God, not for his physical strength but for his faith, David demonstrates that faith. He does not need fancy weapons or armor. God served and will continue to serve as his protector.

Much has been said about David's attitude. Saul first thinks David boasts out of the brashness of youth. Some say that David does not consider the giant's size a problem. Instead, he sees Goliath as a target too big to miss. But consider this. David does not worry about standing in front of Goliath because he knows that God, the LORD of hosts, stands behind him. While the king and mighty warriors of Israel quake on the hillside, David tells Saul, "The LORD, who saved me from the paw of the lion and from the paw of the bear, will save me from the hand of this Philistine." With God as his backup, David feels certain to triumph.

As we go about our daily business, we might feel like the underdog. We might think our challenges are just too big to overcome. But, if we meet them as David did, in the name of the LORD of hosts, we will have the advantage. We can show the world that there is indeed a God who stands behind all who believe.

May we face whatever challenges this day brings with faith rather than fear. Lord, give us courage. Amen.

There's not much scarier than being in a little boat in a big body of water with wind and rain assaulting you. No matter where we live in the world, we encounter violent storms. On the coasts, it's hurricanes. In the plains, tornadoes are common. Blizzards and ice storms can be frightening too. We know that these storms will pass; but while they are in progress, we may be absolutely terrified just like the disciples.

Some of the men who shove off on this boat ride are professional fishermen, and yet they fear for their lives at the height of the storm. Surely, they have experienced such weather before. This lake is known for sudden, violent storms with damaging winds, to use today's terminology. Still, the disciples go out because Jesus requests it. When things get rough, they learn that by calling on Jesus to save them, they have actually invoked the power of God.

Today we just hunker down and wait for the storm to pass. With today's technology, we can watch storms approach on the radar and be ready to take cover if necessary. Spiritual storms like anger, fear, and doubt raise a different issue. They often blindside us. Whether these spiritual storms are caused by natural forces or by other human beings, we can be sure of one thing. God is still in command of all these forces. Jesus is in the boat with us. We believe that we will prevail when we call on God to help us.

Just as Jesus stilled the storm on the lake, we call upon Jesus to address our fears, "Peace, be still! Cease! Go away!"

Lord, when we are afraid, we want to believe you will come to our aid. Help us remember that you are present and that you will respond whenever we call on you. Amen.

It appears that the Corinthian church has some problems. The church "growers" promote a different view of things than Paul, the church planter, even questioning his authenticity as an apostle.

Paul pleads with the Corinthians first to be reconciled to God: acknowledge the magnitude of God's gracious offer! And then he asks that they be reconciled to him. He defends himself and lays out his case. He calls to their minds the many hardships he and his workers have faced to promote the ministry of Christ. They have nothing but possess everything.

Paul pleads with the Corinthians to remember what is important. He speaks to them a with a heart "wide open," challenging them to accept God's grace as well as his ministry: "Now is the acceptable time; . . . now is the day of salvation." The people could be spreading the gospel rather than wasting energy fighting among themselves. Not only do they need to accept salvation for themselves; they need to offer it to others.

Paul took the gospel into pagan cultures of crossroads and port cities of the ancient world. The Christian faith brought different expectations for morality and personal behavior, causing conflict in the lives of new Christians. Usually evangelists used a Jewish community as a starting point. Similarly, today's churches are home base for spreading the gospel of Jesus Christ. Yet, so often, disagreements over everything from doctrine to scheduling sabotage the church's mission.

Paul has done his part. The rest is up to them. "Now is the day of salvation." If Paul were to write this message to a contemporary church, I think he would say something like this. "The ball is in your court. Salvation, just do it—now!"

Lord, help us discern between tasks that are truly important and those that are mere distractions. Amen.

The psalm depicts the speaker as needy, afflicted, poor, and suffering. The psalmist has survived a near-death experience at the hands of those who hate him. But now "the wicked are snared in the work of their own hands." Like David, the psalmist remembers that these people are "only human," and they find that the living God "has executed judgment." The psalmist clearly feels vindicated: "The LORD is a stronghold for the oppressed, a stronghold in times of trouble."

Our challenges differ from the psalmist's, but we often wonder what God has in mind for us. We have our personal struggles, and we are concerned about the needs of others. Daily, we hear of natural disasters, war, accidents, disease, terrorism, and crime. Many of the world's people are oppressed and afraid just as they were in the psalmist's time. The scope of modern human suffering is indeed daunting. Our hearts break when we hear stories told by missionaries and volunteers providing relief after disasters. Has God abandoned those who suffer from poverty and disaster?

We recall the three vantage points and players within the psalm: the speaker who cries out to God, the circumstances and actions of the ungodly, and finally God, the great "equalizer." The psalmist recalls God's actions of the past and now invokes God's help—right now!—to [avenge] blood. Whether we are among the poor and fearful or among those who offer help, we have a special assurance. No matter what happens, remember John Wesley's words on his deathbed: "The best of all is, God is with us."

God, the great equalizer, help us remember those who suffer today. Show us ways in which we can relieve their misery and share your message of hope and assurance. Amen.

Health and Healing

JUNE 25–JULY 1, 2012 • C. MICHAEL GIBSON

MONDAY, JUNE 25 ~ Read 2 Samuel 1:1, 17-27

Saul and Jonathan are dead. David has lost his king and a dear friend as well. In his grief he launches into a lament that is, in a sense, an eloquent testament to forgiveness. David has good reason to be bitter or to feel victimized by Saul. David and Saul have had a turbulent and volatile relationship, but David shows no evidence of any resentment or sarcasm. He praises the strength, courage, and love of both men. Yes, the loss of Jonathan may be more keenly felt, but Saul's death is by no means given short shrift.

How much easier it is for me to bear a grudge than to forgive! It can be easier to remain a victim than to deal with my own "stuff," easier to keep replaying the offense rather than letting go graciously. I stand in awe of one who consistently rejects the easier ways.

Have you ever seen bamboo swaying in the breeze? Even in mighty winds they have a strong chance of survival because of their flexibility. They bend, sometimes very low. One who forgives has the strength of bamboo. To bear a grudge or harbor bitterness increases brittleness. When the mighty winds come, the brittle do not bend, and things can snap.

When we forgive another it does not mean that we excuse or condone the offenses, but it does free us. Forgiveness releases, frees, and empowers both the offender and the offended. David is free by his own choice. He bends low; he rises strong.

God of astounding love, grant me the freedom and grace to bend and forgive. Amen.

Faith & Play Coordinator for Friends General Conference; living in Woodbury, New Jersey

TUESDAY, JUNE 26 ~ *Read Psalm 130*

The psalmist assures us that from out of the depths, when we may feel like a nobody, when everything falls apart, when there seems to be no hope left, we can place our hope in God and wait—and God will deliver us. When we do, say, or think things that separate us from ourselves, from other people, or from God, these failures are not recorded in some heavenly logbook. Rather, God, in steadfast love, stands ready to forgive. If we but wait in hope, the psalmist says, God is trustworthy and will deliver.

This message, however assuring, is becoming increasingly harder for us to hear and practice today. "Time is money," we say, and our hectic lives often reflect that commitment, whether eager or reluctant, to this economy. Waiting may have been fine for people many centuries ago when the pace of life was dramatically slower, but we have grown accustomed to multi-tasking and to ever-newer, ever-faster technologies. We want quick fixes and instant cures, and some of us may be addicted to instant gratification as well. Faster is seen as healthier, happier, and more efficient. We do not have time to wait.

In my journey I have often experienced something wonderful that the psalmist does not mention outright but suggests. Yes, we sometimes have no choice but to wait, but God is with us in the depths while we wait. No abyss lies outside the reach of God's healing strength, power, and grace. Even when God seems absent, the divine hand is touching broken places in us, making things new. Only later may we come to see the miracles of healing that have subtly taken place within us.

God's time is not our time; we cannot afford not to wait.

Healing and forgiving God, teach me what it means to wait for you in hope. Amen.

Health and Healing

Two stories of healing are carefully woven together. A synagogue leader comes to Jesus, kneels at his feet and asks healing for his twelve-year-old daughter. A woman who has suffered for twelve years from a disease that has made her unclean and practically "dead" to religious society comes to Jesus unnoticed, touches him, and receives healing. Then, discovered, she trembles with fear and kneels at his feet. Jesus commends her faith. The synagogue leader's daughter dies; Jesus tells him not to fear but to believe. Jesus goes to his house, touches his daughter, and restores her to life and health.

Coming to Jesus, kneeling, having faith stronger than fear, touching, restoration to life . . . It is no coincidence that the two stories share these elements, these core Christian experiences. Perhaps the number twelve appears in both stories to tease us into looking for these common elements.

Core to our experience . . . I know that God loves me and that Jesus is with me. Because I have long been an active Christian, it is a given that I am a person of faith. I consider myself a contemplative, for goodness sake! But when in the past twenty-four hours have I, in courageous humility, knelt at Jesus' feet, placed complete trust in him, and put my life in his hands? What kind of healing or restoration have I requested in the past twenty-four hours?

I'll be honest. For two days I have been on a private retreat and have been practicing spiritual disciplines, but I have neglected my obvious need. Why, even when on retreat, can I so easily sidestep the essential? These familiar stories call me to mindfulness and to faithfulness today. I have some prayerful business to attend to.

What in you is dead or in need of restoration? Invite Jesus' touch. What does he say to you?

The mighty redwoods of California are nothing less than magnificent. Walking through a forest of these gentle giants I feel awed by their phenomenal age and size. They stand monumental, reaching sunward in majestic splendor.

The first time I saw one of these trees I imagined that its roots must go amazingly deep. *How else,* I thought, *could it stand so tall for so many centuries and through the vagaries of weather?* Later, I learned that the redwoods' roots do not go especially deep. The tree's strength comes because its roots spread out laterally, intertwining with roots of other redwoods and providing mutual support. The mighty redwoods rely on one another.

Paul encourages the church in Corinth to see how Christ's church is strengthened when congregations support one another. Paul pragmatically notes that the strong congregation now may need assistance later on. Giving supports the health and well-being of all.

Paul does not make the giving an obligation, but he advises the Corinthians to move forward on their initial decision, which has now warranted their desire. They are choosing to give of their own volition. Disunity becomes unity. We support one another according to our means because, like the redwoods, it is our nature as church.

We may know in our heads that this is, or should be, true. However, when we are struggling to make ends meet or, conversely, when we have found our stride and are running into a bright future, it can be hard to know this in our hearts and to live it. How easy it can be to defy our calling and focus exclusively on ourselves or on faith communities just like our own! Fortunately, those who understand interdependence set excellent examples.

Reflect on how you have been like a redwood tree. Who has set a positive example of interdependence for you?

Jairus, enjoying the privileges of being the male head of both a synagogue and a household, approaches Jesus directly and confidently as one upright man to another. Although he kneels at Jesus' feet in deference, he does not hesitate to make requests of him repeatedly. While he might be risking his reputation, he nonetheless acts from a position of power. His deepest motives are not stated, only implied. "He" then goes with "him." Does Jesus, moved with compassion, go with Jairus, or does Jairus go with Jesus to continue to plead his case?

The woman with the hemorrhage is nameless. We do not know her marital status. We do know that she has long suffered both from her condition and from the ineffective treatments of physicians and that she has exhausted all her financial resources. She is poor and ritually unclean, an outsider. Still, she is full of faith. In contrast to Jairus, she approaches Jesus surreptitiously from a position of powerlessness and exclusion. She does not address Jesus but suffers in silence. Desperation leads her to act with daring to steal healing from Jesus. He immediately takes measures to give her a voice, to bring her faith to light, and to announce her status as a daughter of Israel. Her methods had been unorthodox, but Jesus offers her not correction but affirmation and blessing.

Jesus honors Jairus's request eventually but on kingdom terms, not his own. The man of power, the synagogue leader, is made to wait until it seems painfully too late. The powerless, unnamed woman, long cut off from religious society (how long she had waited!), is attended to immediately and is revealed as a daughter of faith, every bit Jairus's equal in the kingdom.

God, teach me your kingdom ways. Turn upside-down any values, assumptions, or attitudes that hamper my faithfulness. Grant me your healing, I pray. Amen.

Jewish Christians in Jerusalem have been suffering from a drought and from persecution. The Christians living where the gospel first found expression as the church are impoverished. Paul invites Gentile Christians, who have inherited their faith from these Jewish Christians, to come to their aid.

Paul commends the Corinthians for their faith, speech, knowledge, and earnestness but urges them to excel also in generosity. Paul strives for balance and reminds the Corinthians of this principle with words from Exodus 16:18 that address God's gift of manna: "The one who had much did not have too much, and the one who had little did not have too little."

Paul, as mentioned earlier, makes this offering to the poor in Jerusalem a matter of grace rather than obligation. He does not beat the Corinthians over the head about Jesus' giving himself for them, *therefore*, they should give to others. He makes an assertion and lets the Corinthians figure out the significance.

It is hard to be giving while focusing intently on acquiring, preserving, and hoarding, whether the wealth is comprised of money and possessions, of skills, of intellectual sophistication, of grace, or of anything else. Jesus noted that material things only rust and require vigilance to prevent theft. We might say that, like manna, any gift of God selfishly hoarded putrefies and rots. Just as God provided the Israelites in the wilderness with sufficient manna, God gives each of us and our congregations all that we need, provided we share and do not hoard.

Patient God, I owe my life and health to so many people. Open my heart to deep gratitude for all who have planted seeds of faith in me, to all who have nurtured and tended me over the years, and to all who hold me in love and prayer. Give me a joyous heart and a generous and responsive spirit. Amen.

When I cry out from the depths, Christ says, "Do not fear, only believe." This does not mean "I will take away all your pain" or "I will keep your loved one from dying" or "I will undo all the injustice that has been done in this situation." It means that out of my belief and faithful witness, Christ calls me to life, to hope, and to wholeness and acceptance in the midst of pain, sickness, death, and injustice.

I may not be called to heroic action, but I am called to give, love, and respond according to my means. It may be enough to simply breathe, endure the pain, and get through the night. I may be called to show compassion on my caregiver, or I might be called to be a compassionate caregiver, as fits the occasion. I may be called to respond to the Jairuses who periodically knock at my door in desperation or to people like the woman in the miracle story who slip into my life to quickly grab a bit of something they sorely need.

Faithfully taking the path of compassion involves risk. Fear, often stronger than the actual risk, may surface. If I take action and open myself up to this person, will I be swallowed up in need? Will I get in over my head? Will I lose my privacy, my reputation, my sense of balance? Will this gobble up all of my leisure time? Giving in to fear wastes time and energy. When God calls me to respond to a particular need, things fall into place in ways I would never have anticipated. "With the LORD there is steadfast love, and with him is great power to redeem."

God, your will be done in me. Help me to listen, to discern my call, and to know the measure of my means. Amen.

The Impenetrable Fortress of Faith

JULY 2–8, 2012 • T. ANNE DANIEL

MONDAY, JULY 2 ~ *Read 2 Samuel 5:1-5*

David is anointed king over Israel. Anointing for the office is the protocol for the day. No division exists between sacred and secular. Holding an office in that society is understood as a representation of God to all peoples.

The anointing of King David generates unity among the twelve tribes. The Jacob/Israel covenant is renewed when the tribes declare that they are of the same heritage, same bone and flesh. The God of Abraham and Sarah, Isaac and Rebekah, and Jacob/Israel, they claim is the God who binds them together. For a moment the intertribal conflict ceases. The twelve tribes do not permit themselves to sacrifice security and unity on the altar of tribal or personal differences.

The qualification for the kingly office involved not only might and victories in battle but a relationship with God. God initiates or endorses the position. The recognition of God's presence and power in all that we do makes a difference in the outcome. The process may be long and painful, with many battles to fight, many unjust practices to eliminate, many family principles to construct. When we analyze life, what matter is of ultimate importance for living: to outdo each other or to honor God? A kingdom not made from the penetrable faculty of this world stands on the principle of faith and trust in God.

Lord, give me new eyes to see the materials on which you build your kingdom when we acknowledge your power and presence through faith. Amen.

Member, Conference of the Methodist Church in the Caribbean and the Americas (MCCA); pastor of Wakefield Grace United Methodist Church, Bronx, New York

David takes charge under God. He expands the city. He knows what brings such great success—the God of hosts is with him.

Johanna, an intelligent teenager I know, did not realize that traveling to a more developed country to live would present so many challenges. She applied herself to her studies. In her final examination in her native land she was the most successful student. With her accomplishment came all the accolades and recognition that she took for granted until she had to make major shifts in attitude in her new environs. No one knew about her academic success, her privileges, and her recognition, so no one regarded her. Respect had to be earned again.

Instead of becoming a loner and angry with her new setting, Johanna decides to invest her energy in the activities of her new church. She already has the introduction to church worship and general affairs, but this time she soaks herself in spirituality. She initiates activities for children and teens. She broadens her horizon by attending workshops for Christian education. She fortifies herself through Bible study, and she witnesses by distributing tracts in her community. She takes charge under God. She says in her testimony at worship that God has made her an overcomer. The God of hosts is with her, and she knows it.

Some of us might not have turned an apparent bad situation around to get the best out of it. Some of us succumb to challenges and gloom. It is never too late to start again. Take charge under God and begin to expand your horizon today.

Gracious God, we are grateful that you teach and empower us. Renew our faith today to turn every bad situation into a glorious experience. Amen.

This is not one of the many psalms attributed to David, the shepherd-king, the man after God's own heart. It is one of the eleven psalms attributed to the Korahites, the sons of Korah, the arrangers of the music, the choir. They celebrate the establishment of Mount Zion, the city of the great King David.

What great pride the psalmist attributes to a city and place dedicated for the worship of God! The landscape is described in relation to holiness, beauty, and magnificence. When David becomes king, Mount Zion becomes a symbol of human achievement and an offering to God. The Israelites offer the best of their resources: skills, natural talents, and technical knowledge. The city will attract people of all walks of life and enhance an appreciation for God's goodness and mercy. The city itself seems imbued with God's power.

The psalmist declares that God establishes the city forever. Herein lie durability, resilience, stability, and a witness on behalf of the Creator. Kings assemble to break through the fortification of the city. The city itself astounds them. Without the city's towns-people raising a weapon or exerting God's power on the city's behalf, the assembled kings tremble and fall in panic. How great is our God and how great is God's name!

We proclaim this day that nothing can bring to naught the presence and power of God that we experience in our lives and relationships. We worship knowing that we are the beneficiaries of God's faithfulness. "Great is the LORD and greatly to be praised."

Gracious God, reignite our strength to practice faithfulness in all that we seek to do. Amen.

For the psalmist, the city of Jerusalem is utterly safe and secure. He invites us on a walking tour: "Count its towers, consider well its ramparts; go through its citadels." This safe and secure city is protected by a durable and reliable God!

For all of Jerusalem's greatness, I believe in a church without walls. The basic understanding of church is a building where people worship. But we know that through baptism we become the body of Christ, so you are the church and I am the church.

Is this a rudimentary attempt by the psalmist when he says: "Your name, O God, like your praise, reaches to the ends of the earth"? God's word is not confined to the established place of worship. So let us take our freedom and run with it. Worship anywhere, worship everywhere, and worship in any form. Let not ritual stifle creativity. Let not tradition suffocate ingenuity. Let not formality destroy originality. Be flexible but maintain respect for all that our forebears labored to produce.

Walk around Zion; get out in the open air. Let the community see us at worship, for that may be the closest contact a passerby makes with his or her God. The psalmist enjoins us to tell it to the next generation. Seize every opportunity to make God's name known in public places while we travel by air, sea, or land. Create an aura of peace, and reduce the anxiety of haste while waiting in long lines.

I received my second birth while in high school. When a teacher was late for class, I opened my Bible and read openly. Now I make acquaintances on the train and the bus. When people see me reading the Bible and raise questions, I respond with my testimony to God—and I offer it in praise.

Lord, strengthen me to worship everyday and everywhere that others may have a glimpse of you and develop faith in you. Amen.

If Paul had known that he would cover such a vast audience over such a long period of time, he might have been more selective in what he wrote. Here Paul replies to critics who imply that his life is not "holy" enough. He responds by boasting in his weaknesses, not his strengths.

Paul seems to exercise a vagueness in memory—whether in the body or out of the body—that lends itself to imagination, hesitation, and vacillation. He recounts an experience of a person's going to the "third heaven." Twice he notes that only God knows. God initiates the experience, and God alone holds the true understanding of it.

When our full story of being is told, what is the difference between here and there, the already and the not yet? Whether in the body or out of the body, God knows.

This experience has a subtle effect: it prevents Paul from boasting. Paul resigns himself to the fact that God is ultimate. God is the one who holds all knowledge, the one who allows and disallows.

Paul mentions that he certainly has the credentials to boast: "exceptional . . . revelations." But to keep the focus on weakness rather than boasting, Paul has a thorn in the flesh. He asked for reprieve three times—three times his request was denied. He receives a fresh interpretation for healing—God's grace. It is all sufficient. Paul's very weakness becomes strength for God.

Sufficient for you, sufficient for me, sufficient for all. We adopt an attitude of strength simply through the sufficiency of God's grace. God's grace makes an impact in this body, this world; out of this body, out of this world.

Lord, I thank you for my weakness made strong by you. Amen.

Prophets are without honor in their hometown. Mark uses the Greek verb translated "took offense" elsewhere to depict those who begin but then fall away, those who start walking but then stumble, those who desert. Clearly the Nazareth citizens are having trouble believing that Jesus can be anything more than a hometown kid showing off. Their preconceived thoughts don't allow for their believing that Jesus can embody God's promised rule.

Jesus is not as fortunate as I am in that respect. I gratefully announce that members at Chauncey Methodist Church where I grew up still overwhelmingly support me. In my little country of St. Vincent and the Grenadines I've discovered tremendous appreciation of my ministry. I feel highly esteemed by colleagues in my work setting. But Jesus receives no honor from his folks in Nazareth. He is disqualified because his human credentials do not match his spiritual performance. He is too ordinary, and everybody knows his mother and siblings. Receptivity is low, and he can do no deeds of power there.

I wonder if the atmosphere we create today disallows deeds of power. What more could be done in our lives, our church, our school, our neighborhood, and our country that is currently disallowed because we fail to acknowledge the Christ? What other actions and commitments hamper aspects of our growth? The world is filled with possibilities. We know our spiritual parent. Our heritage is power-filled; we have only to believe.

Dear God, we do not really know what we want. Give us vision to see you leading us to new witness and deeds of power. Amen.

Few persons I know consider this text as a model for evangelism. Jesus leaves Nazareth, his place of rejection, and begins teaching—and he empowers the Twelve to cast out demons and heal the sick.

So why does Jesus give such a detailed explanation of frugality and rapidity? Is time coming to a close? Not really, for this occurred during the first year of Jesus' three years of public ministry. It is early yet.

Does this mission of the Twelve have anything to do with the earlier verses that indicate Jesus' rejection in Nazareth? Maybe, because the unbelief in his hometown seemingly amazes Jesus.

The rejection generates urgency. There is much to be done to encourage people to believe in God and in those God chooses to send. Jesus' concern reverberates rapidity. Go quickly, and see how much ground you can cover. The forces of evil are heavily entrenched. Quick job, move fast. Jesus wants everyone from his home territory to have an opportunity for salvation. After all, charity begins at home. He will soon leave Nazareth to go to Capernaum and make it his headquarters.

Home is still the hardest place to evangelize—family, colleagues, peers, friends, relatives. Familiar territory poses the greatest threat to evangelism. Let us try harder to develop a strategy and get more people on board. We might spend longer time in prayer, searching deeper for the Word in the Word of God. Pull out all the stops. We cannot afford to lose one of those who is nearest and dearest to us. Let us win them by lifestyle and example, for the greatest sermon we can preach is through the way we live.

We don't allow rejection to hinder; we simply "shake off the dust that is on [our] feet."

God, may our words and actions make a difference in the lives of those nearest to us. Amen.

Responding to God's Holiness

JULY 9–15, 2012 • DAVID GREBERT

MONDAY, JULY 9 ～ *Read 2 Samuel 6:1-5*

Stone of Destiny is a film based on the true story of nationalistic Scottish students who, on Christmas Day 1950, stole back Scotland's "Stone of Scone" from London's Westminster Abbey. The stone had been seized by an English king and placed under the coronation throne as an enduring symbol of England's rule over Scotland. Six hundred years later, these students break into the Abbey and bring home this potent symbol of Scottish identity.

As the ark comes to Jerusalem, we need to remember that it symbolizes national identity for the Israelites. Yet it is much more. It represents the very presence of a holy God among God's people. And unlike the Stone, its journey to Jerusalem doesn't take place in secret. Its procession home is a spectacle: thirty thousand hand-picked men of Israel led by their passionate king, David. The mood is festive, upbeat, and celebratory. In fact, scripture states that "David and the whole house of Israel were celebrating with all their might before the LORD" (NIV). They were not *just* celebrating. They were celebrating with "all their might." The sound of songs, harps, tambourines, and percussion filled the air.

How often do we throw ourselves into passionate worship of God? Sometimes our experiences of worship consist of little more than mouthed sentiments and déjà-vu hearts. But when we grasp the immense holiness of the Lord afresh and the fact that God lives in us, we too may start to celebrate with all our might. What an appropriate response to a holy God who dwells among God's people.

Lord, free me to celebrate you with greater passion. Amen.

An elder of Westlake Church, a nondenominational, international church in Nyon, Switzerland

Uzzah dies after touching the ark (2 Sam. 6:6-11). When the ark resumes its journey in verse 12, the men began to carry it with more care and reverence. We don't know if David offered sacrifices after every six steps or just the first six steps of the journey. Either way, David acknowledges the Holy One's presence and walks humbly.

And yet David's humility doesn't fetter his joy; they go hand-in-hand. So as he brings the ark into Jerusalem, he is dressed in a linen ephod and dancing. It's the joyful humility that seems to upset Michal. Her husband, the king, has lowered himself before his people. A king has become a fool.

Michal's bitterness is so biting, so unexpected, that it almost steals the joy from the scene, doesn't it? It feels so out of place. And yet, the fact that the Bible records her derision serves to remind us that not everyone will welcome humble worship of God. In fact, some will stand in stark opposition to it. Like Michal, they won't see people as humble and joy-filled in the presence of God. They'll see fools, cheapening their reputation in the presence of others.

But what is more foolish: to live joyfully and humbly before a holy God or to care only for the opinions of people? God never promises followers acceptance by others. In fact, responding to God's holiness may often reduce us in the eyes of others. We choose our way in life. This story illustrates two possibilities: to dance with humility and joy in the presence of God or to stand bitter on the sidelines, despising those who do.

Lord, point out to me the times that I've cared more about my reputation before others than my reputation before you. Teach me to live with joyful humility. Amen.

The task is done, the job complete. David has solidified political and spiritual power in the new capital city of Jerusalem. The ark of the covenant comes to reside in a special tent-sanctuary there. David offers burnt offerings and offerings of well-being. He offers blessing on the people and publicly passes out food to the people. "Then all the people went back to their homes." At first glance, this passage can feel almost anticlimactic. With the Israelites' return to Jerusalem, has their joy given way to formality? Not at all.

Burnt offerings were solemn, atoning acts of worship, expressing devotion, commitment, and surrender to the Lord of hosts. David and Israel say with this action: "Lord, we give ourselves to you." Fellowship offerings were a more joyful sacrifice that gave thanks for the fellowship God has already offered the people. David celebrates the fact that God desires relationship with them. Sharing a meal is a common feature of this offering; so when the people of Israel go home with bread, meat, and raisins, it does not symbolize David's generosity. It reminds them of the authentic, in-their-midst fellowship with the Holy God of Israel.

Be encouraged by this fact: we too have fellowship with God. Stop and make space in your day to offer gratitude for that and to give yourself anew. As you do so, know that you are echoing voices from long ago in Jerusalem and foreshadowing what we shall all do one day together when we dwell in God's presence forever.

Lord, in response to your blessing, may I live to your glory. Amen.

Recently, our church's junior youth group did a "Mad Scavenger Hunt" around our town with the challenge to get as many photos as they could from an eclectic list of possibilities. Some photos were hilarious, some odd; a few were quite profound. Called on to bring back something that evidenced God's existence, one team took a picture of themselves by the lake. A few of them pointed to the water; some pointed to the mountains; and one pointed to himself. "The earth is the LORD's, and all that is in it." Creation points to God.

Today's psalm celebrates this understanding. Our God is the "King of glory" because the Lord created the entire world "and those who live in it." Many believe this psalm may have been penned for the bringing of the ark to Jerusalem. The psalm begins with an affirmation of God as sovereign. The psalmist then asks several penetrating questions: "Who shall ascend the hill of the LORD? And who shall stand in his holy place?" In other words, who will live in God's reign? Answer: those who are holy in God's sight. Those with clean hands (outward behavior) and pure hearts (inner motivation). Those who choose to live under God's rule, attempting to remain loyal to God's intentions for the world.

God calls us to live holy lives. Our actions (hands) and our intentions (heart) need to be more in alignment with the Holy One. If we live this way, with our lives inclined to holiness, we will experience more of the joy of God's presence. And our lives will point to God's glory, as surely as creation does. Our youth had it right.

Lord, the earth is yours and everything in it. That changes everything. Show me where my hands or heart are not aligned to your will. Amen.

FRIDAY, JULY 13 ~ *Read Ephesians 1:3-10*

Parents who adopt will talk of the deep joy that comes from being able to bring a child into their family—a child who otherwise may not have had the chance to thrive under the incredible love that parents can offer. All children are a gift. An adopted child is a chosen gift.

As you read today's passage, feel God's delight in you as God's adopted child. God chooses you to be "holy and blameless in his sight" (NIV). God offers you forgiveness of your sins and makes the truth of the gospel known to you. You have a future in Christ. God endows us with endless gifts: redemption, forgiveness, wisdom, faith. But here's the thing: God does not do these things reluctantly or contractually. The Holy One offers them freely and with pleasure.

Consider some of the epistle writer's language: God chose us. In love, God destined us for adoption as "his children," freely lavishing grace upon us through Christ. We will become part of the great "gathering up" of God, all done with the deep joy of a father.

I recall the familiar story of Eric Liddell, the Olympic sprinter of the last century, who, in the film *Chariots of Fire*, is quoted as saying, "I believe God made me for a purpose, but he also made me fast. And when I run I feel his pleasure." It's a fabulous line, but falls short of the whole truth. We need not feel God's pleasure just when we use our gifts. We can feel that pleasure in every part of our lives. That privilege comes from being the adopted sons and daughters of a holy Father, who freely lavishes love on us. To the praise of God's glorious grace.

Father God, thank you for adopting me. Let me feel your pleasure in all areas of my life. Amen.

What do you live for? Often the way we live our lives impugns our answer. We say we live to leave a legacy, and yet we focus so much of our time on the here and now. We say we live for others, and yet our first thoughts are usually of ourselves. We say we live for Jesus, and yet so often our prayers reflect a desire for Jesus to live for us.

Now push this further. What were you saved for? In recent decades the salvation story of many Christians has become increasingly about us as individuals. *I* was a sinner (true) but God had a different plan for *my* life. God loved *me*, and Jesus died on the cross for *me*. Now *my* relationship with God is restored. *I* have eternal life.

I. My. Me. Me. My. I. God offers this glorious salvation, an inheritance, and yet our stories of grace carry a strong air of self. And this runs through our Christian culture. Many of us shop around for a church that meets our needs, buy into a burgeoning Christian self-help market, and sing songs about how Jesus' last thoughts on the cross were only of us.

The epistle writer says no. He points to Christ and reminds us that we were chosen from the very beginning to exist for the praise of his glory. Even the reason we were saved, the reason the Holy Spirit comes like a guarantee of our redemption, is not ultimately for our benefit but that Jesus may be more glorified. Our salvation results in glorifying him.

Let this change how we live. In our salvation stories, let us celebrate Jesus. In our decisions, let's look not for the path of greatest personal advantage but for the path that will give him the most glory. Let us live as if Jesus is all that matters.

Jesus, help me live for the praise of your glory—not mine. Amen.

Not a pleasant story to end with, is it? The calculating hatred of Herodias. The pathetic cowardice of Herod. Their actions leave me reeling at the shocking brutality of sin. How could a woman hold so much hatred in her heart? How could a king allow the execution of a man to reward a well-choreographed dance? What stain must Herodias have left on the soul of her daughter? There are no easy answers to these questions.

But against this backdrop of sin, John's righteousness shines so brightly. Consider some of the contrasts in the story: John is prepared to risk his life by challenging the morality of one of Rome's own appointees. That appointee isn't even prepared to risk the disappointment of his party guests to save a man's life. John is so righteous that he is held in awe by his captor. Herodias is so evil that she will corrupt her own daughter into her mission of revenge. John is so holy that some will even wonder if he and Jesus are somehow one and the same. Herod is so morally weak that he will be remembered in history for his cowardice.

And yet, John is the one who is killed.

Responding to God's holiness often means living a life that stands in sharp contrast to the world around us. Sometimes this will win us respect. Sometimes it won't. In some rare cases, we may lose everything. Are we prepared to live a life of holiness, a life of contrast from prevailing culture, regardless of the consequences? The life and death of John the Baptist remind me that I must answer yes.

Lord, may I stand for truth and righteousness, regardless of the cost. Amen.

A Holy Household

JULY 16–22, 2012 • GAIL A. RICCIUTI

MONDAY, JULY 16 ~ *Read 2 Samuel 7:1-3*

By contrast with God's enduring love for us, our love for God is seldom so clear. It is difficult to forget that we live out even our deepest devotion in inescapably public ways and all too easy to remember that others are watching, even evaluating, our witness of faith. The approval of those we admire often powerfully shapes the way we serve our God.

This kind of spiritual Catch-22 is timeless, as with David. "See now," says the king to his prophet, "I am living in a house of cedar, but the ark of God stays in a tent." Not only should the devotee live in no greater splendor than the divine recipient of devotion, but David's building a Temple for the Lord will legitimize his reign.

Both the king and his prophet certainly have the best intentions at heart. If we live in the comfort of houses built of materials like cedar, should not God have a greater house? So the exchange we will overhear later in chapter 7 is counterintuitive, an encounter with One who is perfectly content to live within impermanent tents and tabernacles-on-the-move.

In a sense, King David is a prototype (albeit perhaps an exaggerated one) for a human faith laced with ambiguity—the inescapably mixed motives of the believer. Do we (echoing the apostle Paul's later musings) long to serve God with our whole heart? So too did David. But the unavoidable "creep" of popular opinion, other people's judgment on our walk of faith, sometimes colors the way we strive to serve.

O God, your unshakable love is my strong foundation. May I serve you with uncorrupted singleness of heart. Amen.

Associate Professor of Homiletics, Colgate Rochester Crozer Divinity School; Rochester, New York

With laudable intent, David has proposed to build a better house for the ark of God, since it seems obvious to him that a tent is too flimsy and vulnerable a dwelling for the Holy Presence that has privileged him above all his enemies. And yet David soon learns that the realm of God is not about grandeur! The divine Spirit cannot be housed within walls, but "mov[es] about in a tent and a tabernacle." It seems that this God values the flexibility—the divine capacity to strike camp and be on the move—that tented life affords. While human beings tend to calculate value by size and quality, God estimates a dwelling place according to agility and responsiveness.

God's examination of David's motives rights a relationship turned on its head. "Are you the one to build me a house to live in? . . . [T]he LORD declares to you that the LORD will make you a house." For now, David's eagerness to build a structure for God is too small a concern. To be responsive to God, able to pull up stakes at the divine command—that is the larger calling.

A house for the Lord? Eventually, perhaps, but not now. For now, the Lord will be the house-builder, establishing offspring in the process. The cautionary lesson for us in the exchange between David and Yahweh is that initiative belongs to God, whose prerogative it is to choose a spiritual dwelling place. There, the Holy One waits for us to follow, find, and enter into the divine life already inhabiting the world. In reality, it is a great relief to know that the impossible task of defending, "taking care of," or answering for God is not our responsibility. Ours is to ready our lives for receiving the expansiveness of the promises. Already, then, the promise of verse 11 is fulfilled: from the stress of striving on God's behalf, we are given rest!

God of the continuing journey, make us pliable and responsive to your call, that not even a house of worship may blind our hearts to your promises. Amen.

Having no hope and without God in the world." These words, describing the stark reality of unbelief, are enough to flood any religious community with waves of gratitude by comparison. The writer of Ephesians expresses the contrast represented "in Christ Jesus" simply enough: "now . . . you who once were far off have been brought near."

A friend of mine rescued a dog last year, an obviously damaged, traumatized twenty-pounder named Sadie. The workers at the animal shelter had a hunch that Sadie had been physically abused; but even worse, all the signs indicated that she had been used as a lucrative "puppy mill" breeder to produce litter after litter, vastly weakening her own physical resources. She herself had never learned to play and came into her new family with no sense of what to do with a toy. She had languished in the shelter's fenced confines like a creature without hope until the day she was "brought near"—taken home—by my friend. They are now, at Sadie's particular insistence, inseparable. If animals have knowledge of divinity, her new owner is Sadie's god; the devotion in her eyes says it all.

Sadie remains a damaged pup. She may never catch on to the idea of play; she may never find peace without trailing from room to room close at her owner's heels. But she knows what household is hers—and that she has been brought home.

These words to the Ephesians do not describe some sinless standard but rather a wholly new state of being—undivided from each other, comprising one new humanity, becoming citizens of a household . . . being brought home. With all of our weakness, mistakes, sinful pride, nevertheless the work of Christ has torn down all walls of division that could separate us from the household of God!

God of the outcast, who welcomes strangers, beckon our hearts to the threshold of your loving embrace in Christ Jesus. Amen.

A Holy Household

The epistle writer offers an unsettling contrast but one strangely familiar, in some respect, to every human life. To be "without Christ," he writes, equates to being strangers and aliens: outsiders to a commonwealth and its covenants. Feeling left out, the experience of the outsider, is indeed a common human phenomenon. Whether in childhood with the excruciating wait to be picked last for a team; or sometime in adulthood, getting to know in-laws whose established traditions are unfamiliar and foreign-seeming; or later in life, when the death of a spouse or a shift in circumstances thrusts one into awkward territory as "odd person out" in formerly comfortable social groups; at some point each of us has a taste of being the outsider who does not fit in.

Ephesians lets the reader in on a surprising truth: through the Incarnation—that is, literally with the body of Christ ("his flesh") interposed—peace is proclaimed: not only to those far off but also to those already thought to be near. With the advent of that peculiar peace, God sets up housekeeping. Former strangers and aliens become "citizens" and "members." A household is established, that state of belonging described by the poet Robert Frost as the place where, when you go there, they have to take you in.

We know, intriguingly, in our own bodies the visceral feeling of rest and rightness when walking into the comforting familiarity of our own home. Our own reading chair is there, and our accustomed place at the table. There, we belong; and our whole being senses it. So Ephesians employs this metaphor of a household in Christ Jesus: "In him the whole structure is joined together . . . in whom you also are built together spiritually into a dwelling place for God." The surprising crux of it all is this mutuality—not only that we are at home and at peace together in Christ, but that this household, built with us, is a dwelling place for God.

Thanks be to you, God, for your householding within and among us. May we be your dwelling place forever. Amen.

FRIDAY, JULY 20 ~ *Read Mark 6:30-32*

From talk of Temple, tent, ark, and household, reading Mark now turns us toward a "deserted place." As if to emphasize the significance of the first missionary endeavors, Mark calls the twelve "apostles"—the only instance his account will describe them as such. The account implies that the fledgling missionaries have met with success, telling Jesus with a hint of breathlessness all that they have done and taught. The evangelist adds significantly that with the crowds coming and going, "they had no leisure even to eat."

The words bring to mind too many lunches half-eaten at the crowded desk and seldom tasted or remembered afterward; the "working luncheons" over which the demands of business trump any human connection with servers or cooks, let alone companions at the table; the family suppers missed while working late; the fast-food wrappers piling up in the car after ferrying children to the multitude of appointments already crowding their young lives.

The Twelve returned with accomplishments to show for their time and effort certainly; but it is telling that rather than praising what they achieve, Jesus first addresses the depletion he sees in them. "Come away to a deserted place all by yourselves and rest awhile."

Jesus' model exemplifies a balanced concern not only that ministry be carried out in a needy world, but that those who minister be continually renewed and refreshed. What might balance those two components in our own lives? A rhythm of crowded and deserted places, intensive labor and quiet rest is how we practice the "leisure . . . to eat" that will nurture our own strength as disciples. Come away—and rest awhile!

Holy Spirit, we bring our depletion to your font of renewal and our fast-paced days to your table of transformation. Nurture our strength for discipleship, we pray. Amen.

Many recognized [the apostles], and they hurried there. . . . People at once recognized [Jesus], and rushed about that whole region." From the currency of his own ministry, the Lord knows what is needed to sustain gospel work; but it must not have startled him that they were recognized even before their arrival in deserted places and that multitudes in need awaited them wherever they went. His compassion flows to those he perceives as sheep without a shepherd, no less than to his own overtired apostles; so once again, the healing and teaching begin.

While the nerves of Jesus' disciples sometimes fray, the Gospels never give us a glimpse of anything like frustration or impatience on Jesus' part toward the ever-present crowds. Recognition of the Teacher-Healer ignites a flurry: rushing, hurrying, jostling for a place to position the sick, begging for a look or a touch. Accounts of life in the ancient world juxtapose themselves upon the pace of modern living until the two seem in some ways identical. Yet what is notable is the placement of ministry, the intentionality of where Jesus and his missioners make available the touch of his cloak. "Wherever he went, into villages or cities or farms, they laid the sick in the marketplaces."

The One who would seek out wilderness places for restoration of spirit is the same healer who locates his healing ministry in the marketplace: the nerve center of community life, the public arena. For many Christians, this is great good news: that the call to touch, teach, and heal in Christ's name is not primarily a call to cloister oneself within some sort of consecrated space, as if "sacred" and "secular" could be kept separate. Rather, we are called to follow our Lord into the thick of things, to streets and marketplaces, and thus consecrate the world (and the worldly) with the Spirit's touch.

Christ Jesus, from the quiet of rest lead us into public places, that we might touch the world's hunger for healing. Amen.

A Holy Household

Astrong household is not built primarily with wood, mortar, and shingles—that would be merely a house, as yet uninfused with a living Spirit. No, a household is shaped by those things the psalmist emphasizes here: faithfulness, covenant, steadfast love—the things God promises us, through our forebear David, for all time. That promise, repeated as if to root its foundation unshakably, is to "establish" David's line and his throne: metaphors for the eternal family that will trace its roots to this humanly flawed but divinely beloved ancestor. The promise then is to us as the holy household later reconciled and held together by the mortar of Christ's peace.

God's way of announcing this magnificent act of establishment is powerful: "[B]y my holiness," the Holy One swears "[not to] be false to my faithfulness . . . not violate my [own] covenant, or alter [my own] word." God is willingly bound by God's own promises so that we know for certain that we shall be established as the Lord's household forever. The psalm's soaring lyrics remind us that it would be impossible for our faithful God to be false to that faithfulness.

The promise comes not as license to live any way we think best but as a mandate to walk according to God's ordinances, keeping commandments, holding divine statutes in respect. Verses 30 and 31, two lines embedded in the ground of God's sweeping eloquence here, are a deceptively modest blueprint outlining a lifetime's specifications for the building of a "holy temple in the Lord" (Eph. 2:21). Our task as partners in the covenant is weighty but suffused with joy as we hear our God's voice say, "Once and for all I have sworn by my holiness; I will not lie to David." Thanks be to God!

O God, your faithfulness toward me is the rock on which my house is built. Rest me on this strong foundation, all my days. Amen.

A Holy Household

Staying Focused!

JULY 23–29, 2012 • JORGE ACEVEDO

MONDAY, JULY 23 ~ *Read 2 Samuel 11:1-5*

I have focus problems—but not with my eyes. My focus problems go far deeper than visual ailments. My focus problems are spiritual in nature. I get distracted from keeping God first and foremost in my life. As a youth pastor several decades ago, I used a slogan with our students: "The main thing is to keep the main thing, the main thing!" I so easily lose my focus on the "main thing," my relationship with Jesus!

King David seems to have a focus problem too. Doubtless David loved God. Yet today's story indicates he also had the awful potential to lose his focus on God.

It begins in this story when David gets a bit lazy. In the time of the year "when kings go out to battle," David stays home. Such a small thing—no big deal. Right? Wrong! Then David catches a rooftop glimpse of a beautiful woman bathing. "Be careful little eyes what you see." A glimpse turns into a stare, and lust dethrones God in David's life. Bathsheba becomes easy prey for the lustful and powerful monarch. To top it all off, she ends up pregnant with David's baby.

It all begins with David's losing his focus. Being in the wrong place (rather than on the battlefield) at the wrong time (during war time) with the wrong people (none of David's men confronts him) doing the wrong thing (sleeping with another man's wife) costs the king. Keeping our focus on God is a moment-by-moment discipline. The stakes are high.

Holy Spirit, grant me the discipline to keep my focus on you. Amen.

Lead Pastor of Grace Church, a multisite United Methodist Church in Southwest Florida

In any crisis of life, we get to choose our pain. We can either choose the pain of discipline or the pain of regret. Let me illustrate. A married couple comes to see me because their marriage is in the dumps. Communication is low. Fighting is high. Individual needs are not being met. Though not a trained therapist, I have the experience of being married to the same woman for twenty-nine years and more than twenty-five years as a pastor.

After each spouse shares his or her perspective on what's wrong with the relationship and how they got to this place in their marriage, I always ask, "What are you willing to do to fix this relationship?" Typically, this question catches them off guard, yet it is fundamental to any healing and restoration.

I then tell them that they get to choose their pain. They can choose the pain of discipline by seeing a counselor, joining a small group, attending a marriage conference. Or they can choose the pain of regret—getting a divorce, sharing custody of the children, losing half their stuff! They choose: pain or regret?

David messes up big time by misusing his power as king and getting another man's wife pregnant. He could choose the pain of discipline and 'fess up. It would have been ugly, but resolution might have come. David would have to pay; as a follower of Yahweh, justice and mercy could have been forged. Instead, he chooses more regret. He sets a plan to have the unassuming and innocent husband of Bathsheba killed. His choice multiplies the injustice and pain.

Which will you choose today—the pain of discipline or the pain of regret? Both hurt. Only one heals.

God of justice and mercy, help me to choose the pain of discipline today so that I do not have to experience the pain of regret tomorrow. Amen.

Several years ago, I first heard the phrase "practical atheist" to describe a person who subscribed to the idea of faith but lived his or her life with no real evidence of it. It's the man who declares he is a follower of Jesus but in his life does not pursue the vision that Jesus modeled and taught. It's the woman who announces that she is Christian but does not "practice what she preaches." Truth be told, to some degree we are all practical atheists. We all fall short of the ideals that we espouse. I regularly teach about the importance of being compassionate like Jesus and then find myself heartless and unmoved by the pain of people all around me. I'm a practical atheist in these moments.

The writer of Psalm 14 begins by saying, "Fools say in their hearts, 'There is no God.'" The writer seems sure of his indictment of "foolish" atheists. And honestly, atheism does seem a bit foolish to me. The evidence of a created order seems to point to a Creator. Is it any more or less foolish to say there is no God than to say a God exists who makes no difference in life?

When a local church sign declares a message of radically inclusive love and grace for everyone but in truth affirms an exclusive "unless you are just like us you're not welcome" message, it's foolish. When a Sunday school class studies the treasures of God's Word but practices gossip and backbiting, it's foolish. When a follower of Jesus prays the Lord's Prayer with gusto and then does not trust God for his or her "daily bread" or refuses to forgive as he or she has been forgiven, it's foolish.

In what ways are you being a practical atheist? What patterns in your life might God describe as foolish?

God, keep me from living a foolish life. By your Spirit, help me to live with a sense of your presence and power in my life. Amen.

We all have hopes, dreams, and longings for good for those we love. As a father of two grown sons and grandfather to two young grandchildren, my heart longs for them to do well in life. This prayer in Ephesians 3 is right at the top of my longings list for my sons and grandchildren as well as others whom I love. These verses capture my hopes for spiritual growth for my family, my friends, my church, and myself.

The prayer contains three main petitions. The first petition (verses 16-17) seeks spiritual strength and growth for followers of Jesus in the first century—and in the twenty-first century. It asks that Jesus would "make his home in your hearts as you trust in him" (NLT).

The second petition (verse 18 and the first half of verse 19) for growth makes a more specific request for understanding and for love. The writer asks God to help us grow deep roots into the love of God and that we might understand the immensity of God's love. Wow! This is some prayer.

The brief final petition ("so that you may be filled with all the fullness of God") may seem an afterthought. However, the petition for the "fullness of God" is the fruition and end hope of *all* prayer. That fullness will make concrete the connection among the one who prays, God, and the human family. It is indeed "far more than all we can ask or imagine" (v. 20).

This longing for spiritual maturity in others and us involves not only passionate prayer but also persistent patience. Whether we long for a more consistent prayer life or a more faithful life of service, God is at work in our mysterious life transformation. This is our journey of sanctification toward Christlikeness.

Father, Creator of heaven and earth, I long to grow in my relationship with you. Grant me the patience to stay faithful in my walk with Christ. Amen.

I did not grow up in the church. I never had the privilege of going to Sunday school or summer camp. My first experience of Vacation Bible School came as a pastor in my early twenties. So when my two sons, Daniel and Nathan, were growing up, I learned the children's songs right along with them! One of my favorite songs I learned with them was "My God Is So Great." The song lauds God's great power and affirms that God, Creator of all, can do all. This children's song captures the heart of Ephesians 3:20-21. Our God is an all-powerful God!

Last Friday night, I had the privilege of baptizing David in a horse trough at our Friday evening recovery worship service in our sanctuary. As he stepped into the silver container, I noticed his leg brace. His testimony of life transformation through Jesus was read over the sound system. Drinking at nine years of age, David was lost in a world of alcoholism. More than one hundred trips to rehab could not deliver him from his compulsive and destructive behaviors. A near-death accident that left him paralyzed on one side of his body didn't even wake David up. But David met a God at Grace Church who is able "to accomplish abundantly far more than all we can ask or imagine."

David came out of the water shouting "Hallelujah!" and shot his arms into the air in victory. When we worship at Grace, David dances. It's awkwardly beautiful. Half-paralyzed by his addiction but completely justified by his Savior, David moves in adoration and gratitude to an amazing, all-powerful God. Our God is so great, so strong, and so mighty; there's nothing our God cannot do.

My great, strong, and mighty God, accomplish your life transformation in me. Amen.

SATURDAY, JULY 28 ~ *Read John 6:1-15*

Every Wednesday afternoon and third Saturday morning, the good people of Grace Church, the church I am privileged to pastor, practice the compassion of Jesus in a special way. On these days, our people give away thousands of pounds of food; hundreds of pounds of pet food; haircuts by the dozens; hundreds of articles of clothing; referrals to medical, food stamp, insurance providers, and more; plus everyone receives prayer by one of our prayer team. In these set-aside times we welcome our neighbors to the Grace Community Center. This old grocery store turned into a community center houses our holistic ministries: our GED, after-school drop-in program, homeless ministry, and a host of other works of the center. The miracle of the every Wednesday and third Saturday ministry is that, as our director says, "Every week we pray, 'Lord, fill the shelves.' And every week we pray, 'Lord, empty the shelves.'" And God does!

By all measures, we are a "blue collar" church filled with hardworking people who bring sacks of food to the community center. We work hard to show the love of Jesus in practical ways. Each brings his or her "five barley loaves and two fishes" and, miracle of miracles, God feeds the multitudes, with a bunch left over.

My friend Sharon came last August. In receiving two bags of groceries, she got so much more. Patti led Sharon into a personal relationship with Jesus. Sharon joined our church, made her Walk to Emmaus, and now serves as a host at the community center. It has transformed her life. This is church at its best!

Jesus, thank you for using our five barley loaves and two fish to point people to a God who loves most and best. Use me today to spread your amazing grace. Amen.

I was making my way home from my part-time job in Lexington, Kentucky, in the summer of 1984. My friend Jay and I rode together to save money. About halfway home, we passed an ambulance—not an unusual occurrence because of the hairpin curves on Highway 68. Car accidents happened all the time. I dropped Jay off at his apartment and drove home. As I pulled into my street, my heart dropped. Police cars and other emergency vehicles were in front of our home.

The police told me our sixteen-month-old son, Daniel, had been badly burned in a kitchen accident. The ambulance we had passed was carrying my son and wife. They instructed me to drive to the hospital to join them. I drove the winding road back into Lexington in a blur, my breathing labored and my heart pounding. I shouted at God. "Why, God? Why?"

As I pulled in to the hospital, the waves of shock and anger built to a crescendo. As I ran in to the emergency room, my wife, Cheryl, met me. When I looked into her face, an unexplainable calm came over me. It was as if Jesus had walked into the room.

Like the terrified disciples on the raging waters, we sometimes are reluctant to take Jesus into our boat. But then he speaks: "It is I; do not be afraid," and immediately the boat reaches the shore. Jesus brings calm and rescue. This man who feeds multitudes can care for body and soul. The disciples eagerly welcomed Jesus into their boat, just as my wife and I welcomed Jesus into our intense torrent. Who Jesus is makes the difference between dark and light, terror and peace, death and life.

God, I thank you that Jesus walks into the storms of my life and brings peace. Amen.

Created to Be in Relationship

JULY 30–AUGUST 5, 2012 • AMY L. PROCTOR

MONDAY, JULY 30 ~ *Read 2 Samuel 11:26–12:13a*

We are created to be in relationship with God, the people around us, and ourselves. God established rules for the Israelites to live by to be in healthy, life-giving relationships. David has not lived by these rules. His sins begin small and then escalate out of control as he tries to cover them up. David covets another man's wife, commits adultery and murder, and steals the wife of another man. Israel's greatest king and a man after God's own heart has violated the sacred covenant.

David has sinned and has tried to hide his own cognizance of the sins. God sends the prophet Nathan to hold God's beloved and chosen king accountable. David may waffle, but the moral imperatives of the God of Israel are quite clear. David's moral accountability is all the *greater* because of being the chosen one of God. Yahweh interprets his actions as a rejection: "Why have you despised the word of the LORD, to do what is evil in his sight?"A code of morality exists for all—including the powerful.

Sometimes our human response to sin is to try to cover it up or fix it ourselves. Instead of trying to hide, we need to confess our sins to the ones that we have hurt and to God. The Hebrew word to repent is *shûv*. *Shûv* goes beyond merely confessing sin; it calls for a change of direction in the way we live; we are to turn from sin and turn toward God.

Dear God, fill us with the peace that comes from knowing that when we come before you and confess our sins, we are forgiven, and that our sins no longer separate us from you. Amen.

Certified for ordination as a deacon in the Yellowstone Conference of the United Methodist Church; member of Bozeman United Methodist Church; Bozeman, Montana

Nathan has to stand before the king of Israel and pronounce judgment on him. I do not envy Nathan's God-given assignment to confront David about his sins and hold him accountable for his actions. I imagine that this would have been a frightening encounter for Nathan. If the meeting with David does not go well it, could cost Nathan his life.

Nathan proceeds with the task at hand, telling David a parable about a rich man, a poor man, and a lamb. The story moves David to anger. He passes judgment on the rich man as deserving of death and asks for a fourfold restitution. David does not recognize himself as the rich man in the parable until Nathan states, "You are the man!" In a head-spinning move, the prophet quickly reverses David's place from judge to accused. He then levies God's heavy punishment: public humiliation before all Israel and trouble in the family. David finally admits, "I have sinned against the LORD."

God calls David out about what he has done and holds him accountable for his actions. No one, not even the king of Israel, can hide from sins committed. We cannot hide from our sins. We may think that our sins are not as great as David's, but who among us leads a life free of sin? We confess before God who forgives. Through confession God can "work with us" and transform our lives with love and grace. As a result, we are able to reorient our lives toward God. We can know that we are forgiven and transformed—but always held accountable.

All-knowing and ever-present God, may we invite your transforming love and grace into our lives today. Fill us with the peace that comes from knowing that when we confess our sins we receive your forgiveness. Amen.

This psalm is offered in the voice of David after Nathan's confrontation. We have witnessed the story unfold that leads to the writing of this lament. The psalm gives voice to David and to us. We too find ourselves before God acknowledging grievous failures. The psalmist's words make public David's suffering, allowing us to glimpse the hurt and pain. We sense the depths of despair and confirm the desire for a reconciled relationship with God.

This psalm models an approach to restored relationship with God. Despite his transgression, David does not fall silent, unwilling to address God. He approaches God, pleading for mercy and acknowledging the power of God to cleanse him from sin. He faces up to God's claim in the reading from Second Samuel: "Why have you despised the word of the LORD, to do what is evil in his sight?" His sin has hurt and damaged others, but David knows that his true dilemma is with God: "Against you only have I sinned and done what is evil in your sight." Joy and gladness have vanished from his life, a sign of a disjointed relationship with his God.

But David takes time and creates space to be truly available and vulnerable before God. He sees himself as he really is and pleads for God's transforming mercy and compassion. In this curative space David asks for and experiences reconciliation between himself and God.

Psalm 51 can guide us in the way toward a reconciled relationship between ourselves and God. When we make ourselves available and vulnerable, acknowledging our sin and begging for God's mercy and compassion, we can experience a restored relationship.

God of grace and love, thank you for loving us even when we turn away from you. May your grace transform the ways that we live out our lives. Amen.

Martin Luther once said, "Sin boldly." David knows that he has sinned, but he also knows that God can restore their relationship. In Psalm 51, David confesses his sins humbly and asks for forgiveness boldly. David believes that God will respond to his prayer, and he trusts God to reorient him by giving him a "clean heart" and a "right spirit."

David's bold faith reminds me of the theologian Phoebe Palmer from the Holiness Movement that began in the 1850s. Phoebe Palmer believed that a relationship with God began with a personal decision to lay down one's life on the altar of God and create an opportunity for God to work within, through the Holy Spirit. Furthermore, Palmer believed that it was not enough for a believer to lay his or her life on the altar; the believer had to have faith that God would respond and receive the gift. As Palmer laid her life on the altar she confidently and boldly declared, "Thou hast promised to receive me! Thou canst not be unfaithful! Thou dost receive me now! From this time henceforth I am thine—wholly thine!" Through this declaration, Palmer firmly established her faith in the God to whom she belonged.

We can seize the boldness and confidence of David and Phoebe Palmer as we come into God's presence. We come with a trust that God will renew us, give us a clean heart and a right spirit. Once again gladness and joy will fill our lives. What would living our lives and faith with this type of boldness and confidence look like?

Dear God, we ask for your mercy and compassion. Cleanse our hearts so that we live with the boldness and confidence that comes from our relationship with you. Amen.

FRIDAY, AUGUST 3 ~ *Read Ephesians 4:1-7*

The epistle writer begins with the idea of Christian vocation: "Lead a life worthy of the calling to which you have been called." And we're all called! The ministries of the church are not only the responsibility of clergy but of all believers. By our baptism, all Christians share in Christ's work in the world.

Yesterday we reflected on Phoebe Palmer and the boldness and confidence with which she lived out her faith. For Phoebe Palmer "the obligation to take the service of God as the absorbing business of life, and to regard heaven as her native home, and the accumulation of treasure in heaven is the chief obligation of ambition." The believer's chief reason for living became serving God. Palmer went on to say, "The church is represented as Christ's body. I am one of the members of that body. . . . The health of my own soul and that of the precious body of Christ, of which I am a member, demand its performance." According to Palmer and the epistle writer, believers—as part of the body of Christ—have responsibility for serving the greater body. That is true for us as well.

The Message translates Ephesians 4:7: "But that doesn't mean you should all look and speak and act the same. Out of the generosity of Christ, each of us is given his [or her] own gift." Each of us has unique ways to serve. How are you being called to serve in ministry? How can your unique gifts support the body of Christ?

Dear God, help us become the people you created and called us to be. Give us the strength and courage to use our gifts in ministry in the body of Christ. Amen.

The saying, "One for all, all for one" no longer has to apply only to the Three Musketeers. This saying could be the motto for the body of Christ. "You have one Master, one faith, one baptism, one God and Father of all, who rules over all, works through all, and is present in all. Everything you are and think and do is permeated with Oneness" (Eph. 4:5-6, THE MESSAGE). As baptized believers we are all "called"; but as the writer points out, each of us has a special talent or skill that we bring. All our gifts come together to build up the body of Christ. This list expands the work of ministry from a few to all. All gifts enhance the greater work of the church.

Not all of us may find our ability to serve in this list of gifts. Few of us may perceive ourselves as apostles, prophets, evangelists, pastors, or teachers. However, ministry is not only for the select few. These gifts exist to enable the work of ministry, in which we all are called to participate.

Despite the differing gifts, this text stresses unity, oneness, and working together. We come together and live out this oneness in community. By entering into relationship and solidarity with one another we no longer live isolated lives but become community. In the unity of faith we tell our stories and share what Christ has done in our lives. By listening to one another, carrying one another's burdens, and serving together, community develops.

Recall David's sense of disjointedness in regard to his relationship with God. We, the body of Christ, can experience a similar discomfort unless we find ourselves "joined and knit together by every ligament . . . , as each part is working properly." Only when we bring our individual gifts together will the body build itself up in love. "In the body of Christ we are made one with Christ, one with each other, and one in ministry to all the world."

Dear God, unify us in our faith and empower us to use our gifts for the work of ministry. Amen.

This chapter begins with Jesus feeding five thousand people from two fish and five loaves of bread. Naturally the crowd returns the next day to the source of yesterday's meal. The people want nourishment for their physical hunger. However, instead of feeding the crowd again, Jesus talks to them about the spiritual nourishment that only he can provide. But they don't understand.

The previous day Jesus has fed five thousand, and the questions raised today are, "What sign are you going to give us then, so that we may see it and believe you? What work are you performing?" The manna that the crowd mentions in the text only provided nourishment for one day; Jesus, the bread of life, provides nourishment for eternity. Jesus points out that God not only "gave" manna, but God "gives" the true bread of heaven. Jesus can provide a much more lasting nourishment and fulfillment than the crowd seeks.

We too want to perform the works of God, and at times we too ask God for signs. The work of God comes in believing in Jesus. The miracle that matters is not the feeding of the five thousand but the miracle of faith itself. Jesus is the bread of God who gives life. He satisfies our spiritual hunger.

Christ provides for our spiritual nourishment through Holy Communion. Today, the first Sunday of the month, is a time that many churches celebrate Holy Communion. Communion is a channel by which God shares divine grace in the life of a believer. Christ serves as host at the Communion table and through his presence we experience the grace of God. "Whoever comes to [Christ] will never be hungry, and whoever believes in [Christ] will never be thirsty."

Loving God, on this sabbath day of rest and holiness, may we experience the presence of Christ in our lives. Enable us to go out and be bread for the world. Amen.

Sustenance for the Journey

AUGUST 6–12, 2012 • ANDREW C. THOMPSON

MONDAY, AUGUST 6 ~ *Read 2 Samuel 18:5-9, 15, 31-33*

David's lament upon hearing of Absalom's death expresses pure parental bereavement: "O my son Absalom, my son, my son Absalom! Would I had died instead of you, O Absalom, my son, my son!" David's sin has indeed borne deadly fruit.

Parental disarray results in a conflict that pitted father against son. David experiences some of life's worst calamities: rejection by his own flesh-and-blood (Absalom), a violent conflict he wants no part of (civil war), betrayal by a trusted comrade (Joab), the death of one of his children (again, Absalom), his very life and vocation called into question (as anointed king over Israel).

Our world sometimes confronts us with terrible calamities, but we seldom have to face them all at once. David experiences desolation. His anguish echoes that of Job, "I have no peace, no quietness; / I have no rest, but only turmoil" (Job 3:26, NIV). It even echoes Jesus' cry from the cross, "My God, my God, why have you forsaken me?" (Mark 15:34).

David's food in that season is the bread of affliction. But the bread of affliction is not his sustenance. He will only find true sustenance in the place where we all find it: "The eternal God is your refuge, and underneath are the everlasting arms" (Deut. 33:27, NIV). In our own dark nights of anguish, we remember the words of the psalmist: "Weeping may linger for the night, but joy comes with the morning" (Ps. 30:5).

Heavenly Father, abide with me in times of desolation. May I sense the presence of your Holy Spirit especially then. Amen.

Teacher in the areas of historical theology and Wesleyan studies at Memphis Theological Seminary; Memphis, Tennessee.

God's story with us in scripture is—over and over—a story of moving from pain to healing, from exile to restored communion, and from death to life. Think of the Hebrews, groaning under slavery to Pharaoh. God raised them up with a mighty hand and an outstretched arm and brought them safely across the Red Sea. He fed them with manna in the wilderness and gave them the Law for their good. Then he brought them finally to the Land of Promise so that they might have a home forever.

Later in Israel's history, Babylon destroyed the holy city of Jerusalem and burned the Temple to the ground. Even then, God did not leave the people to suffer alone but brought them back from exile. God gave them leaders to oversee the rebuilding of the city, and the Temple itself was restored.

Psalm 130 seems expressive of David's anguish in the death of his son Absalom. The psalmist too cries out from "the depths," a place so deep that we marvel that he can articulate the words. The psalmist assumes forgiveness—not by virtue of his actions or words or through his devotion to the Lord—but by the actions of a God who is revered.

The psalm captures the experience of moving from death to life in just eight verses: from the pleading cry from a place of despair to God's forgiveness of us despite our unworthiness. Notes of hope and waiting then culminate in a closing affirmation that is the very opposite of the psalm's opening: "O Israel, hope in the LORD! For with the LORD there is steadfast love, and with him is great power to redeem."

From despair to hope. And from hope to promise. This exhortation will serve the church today: God will provide.

Blessed Redeemer, give us the assurance of your love for us. Help us in our time of need. Amen.

Living as a Christian means living as a new creature. "So if anyone is in Christ," the apostle Paul writes, "there is a new creation: everything old has passed away; see, everything has become new!" (2 Cor. 5:17).

Ephesians offers examples of what that new lifestyle means. Do believers lie to one another? No, we will tell the truth. Do they refuse to be reconciled with one another? steal? speak with unbridled tongues? act out of malice? No, we will live differently, showing love and consideration to one another. And we do these things because we know we have been forgiven.

This is not simply a list of moral "dos" and don'ts." It's about the life that is possible for us, because we have died and risen with Christ. It is about the vulnerability we are able to accept with one another, knowing that the only reason for fear has been dismantled on the Cross. Our lives now are "hid with Christ in God," which means that we can live differently than the ways we knew in the world.

Equally important with affirming this new life, however, is affirming the community that makes it possible. We can live in this new way because "we are members of one another." We have been woven together into the body of Christ. We are the church; we know we cannot go it alone. If we want to learn to forgive, to speak rightly, and to act out of love, we must learn those things in a community of believers—guided always by the Holy Spirit.

Accepting our place within a community is not always easy. We live in a world that tries to make us think and act as individuals. An individual Christian cannot make it alone; in the church we find our sustenance of grace.

Lord Jesus Christ, I thank you for your gift of the church. Help me to find my home there. Amen.

THURSDAY, AUGUST 9 ~ *Read Ephesians 5:1-2*

The great medieval spiritual writer Thomas à Kempis begins *The Imitation of Christ* by saying that the words of Jesus "teach us how far we must imitate His life and character, if we seek true illumination, and deliverance from all blindness of heart." "Let it be our most earnest study, therefore," Thomas says, "to dwell upon the life of Jesus Christ."

When we read in Ephesians that we are to be imitators of God, it seems at first like an impossible task. How could we ever imitate perfect knowledge, perfect power, and perfect holiness?

We can't do those things, of course. But the scripture says we should strive to *imitate*—not take on all of God's attributes. Ephesians speaks of imitating God as walking in love. And the love to which he refers is Jesus' own love. First John 4:16 says, "God is love, and those who abide in love abide in God, and God abides in them." We can love in this way because we have been loved ourselves by the One who came to bring light and salvation into the world.

A bumper sticker I saw recently says, "Christians aren't perfect—just forgiven." That's not exactly true. We're not just forgiven. We have been loved with the love of forgiveness, but we're also continually loved with the love of healing. We are being changed as we receive grace each and every day.

Paul counsels us elsewhere, "Not that I have already obtained all this, or have already been made perfect, but I press on to take hold of that for which Christ Jesus took hold of me" (Phil. 3:12, NIV).

If we have not yet been made perfect, we still know that perfection—which in the Bible means "completion"—is where we are headed. And imitating the God we know in Jesus Christ, by walking in love, is the vehicle that will take us there.

God of grace, give me your love that I might worthily imitate you in all things. Amen.

Anyone who has experienced what it means to be in "the depths" can relate to how terrifying a place that can be. I don't mean a case of the blues or even a few days in a row of depressed feelings or sadness. I mean *the depths*, the kind of experience that involves depression or anxiety in their fullest sense and that lasts for months or years.

We find ourselves in the depths when we experience hardship without a sense of God-with-us. As creatures who have been made for communion with God, our experiences of God's absence can result in profound debilitation.

The psalms understand this facet of our nature, and that is why their subject matter covers the full range of human experience, from rejoicing and celebration, to fear and desolation, to hope and anticipation.

In expressing the hope of renewed communion with God even while suffering in the depths, Psalm 130 says,

> My soul waits for the LORD
>> more than those who watch for the morning,
>> more than those who watch for the morning.

People who kept watch were a common and necessary part of civic life in the ancient world. They stood stationed on a city's walls to watch for any sign of danger, whether from a foreign army or approaching storm. They kept their watch on the walls at night as well, to herald the coming of dawn every morning.

Those watching remind us of our hope as children of God—hope that goes deeper than any depths to which we can sink. Waiting on God, like watching from the walls, requires discipline and patience. We can wait, though, when we know that the Lord's coming is assured. And assured it is, just as much as the coming of the dawn.

Holy God, help me to maintain a hopeful watching for your coming. Quench the thirst of my soul by your Spirit. Amen.

When we pray the Lord's Prayer, we say, "Give us this day, our daily bread." In a land of abundance, where food is plentiful and cheap, we can easily forget the necessity of daily bread. And yet, necessary it is. Without nutritious food and clean water, we will die.

Our supplication for daily bread in the Lord's Prayer is a recognition that what we need for life ultimately comes from outside of us. To live, we must eat. And to eat, we must have food. The trees and green plants of the earth can make their own food through photosynthesis, using only air and water and sunlight. But not us. We require sustenance that comes from somewhere besides us. We are dependent creatures.

As with life, so with life eternal. Daily bread saves us from starvation, but we need bread of a different sort to be saved from the bodily death that eventually claims all living things. Jesus tells us that he is that bread. Manna in the wilderness may have sustained the Hebrews day to day in their journey to the Promised Land, but only the Bread of Life can sustain God's people eternally.

Accepting Jesus' words means doing something we're not always good at doing. It requires admitting that we don't have what it takes within us to survive. We are dependent creatures from start to finish. We are born helpless out of the water of our mother's womb, and we are born again in the waters of baptism under the care of Mother Church. We must eat our daily bread to live from sun to sun. And we must receive, with praise and thanksgiving, the body and blood of our Lord that we might live forever in his kingdom.

Lord Jesus Christ, you who are the Bread of Heaven, feed me by your grace so that I may live with you forever. Amen.

Paul says in 1 Corinthians 13:12, "Now we see through a glass, darkly; but then face to face" (KJV). I often think of these words when adversity—large or small—confronts me.

Even those of us raised in the church—baptized and formed by years of instruction, preaching, prayer, and sacrament—encounter much in life that seems contrary to God's will. Even worse, we sometimes find that what is contrary to God's will is *in us*. Our own thoughts, words, and deeds betray us. We cause pain and harm to ourselves and others. We sin.

Jesus' neighbors struggle to know how to respond to his words. They've known Jesus all his life. They know his parents: Mary and Joseph. To them, Jesus is just a hometown kid. So how can he be making such grand claims?

Our struggle differs from theirs. We *do know* who Jesus is. When Jesus refers to the prophet Isaiah in verse 45: "And they shall all be taught by God," we know that Jesus himself is God in the flesh teaching us. So why do we doubt? Why do we give in to evil desires and turn to anger and lust and greed?

Until that time when we see face-to-face, we remind ourselves that God's purposes truly are being unfolded, for us and for all creation. And grace does heal, which we discover to our great joy as we live the life of faith.

Hebrews speaks hope to our frustration over our present circumstances. Though we do not yet see clearly, Hebrews 2:9 says, "We do see Jesus, who for a little while was made lower than the angels, now crowned with glory and honor because of the suffering of death, so that by the grace of God he might taste death for everyone."

Jesus has been revealed to us that, through his death, we might be saved. That is sustenance for our journey.

Eternal Holy Spirit, draw me ever toward Jesus until I am finally able to see him face to face. Amen.

Faith Seeking Understanding

AUGUST 13–19, 2012 • G. KEVIN BAKER

MONDAY, AUGUST 13 ~ *Read 1 Kings 2:10-12; 3:3-14*

Sitting with a couple in my office during one in a series of premarital counseling sessions, I began to address the subject of finances. I started with my usual opener: "A budget is a moral document." My statement was followed by a quick question: "What do you mean by that, pastor?" I replied that how a person or family spends money says something about who they are, what they love, and where their priorities are. I then encouraged the couple to go over the past twelve months and take an inventory of their spending and giving habits.

We could take a similar spiritual inventory of our prayer life. Look back over the past twelve months of your time in conversation with God. Did you take time to listen as well as speak? Who or what did you pray for? Our prayer life too often betrays a preoccupation with self-serving agendas. Do our prayers express a deep longing for God's will to be done on earth as it is in heaven?

Solomon's conversation with God in his dream is a good example of that deep longing. Despite his awareness of the enormous challenges that face him as the new king of Israel, his prayer has less to do with his own agenda and more to do with his vocational calling and mission to lead God's people: "Give your servant therefore an understanding mind to govern your people, able to discern between good and evil; for who can govern this your great people?"

God of wisdom and love, give me not what I want but what I truly need to help me fulfill your divine purposes for my life. Amen.

Lead Pastor of Reconciliation United Methodist Church; Durham, North Carolina

People today don't put much stock in dreams; but historically and biblically speaking, generations of people who have gone before us thought otherwise. Sure, many dreams probably have no significance—perhaps the result of eating something odd the night before. But there are also dreams that communicate important truths and spiritual insights.

Take Joseph, who dreamed about how God would one day make him a great leader in Egypt; Daniel, the great interpreter of dreams; Joseph, the betrothed of Mary, who was told in a dream that Mary would conceive a child from the Holy Spirit; or the Magi who were warned in a dream to return home a different way. Some might say that God often chooses to speak to us in dreams because that is a time when we are more susceptible to God's direction and guidance. Perhaps when we dream, our human will is less prone to resistance and obstinacy.

Solomon's prayer for wisdom is so powerful and worthy of our prayerful imitation that we often overlook the fact that his entire conversation with God happened while he slept: "Then Solomon awoke; it had been a dream" (1 Kings 3:15). I often wonder if God came to Solomon then because that was the best time to try and get a busy king's attention. As far as dreams go, I rarely can remember my own. But I do think that to hear God, to speak to God, and to seek God's will for my life often require slowing down, taking time out from my busy schedule, and turning off all the distracting sounds and voices that so easily get in the way. At least that is often how God gets my attention—when I take time to be still, pray, and read scripture on a daily basis—whether I am dreaming or not.

Lord of both my waking and my sleeping hours, help me be still long enough to hear your voice and discern your will for my life. Amen.

My daughter is learning to play the piano by using tutorial videos on the Internet. I wasn't sure how far a person could progress with nothing but a keyboard in her lap and a computer screen in front of her, but she now has three or four tunes under her belt that have become permanently etched in the heads and memories of every family member. They play incessantly on a repeating loop that continues even during sleep.

As my daughter began learning the notes of the treble clef, she pulled out an old, familiar acrostic that I remembered from my own piano lesson days: EGBDF ("every good boy does fine"). Acrostics are helpful like that. This technique is nothing new; it is thousands of years old. As today's scripture illustrates, acrostics not only help in learning the notes on a musical score; they can also help transmit and foster the memorization of the ABCs of praise.

Psalm 111 is an example of an ancient acrostic poem, which we easily miss because few of us read it in the original Hebrew. Each half line of this ten-verse psalm begins with a letter from *alef* to *tav*, with a line of praise for each of twenty-two letters of the Hebrew alphabet. This is not the only place in scripture that uses letters of the alphabet in a unique and instructive way. Most of us are more familiar with the first and last letters of the Greek alphabet, used together to describe God as the one who is both the beginning and the end (alpha and omega, Rev. 22:13).

Psalm 111, a psalm worthy of memorization, can become a model for our own poems of praise. The next time we want to praise God for all that God has done in our lives, we might try starting with *A* and ending with *Z*.

Almighty God, Blessed Savior, and Covenant-making Lord, may we find new ways to expand the way we praise you each day for all your wonderful works. Praise the Lord! Amen.

In an old comic movie, students were touring a scientific research lab. Throughout the tour a man in a padded cell screamed at the top of his lungs as if experiencing extreme pain. After the intermittent and disturbing screams continued for some time, one student finally asked, "What on earth are you doing to that poor man?" The professor replied, "Oh, him. Well, he is a clock watcher. We are experimenting with time deprivation. We are trying to see how long he can go without looking at a clock."

The student looked through the window at the tortured form huddled in a fetal position against the wall. As the students depart, it becomes strangely silent. The camera zooms to the bare wrist of one of the students who no longer has his wristwatch and then cuts to the padded cell where the man sneaks a peek at his newly acquired watch.

If that scene is funny at all, it is only because it comes so close to the truth. Time is very dear to us. Most of us tend to hoard it and protect it. We do not give time away easily. Our generation has no time to spare. To us clock watchers, to those of us who are lost in a sea of busyness, the writer of Ephesians has a strong and powerful word. Stop. Just stop. Make the most of your time, for the days are evil.

What we need not do is to kill time, to fill it up; rather, we need to *fulfill* time, to *redeem* time. The epistle writer warns us not to be foolish but to understand what the Lord's will is: Jesus not only wants our life, our giving, our hearts, and our minds. Jesus also wants our time. To learn to live wisely, to understand the will of the Lord, is to recognize that everything we have is God's—even our time.

Lord of all things, including time, help me to live wisely, making the most of the time you have given me. Amen.

Biblically speaking, "giving thanks" is the primary speech of humanity. God's Word reminds believers that when we say "thank you," we become more fully human and we enter more deeply into divinity. Gratitude is key to the spiritual life. Without it we cannot grow in the grace and knowledge of God. Without it we are diminished as people, and we live a diminished life in the world. Gratitude is essential to a life of joy, a life of compassion, a life of fulfillment. Deep down, most of us already know this. Most of us are aware that the ability to express thanksgiving is part and parcel of what it means to be Christian. But gratitude does not come naturally; it must be cultivated.

We cultivate this posture of gratitude most explicitly in worship. Worship reminds Christians that our expressions of thanksgiving are really answering speech, responses to what God has already done in us, for us, and through us. It is no coincidence that when followers of Jesus gather around the Lord's Table, they gather to pray "The Great Thanksgiving"—a prayer that expresses gratitude for all of God's mighty acts in salvation history.

The writer of Ephesians expresses this biblical truth clearly, reminding us to cultivate gratitude in our worship and exhorting us to do so regardless of our present situation or current life's circumstances: "Be filled with the Spirit, as you sing psalms and hymns and spiritual songs among yourselves, . . . giving thanks to God the Father at all times and for everything in the name of our Lord Jesus Christ." The alternative is to give ourselves over to a spirit of cynicism and ingratitude, which when left unchecked does more than diminish our joy and contentment—it erects obstacles to our relationship with God.

God Almighty, giver of all good things, help me count my blessings each day and give thanks to you at all times for everything. Amen.

SATURDAY, AUGUST 18 ~ *Read John 6:51-58*

Some people call them the "hard sayings of Jesus": those difficult teachings of Jesus, particularly those that cause offense and lead many to turn away from him, forsaking their initial enthusiasm for the wandering rabbi from Nazareth. It is an unsettling, familiar biblical theme. Jesus' words can save and heal—but often enough, they can also shock and offend.

John 6 provides a case in point. Jesus gives us his flesh to eat? Jesus gives us his blood to drink? Even if spoken metaphorically, these words seem inappropriately graphic. If taken literally, such words were an offense against Jewish law and Torah teaching. Either way, Jesus' words are hard to swallow. "When many of his disciples heard it, they said, 'This teaching is difficult; who can accept it?' . . . Because of this many of his disciples turned back and no longer went about with him" (John 6:60, 66). Of course not everyone pushes away from the table. Jesus turns to the Twelve and asks if they wish to leave also. Peter answers, "Lord, to whom can we go? You have the words of eternal life" (John 6:68).

Do you find the words and teachings of Jesus hard to swallow at times? You are in good company. Many have found the cross-bearing road of discipleship a difficult one to travel. But do not let that deter you from following Jesus. Do not let "hard sayings" cause you to push away from the Lord's table of grace. Jesus' words are true: at this meal Jesus promises to abide in us, feeding us with the bread that leads to eternal life. At this meal we can take our time chewing on Jesus' teachings, digesting his love, savoring his grace, tasting his forgiveness, and feeding on his mercy. Come, taste and see that the Lord our God is good.

Gracious God, help me so to eat and drink the body and blood of Jesus that I might digest his truth and savor the goodness of his eternal life dwelling within me. Amen.

I remember the day a pastor was leading worship and came to that part of the Communion liturgy where he recalled the words of Jesus: "This is my body broken for you" and "This is my blood shed for you." An audible "eewww!" came from a youngster in the congregation who was attending for the first time. She, like the people in today's Gospel story, had taken offense at these words. Eat flesh? Drink blood? . . . Really? . . . Seriously? You are kidding, right?

I feel sure that some well-meaning adult quickly sat the youngster down and explained that certain matters in worship really aren't what they seem. I imagine someone telling her, "Honey, in the church we say 'body' but what we really mean is bread. We say 'blood' but what we really mean is grape juice. Don't get upset; it is the same stuff you buy at the grocery store." And just like that, good, well-meaning adults throw away the gospel medicine Jesus offers and quickly exchange it for a load of rational, safe, and nonthreatening spiritual rubbish.

What would happen if the church decided to learn something from the faith and the probing questions of children instead of rushing to correct them and reassure them that there is nothing to be worried about when we come to the Lord's Table? What if the little girl had it right, and we adults have it wrong? What if she was right to take offense, to realize that Jesus' teaching is difficult, and that the way of discipleship is less about feeling safe and comfortable and more about sensing the real danger Jesus poses to our ways of living, our ways of thinking, our ways of relating—and, yes—our ways of eating?

Lord, help us so to eat and drink your body and blood that your very life may dwell within us, challenging and changing us into your faithful followers. Amen.

Dwelling

AUGUST 20–26, 2012 • REGINA M. LAROCHE

MONDAY, AUGUST 20 ~ *Read 1 Kings 8:27-30*

Solomon's declarations around God's dwelling in and beyond the infinite articulates a realization of a vastness of view beyond the human mind's capacity. His inability to grasp God's willingness to possibly dwell within the limits of earth or an earthen structure reflects our doubts about God's ability or desire to be in the smallness of our lives. So, later, God chose to dwell in a womb, in the arms of a girl, in a house fashioned by a carpenter father. God chose to dwell in the pettiness of human squabbles and perspectives and within the grandeur of human sorrow and love.

But long before Jesus' foot touched Nazareth's dust, Solomon, in spite of his incomprehension, stepped into the mystery and invited, welcomed, and pleaded God into the finite places.

And God entered in, perhaps recognizing the infinity that exists in the microscopic or perhaps acknowledging the infinity that exists in Solomon's dreaming, prayers, and visions, as well as our efforts and endeavors. Perhaps God enters the infinity of spirit and love that yields tiny manifestations: a wrong righted; a new baby; shelter, clothes, food for a stranger; tending of soil, water, and creature.

We view God through lenses shaped by our environment—by the vastness and limits of our experience, our hurts and joys, and our abandonments. As we dwell in the infinite God, do our vision and selves grow more infinite with greater space into which we invite God to dwell?

God, smile upon our audacity to believe we have room for you; then enter us, expand us, dwell in us. Amen.

Storyteller living in family and community on an island in Lake Superior

For days when I was a small child, Mother, Father, Uncle and Aunt took turns raising and dropping a lever handle by hand to dig a well for our new home: "thud-ringgg, . . . thud-ringgg." Dad accidentally dropped a pair of strung-together pliers down the well pipe in one of his many attempts to repair the hard-working equipment. When they fished the pliers out, the string was wet. Adults cheered and laughed, men shouted in Haitian Creole. We children danced and clapped without fully understanding the celebration.

Four years later, my family accompanied my father to his hometown of Cape Haitian after twenty-five years of political exile from the troubled island of Haiti. Once there, he hired men off the street to dig a well with the pipes he had transported and the equipment from our home well. Again: "thud-ringgg." His parents' neighborhood had been dry for months, so the crowd that gathered around my father and his water project was large and festive. And when water was reached: "Eh-ay-ay!"

Reading of springs and pools calls forth the vibration and aural memory of the ringing pound. I have seen firsthand a man make a dry place a place of springs. I have seen footprints in the construction site's clay soil fill with rain water. I connect with images of crossing difficult, desert-dry terrain and bringing life-water. It takes strength, sweat, endurance, digging, conviction, laughter, bloodied fingers, and intense caring. As for pools . . . stand, walk uprightly allowing your own weight and the strength of what God pours into you to become an impression, an imprint on the surfaces, people, situations you encounter. It means entering deeply into life and allowing your presence and God's presence in you to leave a mark.

God of water and life, pour yourself into us with such love and promise that we will walk through, stand in, and dig into the hardness of life with fervor and joy. Amen.

As the first day of school loomed close, my young five-year-old friend Tunzai got increasingly nervous. Throughout his preschool years he and his father often played a game to ease his fears. His father would give Tunzai a mission to focus on rather than his fear. Then Tunzai would name the mission and don the gear he needed to accomplish it.

His father employed the game again. In this case, Dad stated the mission: to meet the teacher, to meet new kids. His gear included new school shoes, backpack, sweater. The plan of action: arrive at school; stow backpack in cubby; hang sweater on hook; park bottom on chair; sit at attention.

It worked. Tunzai didn't focus on his anxiety. He came home announcing that school was easy! But he had forgotten his sweater in his end-of-school-day rush to ensure that his cousin boarded the school bus safely. Tunzai had added another mission that superseded even remembering his gear: caring for someone he loved.

Gear, or armor, is important. It drew Tunzai's attention in the preparation. My volunteer firefighter husband knows his gear could save his life: it must be worn to battle a blaze. Our armed forces and many others rely on various shields of protection that allow them to enter dangerous situations with some degree of confidence. We armor ourselves with stylings, colors, and fashion statements that help us maneuver a sometimes hazardous society.

Ephesians notes a reliance on a strength and power outside ourselves: the strength of God's power. Every piece of equipment mentioned serves a specific purpose. But perhaps the young kindergartner discovered the ultimate mission, the ultimate "gear": love. Love summons strength, truth, righteousness, peace, faith, prayer, and boldness.

Dear God, outfit me for life with you. Amen.

My family was newly arrived from the city. Stu Swenson came one day with his tractor to turn the earth, to plow our field so we could plant seeds, plant a garden—plant ourselves in soil, in a process that reminded my parents of home.

Not a big deal. That's what neighbors do, right? But my family's skin was brown; our hair was dense; my father's accent was thick. In this rural white farming community we were the stranger, the alien, the foreigner.

Stu Swenson, an old farmer plowing fewer of his fields every year, mustered up the energy to tend the foreigners a mile down the dirt road. Perhaps the years of farming, of attending to the mystery of life and sustenance rising from the earth beyond his control encouraged him to receive gifts. In the face of the unpredictable, he knew how to have faith. Perhaps this faith taught him gratitude powerful enough to yield generosity and hospitality.

We humans tend to provide for self, family, tribe, or clan—maybe for one's nation or race. But for the outsider, the foreigner? It's not just with food, shelter, or jobs. We even attempt to hoard God's favor, mercy, and grace, binding it around ourselves and our particular loyalties.

In this prayer from First Kings, Solomon beseeches the people to offer hospitality to the foreigner, a hospitality that extends to worship. The Israelites are to respond favorably to all requests, not simply out of kindness but to evangelize the foreigner for the God of Israel. In that way, "all the peoples of the earth may know [God's] name."

So whether plowing a field or inviting to worship, we offer gifts and extend hospitality generously out of faith and gratitude for having been gifted ourselves.

God, for both gift and giver, I thank you. Amen.

Two thousand years ago a mix of folks mingled about and argued, perplexed and offended as Jesus offered his body to be eaten and drunk as a source of life. These men and women had firsthand experience in gutting fish, butchering goats, uprooting vegetables, smashing fruit, and crushing seeds in order to eat.

Today many in our society are distanced from the reality that things must die for even the most careful among us to live. I would think that the agrarian Middle Easterners could stomach Jesus' meal offering better than many of us today. But maybe their familiarity with carcasses and blood and pain made Jesus' offer too graphic—this miracle-working rabbi crushed, suffering, dying.

Perhaps the notion of digestion seemed offensive. Few of us understand or talk about what happens in the dark, in the juices and bacteria of our stomachs and intestines. The details of digestion are off-putting and often embarrassing. Associate this near-celebrity holy man with the dark recesses of ourselves?

And could they or we allow this intriguing but disruptive man to permeate our being in those dark unspoken-about places? When the life and energy of a morsel of bread made from our own hands enters our bloodstream, fine! But how could we permit this enigma man to carry his pain and death, his life and holiness into every one of our cells, transforming us in him and himself in us? Too much!

It is too much unless we're at home with the distasteful and disturbing, unless we realize we're at home nowhere . . . with nowhere else to go, no one else to turn to.

We are, after all, what we eat. The disciples and folks who did not and do not turn away in confusion at this sacrifice become spirit and life.

God, help us know the necessity and gift of your offering. Amen.

As I wait at the airport, I study the welcomes. Some thrust flowers, some rush forward. Almost every third "welcomer" does something with spread-open hands. Some hold them on either side of their face, ducking in shy delight. Others wave them in front of themselves at shoulder level in excitement. Still others open palms upward, reaching. After years of playing with dance, movement, and cultures, I wonder at the universality of this open-hand welcome, open-hand rejoicing. A few thousand years ago, before miles-long airports of glass, steel, and concrete, a man stands before an extravagant Temple. All of Israel watches as their king "spread out his hands to heaven"—welcoming home the ark of the covenant, "the glory of the Lord," "the name of God," and the very being of God.

Hands spread. From dance, airport arrivals, and life I've learned that spread-open hands usually indicate a spread-open heart; opening the hands is often the beginning of the dance. I've learned that mirror neurons exist in our brains: whenever something around us moves, something in our brains, in our bodies, moves with it—experiencing the movement as our own. Hence, when I dance through space, when the officiant dances bread and wine skyward, when a tree dances the cycle of life and falls to earth—all present, even those who refuse to dance or are afraid to dance, dance along internally.

As Solomon spread his hands and his heart in celebration and welcome, in pleading and covenant before all of Israel, did these witnessing people of ritual and celebration feel their hearts open, spread, and dance? Did their hands actually lift—thousands of palms blossoming beneath the heavens?

Creative God, teach us to open our hands and hearts that we may dance our adoration and prayers. Give us the courage to dance-pray on behalf of and in invitation to your world. Amen.

Softness of feather, heat of breast, turning of small bird body. . . . These work on the mud, leaves, twigs, and incidental matter to shape a nest for mother to sink into, for eggs to emerge into, for babies to break into.

Human parents shape space to sink into, blanketing it with comforting colors and textures; burrowing into the heart of a watching, protective community as they prepare a resting place for the expected young one. Similarly, spaces of shelter and care are shaped for the elder at the other end of life.

In good circumstances, humans shape a cushioning nest place for their vulnerable and frail. Is that the truest home or dwelling place? A place shaped around our most defenseless and breakable (sometimes broken) pieces and selves? When those pieces are held and honored, we can sing our contentment: lullabies and praises, as the swallow in a sheltered place.

We begin to learn from these how to shelter our souls in the house, altar, hand, love of God. We begin to learn to draw around ourselves the things of God. We begin to learn how to dwell, turn, burrow into the presence and person of God.

As we begin to dwell and sing, how do we remember the unsheltered, the endangered in body and spirit—those needing housing, community or companionship or respite from warfare? How do we dig, shape, turn out home places with room enough for all, including those with brokenness so close to the surface it frightens us?

Sometimes this means actually sinking our hands in the mud and concrete of a building project or sinking our hearts into the dark places of another's story. Perhaps in the sinking in, in the turning and dwelling, shelter is created.

Homemaking God, teach us to dwell in you with total abandon and release. Empower us to fashion space from who you are for all your children and creation. Amen.

Dwelling

True Worship

AUGUST 27–SEPTEMBER 2, 2012 • JERRY KEARNEY

MONDAY, AUGUST 27 ~ *Read James 1:17-25*

All of us are accustomed to looking into the mirror. *How is the hair? Do I look good in this outfit?* We use the mirror to reassure ourselves that all is well—or at least as well as can be expected—and that our external image is sufficiently presentable to the world.

Less frequently do we gaze into the mirror of our souls. The view is frequently less flattering than we would like. In times of honest reflection we see both beauty and warts. Sometimes the ugliness overcomes us, and we work hard to forget what we have glimpsed.

Like our spiritual mirror-gazing, most of us give a cursory glance at God's word. We take a quick peek now and again, maybe even fairly frequently. But often we engage simply with the most immediate image of the words. A deep listening to God's word challenges us to look beyond the shadows of personality, beyond the shame of mistakes, beyond the perception of failures to see the face with which we were born—a face that radiates and mirrors the very image of God.

That image calls us to remember what we look like as images of God when we leave the confines of home and safety and head out into the world. We move beyond an integrity of thought and speech to an integrity of hearing and doing. As long as we keep that image in mind, we look into the mirror to see an authentic and persistent image. Our commitment to "the perfect law" makes us "doers of the word."

O God, may we never forget what we really look like and who we truly are. Amen.

Vice President of Mission, St. Thomas Hospital; Nashville, Tennessee

I go to church every week." "I sacrificially tithe." "I have undertaken numerous terms of service in various congregational ministries." "I have been largely faithful to my commitments." "I have not consciously offended or turned a deaf ear to my neighbor." "I have not been fraudulent in affairs that matter." "I have worked hard and have earned respect and admiration."

I suspect these statements may summarize the reality of most of us, as well as the Pharisees who confront Jesus. These words convey a justifiable righteousness, a sense of serenity and security. Yet true worship requires that we intently and penetratingly engage God's word and presence. The encounter with God, while soothing and enriching, is also always disquieting. Just when we think we've got things figured out, we are thrown from our comfortable assumptions and confronted with inescapable realities that challenge our worldview. The encounter demands that we identify our continuing need for repentance and interior transformation. As Jesus reminds us, "Nothing outside a person that by going in can defile, but the things that come out are what defile." Interior transformation matters.

Culture tells us to do good to those who do good to us; love those who are like us and those whom we like; don't cheat friends; share what is left over—these behaviors are relatively easy. They ultimately distract because they permit us to avoid the really hard work of understanding our motivations and changing our hearts and, consequently, our behaviors.

Gracious God of comfort and discomfort, prevent me from becoming complacent and allowing my relationship with you to become stagnant. May my worship be dynamic and transformative and therefore pleasing to you. Amen.

True Worship

Why do good people do bad things? For committed Christians, this is an absolute embarrassment but also an inescapable reality. We, whose eyes have been opened through the revelation of scripture and by reflection upon the multiple experiences of God's incredible beauty and love in our lives, persistently make poor choices. Often our actions, attitudes, and acquisitions divide rather than unite us.

We do these things because we allow ourselves to be lulled into the perception that these things are good for us. We allow self-centered narcissism and desires for self-satisfaction to influence us. We develop habits and patterns of behavior that reinforce and entrench that perception. The deep recesses of our hearts are infected by a viral enemy that has the capacity to consume and overtake us. The Pharisees and scribes, understanding this capacity of the human mind and heart, have enforced long-standing laws of ritual purity in order to "fence in" the commandments. But Jesus upsets the apple cart by stating that eating with unclean hands isn't the problem: "All these evil things come from within, and they defile a person."

Two qualities can combat these "wicked designs that come from the recesses of our hearts." The first is a firm and compelling desire to grow more deeply in relationship with God. And the second is courage to respond wholeheartedly with choices and changes necessary for conversion. Patience with ourselves and a deep awareness of God's incessant forgiveness support the many fits and starts of our weak spirits. Fidelity to the struggle is most often the best we can do. Our willingness to expose our self-deceptions gives God's grace an opening.

Ever-present and sustaining God, open my eyes, mind, and heart so that I might clearly understand the immensity and wonder of your love and be drawn by ardent desire to live in your presence. Amen.

True Worship

The most salient and consistent characteristic of believers that emerges from the Judeo-Christian and most other major religious traditions is care for orphans and widows—the helpless, the vulnerable, the marginalized of society. Love of the other serves as a litmus test of the true measure of our love of God. This concern and action are not merely options for when we have spare time or some extra change. They are absolute imperatives. In fact, the only judgment scene in all the Gospels clearly conveys the message that inclusion in the kingdom is based on fidelity to works of mercy.

We cannot assume that our churches, humanitarian agencies and dedicated missionaries are taking care of this responsibility for us. True and pure worship demands personal engagement with those who find themselves alone, cut off, or shunned by family, friends, and neighbors because of mental illness, addiction, mistakes, disagreements, resentments, differences. We keep ourselves "unspotted" by honoring and celebrating the richness of the differences among us; by dropping narrow, self-victimizing resentments; by generously setting aside disagreements; by quickly forgiving mistakes; by persistent companionship with those on the painful road to recovery; and by understanding and actively supporting those whose lives are filled with the demons of emotional fragility.

Vincent de Paul, who lived in seventeenth-century France, dedicated his life to care for those on the margins of society. He admonishes those who seek to live in imitation of Christ that if at the time for worship one is called to provide for those in need, "then one should leave peacefully." "To leave for God; that is, to leave one work of God to do another of greater obligation, is not to leave God."

Loving God, may our service to others genuinely help them and signal our true worship raised up to you. Amen.

True worship demands that we clearly understand the nature, dynamism, and attraction of the one whom we worship. The notions we have of God are many and varied. Our encounters with God through reading of the scriptures can be ones of vengeance, retribution, surprise, mystery, loving-kindness, justice, absence, imminence. The language and images we use to describe the relationship also affect our understanding of God.

This scripture moves our appreciation of a relationship with God to an entirely different plane. It presents the God we worship and serve as the one most intimately related to us. We frequently segregate our intimate lives from our spiritual lives. Somehow we fear that physicality and sensuousness are antithetical to relationship with God. But this passage encourages us to go to those places where we have felt our greatest intimacy, warmth, and self-approval. Where have we had these experiences—in the warm embrace of a beloved, in the sharing of deepest secrets, in a child's clinging, in the final grasp of a dying loved one?

We know the intensity and struggle that are part and parcel of everyday relationships, and we hope that somehow our relationship with God is more mystical and magical. But the reality is not so; our engagement with God is just as tangible, just as intimate, and just as complicated as our relationships with one another. God as intimate lover calls to us to "arise, my love, my fair one, and come away." If we do not permit ourselves to feel the sensual lure of God's call, our relationship may remain cold, sterile, and insignificant. In this case our worship is perfunctory at best: our card may be punched, but our hearts are not changed. The God who loves us with an incredible, unjustified, unqualified, unconditional love wants to enter into the deepest of intimacies with us.

O God, the time of singing has come. May I respond to its sweet melody. Amen.

The kingdom of God contains all that is good. The psalmist sings of the convergence of all the conceivable yearnings of the human and divine heart: justice, good judgment, peace, equity, sufficiency. Some scholars suggest that this psalm might have been penned for the enthronement of David as king, the human representative of God in the world, the embodiment of those godly characteristics that make for righteous rule.

The image of justice and peace differs greatly from the world in which we live. All too familiar to us are images of wars, oppression, human trafficking, malnutrition, homelessness, exploitation, rejection, and shattered dreams. The vision of the psalm seems far removed from our reality.

The reign of kings after the fall of Jerusalem became a more political position. But we, the followers of Jesus, have been given the daunting mandate to extend God's reign. Jesus has told us that the kingdom is in our midst. Our challenge is to look deeply into the events that occur around us through the lens of faith in the resurrected Jesus and to identify the signs of hope and glimpses of the kingdom. This takes penetrating, painstaking, and reflective searching and understanding. It requires a deeper engagement in and with the world than our usual casual and fairly superficial daily encounters. Only through this process will we see the threads of the unfolding of God's creation drawn together.

Informed by this faith perspective, we can see and understand the deeper meaning of the moments of our lives and feel more compelled to engage ourselves in behaviors and actions that hasten the coming of that time when God will be all in all.

Blessed may you be forever, O glorious God, and may the whole earth be filled with your glory. Amen.

Interaction with God is both wonderful and problematic. Let's deal with the problematic first. Our usual methods of sensory communication are not in play, and the mechanics of our customary daily interactions cannot be relied upon. For centuries, humans have attempted to understand and interpret the experience of God in terms that make sense and are consonant with all other experiences of our lives. All our "God-talk" only approximates our experience and the reality of God.

The wonderful part is that our relationship with God does not depend on the usual and customary constructs. God loves us, not for anything we have done or deserve but only because we exist. We receive absolute and complete forgiveness of our transgressions, not because we have made restitution or worked off our guilt but only because we exist and have been freely saved by the selfless sacrifice of Christ Jesus.

The "tradition of the elders" will not keep us from defilement. Lip service without heart service will not save us. Holding to the trappings of human tradition will not cleanse us. Thus, our mutual attraction and entwinement with God demand our capacity to willingly suspend the categories of everyday relationships and to allow ourselves to be transposed to another plane of interaction. Herein lies the ground of "true worship."

It is insufficient simply to cry, "Lord, Lord" (Matt. 7:21), and observe, even slavishly, the external trappings of religiosity. True worship occurs through an intimacy with God whom we experience as personally embracing and loving us. When we take that love seriously, we understand that encounter with such love can do nothing but propel us to extend that love to others. It's a heart thing!

Lord, give depth to my devotion and help me to love you with all my heart, all my mind, all my strength. Amen.

Downside-Up Gospel

SEPTEMBER 3–9, 2012 • LARRY JAMES PEACOCK

MONDAY, SEPTEMBER 3 ~ *Read Proverbs 22:1-2*

One-line proverbs, appearing on T-shirts or bumper stickers, are often cute, frequently trite, and occasionally wise. How would it feel to wear this one: "A good name is to be chosen rather than great riches." Or, "Favor is better than silver and gold." Some scholars believe the Proverbs and other wisdom books in the Old Testament arose during a time of social dislocation and confusion in Israel's history. Maybe the similarity of our times to theirs encourages us to turn again to the Proverbs, which provide anchors in the midst of cultural ambiguity. Proverbs offer guidance and point us in good directions.

Riches and power tempt and lure many to lay aside family traditions, solid reputations, and one's "good name." During these autumn days, stories of baseball players who used drugs to bulk up and to pad their numbers of home runs or strikeouts can still make the headlines. Record books list names followed by an asterisk, the small symbol that tarnishes a name and diminishes an accomplishment.

A good name was valued in ancient Israel—not just as a personal issue of identification but more closely allied with defining a reputation, giving a glimpse of character. The choices we make can shape and build a reputation. Not all paths chosen are equal, though God works with our decisions to bring something good.

Think of comments you have heard. "He is kind and generous." "She is always willing to help." These are "good-name" statements. They need no asterisk.

God, give me courage to make wise decisions. Amen.

Executive Director, Rolling Ridge Retreat Center; North Andover, Massachusetts

Jesus has a good name, a renowned reputation as word has spread about this teacher, healer, and miracle worker from the backwaters of Galilee. The feeding of the five thousand (Mark 6:30-44) had reverberated and "people . . . rushed about that whole region and began to bring the sick on mats to wherever they heard he was" (Mark 6:54-55).

Jesus needs a break, a little retreat space, a vacation. He chooses a hiding place in the region of Tyre, a mostly Gentile place not frequented by Jews. We understand the need to get away, often to a foreign country or a monastery or a retreat house—a place set apart for reflection, rest, and renewal far from the reach of cell phones and beepers.

"Yet he could not escape notice." Even in that safe house, the needs of the hurting world reach Jesus. A Gentile woman sneaks into the house and falls at Jesus' feet. Having people around your ankles is disconcerting, as any football player knows. Tripping and falling frequently result. This woman with an urgent plea and a quick tongue trips up Jesus' solitude. He cannot easily shake her off or kick himself free.

Some scholars and commentators try to soften Jesus' not-so-meek-and-mild response. Yet Jesus clearly sees his ministry to the children of Israel as a first priority; and so did the early church, as Peter and Paul symbolized the polarities of the mission. Here in Mark's account, the door opens and the Bread of Life is given to one not a Jew, a crumb that will in time become loaves blessed and broken over the whole globe. Here in this healing story Jesus begins to see not just a problem person to be shaken off but also a people to love.

Loving God, open my heart wide to see beyond my limited perspective and to move through preconceptions that hinder your all-embracing grace and compassion. And help me discern my own need for a renewing retreat. Amen.

Look at this story through the eyes of the Syrophoenician woman. She comes on a mission, a maternal imperative, willing to beg at the feet of a foreigner to seek healing for her daughter. Yet, she carries heavy baggage as she crawls into the hiding place of Jesus. She is a Gentile, a woman, and as in other stories in the Gospels (see John 4), she should not be in the company of a male Jew.

Prior to this story, Jesus has addressed the issue of what is clean and unclean and turned the traditional Jewish notions of purity upside down. This woman would be one of the untouchables, but this Gospel story shows the persistence of the forgotten, the unclean, and the little ones in seeking and claiming God's care. Often the bottom-rung folks, those of low rank, receive God's attention and raise the gospel to new heights of inclusion and love.

Soon many churches will recognize the new school year with Rally Day or Christian Education Sunday. Do not shy away from using this story, for in many ways children are like the Gentile woman. Children crawl into our lives, cling to our ankles, climb into our laps, and say, "Pay attention," "Learn from me," "Love me," "Take care of me." Such simple and strong words need to be said and heard because all too often children, like the Gentile woman, are ignored, put down, forgotten.

American painter Norman Rockwell painted six-year-old Ruby Bridges carrying her books to school. In 1960, Ruby was the first African-American student to attend an all-white school in New Orleans. The painting shows her walking with her head up, eyes forward, between two sets of marshals. I look at the painting in my office and try to pay attention to the children, the forgotten, and the vision of a community of inclusion and love.

Computer search "Ruby Bridges" and find the painting by Norman Rockwell. What stories of children give you hope?

Like the Syrophoenician woman seeking healing for her daughter, some friends bring a deaf man with a speech impediment to see Jesus. Thank God for family and friends who tell us about God or bring us into Jesus' presence in the community of faith. Give thanks that we can pray on behalf of others and work for justice and healing for those without voice.

Jesus is back in familiar territory, and his reputation is known. Yet even now he seeks to contain, limit, or even silence the growing acclaim. He draws away from the crowd to a private space to touch the man and to speak the word *ephphatha.* Jesus speaks to us, "Be opened": open to seeing the needs around us, open to the whispers of grace within us, open to raising our voices in praise or in speaking a prophetic word.

An elderly man asked for a prayer of healing and anointing with oil during a worship service. It was not my church's custom or tradition, but I said I would preach on healing and then invite him forward one Sunday morning as a special favor for him. As I told the congregation what was going to happen, I timidly opened the invitation to others who might want to come forward for the laying on of hands and anointing. The long line of people coming to the altar surprised me, shocked me, and thrilled me. One person asking for a special prayer for healing had opened the doors to a new ministry. One person not wanting to keep silent about his need had uncovered the depth of hurt and pain we all carry. That one elderly man, with his request for healing prayer and anointing had turned our community of faith toward Jesus, who heals and who does all things well.

Gracious God, open us to your touch. Open us to new possibilities even in familiar places. Open us to reach out to those in need. Touch us with your healing love. Amen.

I took a class called "The Downside-Up Kingdom." The teacher believed the new reign of God was better viewed from the underside of life, from the vantage point of the poor and under-privileged. She advocated getting to know those in society who are ignored or oppressed, those on the fringes of our socially stratified culture.

James notices the poor and the forgotten and calls to pain-ful attention what happens in church gatherings. The well-to-do get the best seats in the new sanctuary, get to go first in the potluck line, get more visits from the pastor. On the one hand, James says God shows no partiality, has no favorites, and makes no distinctions between people. Yet equally, God denounces any discrimination that demeans and oppresses the poor.

Observing the early Christian community, James notices the poor receive no seat; even in the courts the rich treat them badly. God *does show* a partiality to any who are treated unjustly. God makes an option for the poor and oppressed, and Jesus says they have a special place in the new reign of God. (See Luke 6:20.)

Thought to be a quiet and safe choice for archbishop of El Salvador, Oscar Romero became an outspoken critic of policies that oppressed the poor. Saint Frances of Rome, born to an afflu-ent family and married to a wealthy man, cared for the needy and often disguised herself in order to sneak out of the palace to distribute goods to the poor. Canadian Jean Vanier came from a prestigious family yet committed his life to care for persons with mental disabilities and formed the L'Arche community where able-bodied staff live side by side with the differently abled.

Whom do you remember as a champion of the oppressed? Read about some saints in history. How are you and your church community reaching out to the poor?

James can make us feel uncomfortable by exposing our shallow words that do not change the problem. He uncovers our good but faulty intentions that often end up lacking concrete action. He shows our lame attempts to sound wise and talk big but do nothing. We stand confronted by an all-too-often truth that our words simply cover up our lack of action.

Faith for the epistle writer does not involve a system of belief but a way of life. What we do is as important as what we say. Words gain integrity when they are matched by consistent, loving action.

Paul wrote that we must be saved by faith alone and not by works (Gal. 2:16); he views works differently than James. Obediently carrying out the works of Jewish law will not win salvation according to Paul; but for James, works flow from the love and grace of God who has saved us. For James, works of charity clearly signal our faith in God and are essential to back up words of kindness.

A pastor friend of mine noted that his congregation said they were open to all people but did little to back it up. He invited four couples of his white country church to pair with four couples of a nearby African-American city church. Each foursome would commit to eating dinner in each other's home and to attending each other's church. Understanding and friendships grew; walls and barriers were broken down. Being open to others in particular gave way to being open to others in general.

In the beloved community of God, people different in color, background, documentation, nationality, or orientation sit side by side and feel at peace.

Challenging God, stir us to loving deeds that match our good words. Remind us that our mission is to clothe the naked, feed the hungry, and be peacemakers. Amen.

These last verses from Proverbs tie up the ends of our week of weaving the deeds of justice and healing into the fabric of faith and reputation. The wisdom writer makes it clear. Sow injustice, you reap trouble. Be generous and be blessed. The simple acts count, like sharing bread with the poor or contributing to a food bank.

Compassion goes beyond the personal but does not forget the importance of good and kind deeds—remember the instructions of James to back up words with acts of caring and sharing. "At the gate" refers to the public system of justice widespread in ancient Israel. The judges heard evidence in cases at the gates to the city, in the presence of many witnesses. The rich might have money and power to persuade, but the poor have an advocate, God Almighty, who pleads for them and stands by their side.

Clearly we are to feed the poor and use the political and legal avenues to end injustice. Social service and social justice must be woven together. Bake a casserole and write to support legislation to address national and global hunger. It is both-and, not either-or.

Justice themes also weave throughout the Psalms, but our text hovers in Jerusalem, where trouble camps at the walls. The psalmist looks at the hills and Mount Zion and pens a word of hope. Those who trust in God are not moved or dissuaded from the cause of justice. God encircles them with love and goodness. But wickedness lurks, and he expresses some concern that foreign powers might tempt or lead the community to "stretch out their hands to do wrong." The psalmist concludes with prayer. "Do good, O LORD." Bring peace.

Holy God, hold us firmly in your embrace. Fill us with courage,
and keep us steady on the paths of justice. Amen.

Teachings and Teachers

SEPTEMBER 10–16, 2012 • CYNTHIA HIZER

MONDAY, SEPTEMBER 10 ~ *Read Proverbs 1:20-33*

The hike began late. We were headed into a sacred canyon, and our guide had suggested we start early. But getting nine teenagers and four adults up and fed and to the trailhead made it late morning before we entered the canyon.

Did we have enough water, our guide asked? Did we have sunscreen and long-sleeved shirts, hats, and water shoes? Water shoes? I dimly remembered something about that in one of the crackly telephone calls, but we were headed to the desert, after all. We didn't take seriously the wisdom offered by someone who had lived in the canyon the length of his life and knew every step of it intimately. He carried the wisdom of a people living in this canyon for eight hundred years. Wisdom was crying out in the street, but we didn't listen.

We had packed light; each had a bottle of water and sunscreen. Most had hats. Fewer had long-sleeved shirts or long pants. No one had water shoes. Still, we forged ahead and soon descended one thousand feet down a rocky trail. Red boulders and vistas buoyed us for hours. By the time we stopped for lunch, most were out of water. We gobbled our sandwiches and collapsed in the shade, and napped.

Our guide quietly unlaced his hiking boots and slipped on water sandals. For the next four hours the river became our trail. Our bare feet struggled against slippery, jagged rocks and downed branches. The wisdom of God sometimes looks like simple practical advice.

God, may we listen as you pour out your wisdom in so many unassuming ways. Amen.

Associate Rector of the Episcopal Church of the Epiphany, Atlanta, Georgia

The book of Proverbs is one of several "wisdom" books in the Bible, along with Ecclesiastes and Job. Its parallel in the New Testament is the book of James from which we also read this week. Both Proverbs and James are eager to instruct us, even with information we already know or should know.

We already know that wisdom abounds; and every street corner, every checkout line, every radio and television airwave tosses out nuggets on how to live the good life.

The prophetess Wisdom takes her assertions to the town square. There she shouts from the corners at scoffers and fools. Her advice? "Give heed," which literally means "to return." God graciously offers wisdom to the people. They, like we, have the ability to perceive what God desires of us. God has so ordered creation that our study of it gives us insight into God's nature. God's wisdom comes to us from the treetops and flies in on every seedpod and blade of grass. We hear it in the pulse of birdsong and street traffic and marketplace. It's the life force that flows. It is lived experience.

God's wisdom is everywhere and in everything. It involves imagination and expression. It is the natural abundance that comes from creation. Our bodies and minds and spirits are created chock-full of this wisdom, this spirit of God, this truth and knowledge; it is so close at hand we can turn our attention to it at any time.

Woe to those who fail to be wise: they will call and receive no answer; they will seek and not find. Those who live within the realm of Wisdom will find themselves secure and at ease. Being wise to God's ways brings abundance and happiness. At Wisdom's foundation is a flowing, unbounded love that orients us toward mercy and empathy.

God of Wisdom, open our eyes to your life-giving wisdom. Amen.

I stood in a circle with others and saluted each of the four directions, praying in each direction. We started with the East, then turned to the South, then the West, and ended with the North. Then we turned to the East again, to indicate the completion of the circle.

In the direction of the East we prayed to the energy of beginnings, of spring, green grass, and all that is new. In the South we prayed to the fiery heat of love and a high-noon blue summer sky. We turned to the West and gave thanks for a golden harvest at the end of the growing season, and we honored wisdom born from experience. As we turned to the North we saluted a time of rest, of dream time, and a time for regeneration of ourselves and the birthing of new ideas.

Where was I? What religion was this? I have prayed in this format, to these directions, to these essences of truth through Native American prayers, Celtic, Chinese. I have saluted the directions, the sun and moon and earth in English, Irish, Gaelic, Hebrew, Chinese, Sioux, and Creek. In a church on the Navajo Nation, I was taught to walk around the altar always in clockwise fashion, in the direction of the sun.

This is the time-honored understanding of the very energies of the universe. God is everywhere, not just in the East or North. It is the logic within which the universe operates—this unfolding of day to night, season to season, place to place, age to age, "one day telling its tale to another" (AP). As we step into this fundamental teaching of how things are, we find restoration and comfort. "The law of the LORD is perfect, reviving the soul." This same understanding also revives my trust. The circle is God speaking truth.

Creator, help me step into the harmony you have created. Amen.

THURSDAY, SEPTEMBER 13 ~ *Read James 3:1-2*

The September garden, to my mind, is the best. It is a collision of every luscious thing the garden can grow: late summer squash, peppers, and eggplant now mingle with fall onions and radishes and the first cuttings of arugula. Figs and grapes are ripe, and peaches linger a few more days.

The September garden also holds potential for our redemption. As we wrap up the harvest and prepare the garden for winter, we step back to reflect. Now we take time to consider if we planted the right variety of tomato for our region or if we should have planted them on the ridge instead of the valley. We will take note of that for next year. We will build deer fencing and consider rain barrels for times of drought.

But to get to redemption, our reflection must go deeper. Since we have sold produce, now is the time to ask ourselves if we charged a fair price. Were our bags really a full pound? Did we gossip and judge; did we respect the dignity of every person? September is the time to consider our mistakes and make amends for the coming year.

Since the Jews following Jesus were not yet excluded from the synagogue in these early days, it is likely that the epistle writer and his family would have continued to observe Jewish holy days. In September he and his family would have been preparing for Yom Kippur, the Day of Atonement. He too would have been in a period of stepping back and reflecting and asking forgiveness.

In the midst of the epistle's caustic admonishments toward teachers and unbridled tongues, we can easily miss in this passage the small but forgiving and even redemptive September moment: "all of us make many mistakes."

God of all seasons, help us to use this season of September to reflect, ask forgiveness, and wait upon you to reorient and redeem our lives. Amen.

Teachings and Teachers

FRIDAY, SEPTEMBER 14 ~ *Read James 3:3-4*

My prayer shawl hangs on a peg that I see as I wake up each morning. There it is again in the nighttime when I retire. It is not exactly waving to me, but I notice its movement from the autumn breeze coming in the window. I could say Morning Prayer and Compline, these two times, morning and night. I could postpone activities of the ego, of the active life: the morning coffee, feeding the dogs, checking the computer for traffic problems along my commuting route. I might postpone or even eliminate the anxiety of the day. I might instead wrap the shawl around my arms and fold myself down onto my mat in the presence of God. If I did this, I could allow myself to be available to receive support, teaching, wisdom.

Especially now, in September; the morning light comes later and holds the days' activities back a while longer. Evening dusk comes earlier too. Morning light and evening dusk press in toward each other to create a shorter day of busyness and a longer period—an opportunity—to turn our attention inward.

These opportunities to set aside time for prayer become like a bit in the horse's mouth or a ship's rudder. They gently draw us near and guide. They discipline our minds.

They are teaching moments too, not of words that can be said hastily, which we later regret but a knowing of the unfathomable seeping love that surrounds us in the air we breathe. They are the gift of wisdom, even mercy. In these God-directed moments the divine Presence can direct our course and bring us to mindfulness of how we speak and act and treat one another.

Morning and evening prayers, time on our mat or in our prayer chairs, time spent allowing wisdom to form us and inform us: these are bits and rudders. They rewire our brains toward seeing and knowing the whole world as Christ does.

Guiding God, I ask to be directed and drawn near to see the whole world as one. Amen.

As the epistle writer notes, the tongue and its language can limit, can hurt from words withheld or spoken. Once uttered, they cannot be retrieved. "No one can tame the tongue." And it can offer both blessing and curse.

It is my job to put art materials in the Sunday school rooms. The children employ the art materials after hearing a Bible story. They offer a kind of silent language for the children to respond to God—hidden and found, finite and infinite. Our role as teachers is to prepare the space for the child's own discovery of these qualities. There is wisdom in this curriculum: our tongues are generally silent. But through silence or words spoken aloud, the emphasis is placed upon blessing "the Lord and Father," as well as those "made in the likeness of God."

James 3:1 holds teachers to a high standard. The translation from the Vulgate even refers to them as masters. To that end, I choose art supplies for my students carefully. I have fresh play dough for the younger children and modeling clay for the older ones; beautiful pencils, markers, and watercolors. I have several sizes and types of paper, scissors, glue, and even glitter. These are nice art supplies, but finally, somehow limiting. What seems to be missing is something from nature.

So I gather fresh green leaves one week and golden leaves the next and then sweet gum balls. I am enchanted with the small twigs that fall to the ground in my yard, especially the ones covered with mosses and lichen. But the leaves wither. The sticks break. The lichen fall off. These too seem limiting, unlike God.

What I would really like to bring into the classroom are clouds. Clouds would not be limiting. With clouds children could learn the language of mystery, of God hidden and found, finite and infinite—of blessing.

Infinite One, come close and teach us your mysteries. Amen.

Several renowned theologians recently have written autobiographies. One of them even wrote a second one, ten years after the first. It is as if, after years of writing and teaching, after years of making their mark on the world, they have finally asked, "Who do you say that I am?" The answer they get back is not big enough. As they get closer to their fulfillment and the maturity of their work, they feel the necessity to redefine who they are.

Jesus is refining and redefining his identity as he asks Peter, "Who do people say that I am?" Jesus is the Messiah, Peter says. But maybe Peter's idea of Messiah is smaller than that of Jesus'. Perhaps Peter is blind to the full revelation of Jesus. This conversation comes after a spate of miracles and healings, most particularly after Jesus' healing of a blind man in Bethsaida. Now Jesus will open Peter's eyes to the true meaning of Messiah.

Jesus and the disciples are traveling from Bethsaida to Caesarea Philippi. While on the way Jesus asks them who people think he is. But even as they travel and move, our concept of Jesus' identity is moving. Instead of becoming all-powerful, Jesus turns it around. Instead of becoming the masterful David figure who will return power to the Israelites, Jesus defines who he is and how salvation will come about.

Peter gets the answer right and then is the very one who rebukes Jesus' understanding of Messiah. Jesus goes on to discuss the nature of Christian life: "those who . . . save their life will lose it, . . . those who lose their life for my sake, . . . will save it." Peter is moving down the path to maturation and understanding. We constantly refine and redefine our understanding of God as we mature in our faith walk, but our journey will follow that of Jesus. This much we know.

Jesus, as we blossom in our faith, let our refining of you blossom. Amen.

Choosing Life with God

SEPTEMBER 17–23, 2012 • PAUL L. ESCAMILLA

MONDAY, SEPTEMBER 17 ~ *Read Proverbs 31:10-31*

Proverbs 31 is a strikingly vivid picture of a woman who is, in her own right, a "renaissance woman" of sorts. Securing food, growing produce, making wool and linens, trading, merchandising, clothing her family, discharging orders for her household staff—this is a woman of some means.

But clearly the woman's means are not merely material. Her success derives from an inner sensibility or character rather than from an outer set of resources. The text profiles this character beautifully.

First, the woman's hands (mentioned seven times) figure prominently as an extension of her inner intentions and motives. Not only do they craft and sew and plant and reap; they also clothe and feed and respond to the poor, always exuding self-assurance and confidence. Not to be missed is the fact that they serve the woman's own needs as well as those of her household and the needy.

Other verses demonstrate the balance and well-roundedness of this woman as well. She has dignity in her person but also laughter. She is wise but also kind. She seeks opportunities for generosity no less than for gain. She is clearly a beautiful person, but charm and physical appearance are irrelevant to her beauty. Finally, she knows the dimension of life from which all other dimensions derive their meaning: knowing God. Indeed, "her works praise her."

Think on the life of this person in Proverbs as a model of virtue.

Senior pastor of St. John's United Methodist Church; Austin, Texas

TUESDAY, SEPTEMBER 18 ~ *Read Psalm 1:1-2*

The first verse of Psalm 1 introduces us to a word that has not appeared to this point in the Hebrew scriptures: *blessed*. We've seen words like *bless* and *blessing* before, of course, but those particular Hebrew words refer to the act or experience of anointing, affirming, or exalting. (For example, see Genesis 48:8-22.) This word *blessed* has more to do with an outlook or disposition toward life. The closest translation for the word is probably *happy*.

Happy is about as washed out, watered-down, overused, and undernourished as a word can get. Yet Psalm 1 lifts it up and applies it with remarkable freshness, substance, and depth. And what is the source of this state of happiness? It takes a while to find out, following the sentence to its conclusion; but the search leads us here: "Blessed are those . . . whose delight is in the law of the LORD."

The psalm, which serves as a prelude or preamble to the whole psalter, spells out in simple terms the way a good life evolves: happiness is a matter of finding good instruction (while avoiding poor instruction) and living by it.

As it turns out, the good instruction is not a package deal. No formulas or "secret steps to happiness" apply. We could translate "the law of the LORD" as "the Lord's instruction," which clarifies something extremely important about the biblical understanding of happiness: it involves being in relationship with God, who teaches, guides, and directs our paths. Happy are those who delight in their teacher and whose teacher's name is the Lord.

God, I wish to know you in all your delightfulness and to learn your instruction that my life may be blessed. Amen.

If verses 1 and 2 of Psalm 1 explain the means to happiness in God, then verse 3 has something to say about its effect on our lives. In essence, to be related to God is to become as trees. This metaphor occupies the whole of the third verse.

The trees depicted here are not cut down for firewood, used up once, and discarded as ashes. A person of faith is meant for greater and repeated resourcefulness—a lifetime of giving, serving, growing, and prospering. That these trees are planted by streams of water suggests that not only do they nourish others, but they receive nourishment. Further, their fruit-bearing is seasonal, rhythmic, and natural; not erratic, hyperactive, then finally, spent. Trees are not fruit factories but fruit bearers. The fruit they yield is not an unrelated "product" but an expression of their own organic makeup.

Of course, the trees envisioned by the psalmist are grounded. By their nature, they will reach outward and upward, toward water and sunlight. And in season, their boughs will bend earthward with the weight of their fruit. But not all their activity is so visible to the eye; at the same time, they will always be developing roots deep down, drawing continual nourishment from both earth and stream.

Nourishing and drawing nourishment. Giving, yet maintaining identity. Growing and reaching, yet firmly grounded. Persons whose lives are rooted in God's presence and instruction reflect these characteristics.

Think of yourself in terms of Psalm 1. I am like a tree, and my life is grounded and watered. I am reaching, providing shade, and bearing fruit; for I delight in God's instruction.

O God, you are rain and sunshine, river and soil to the tree that is my life. I rest in your provision and delight in your care. Amen.

Verses 1-3 painted the blissful picture of a life of happiness in God in all its substance, creativity, and beauty. Verses 4-6 draw the contrast. And for this purpose, the psalmist employs another metaphor, this one based on chaff.

The hues and tones of this metaphorical picture are somber and bland. Gone are the images of streaming sun and the shady boughs of green leaf and robust fruit, flowing stream, and cool, sweet-smelling earth. Here we have chaff—weightless, tasteless, void of substance or texture or color. The only thing said of it is that the wind drives it away. At winnowing time, its only value is in its absence.

The psalmist's artistry becomes clear. Even as the lessons of the good life, that is—life within God's instruction—are being spelled out, two pictures have been painted that affect our senses in very different ways. Life with God tastes sweet; it is joyous and abundant. Life apart from God, that is, lived to oneself, is husklike, bland, and dry; in other words, it is tasteless.

Likewise, the sense of footing differs in the two pictures. The "way of the righteous" is well-grounded, even while allowing for growth and movement. The "way of the wicked' is shifty, flighty, and completely without bearing.

In terms of contrasts, we could draw no greater. Of course, life does not always present such obvious differences between choosing life with God versus life on one's own. That is precisely why Psalm 1 is so valuable; it sees with a clear, spiritual eye the way life with God and life on one's own really are. Then it invites us to choose life with God.

Guide me, O God, in choosing always that which is good and worthy and deeply delightful over that which is banal and tasteless and dry. Amen.

FRIDAY, SEPTEMBER 21 ~ *Read Mark 9:33-37*

We know Mark as the freight train evangelist. Just reading his first chapter without pause can leave us nearly breathless. By the time we get to this point in the Gospel, not only have many actions been recorded but the word *immediately* has been peppered throughout. This is no sit-down story. Jesus is on the move—healing, teaching, exorcising demons, feeding the hungry, and on and on.

Then something happens to bring it all to a halt. Is it a run-in with Pharisees? A scrape with the Sanhedrin? Is it fatigue or weariness or disillusionment? It is none of these things. In the middle of chapter 9, which is in the center of the Gospel, everything comes to a halt because Jesus perceives that his disciples are talking about their own greatness. Jesus sits down—one of the few times in the entire Gospel—and teaches his disciples.

It is very important to notice that the one thing that slows down the pace of this Gospel is the evidence of selfish ambition on the part of Jesus' disciples. Who is the greatest? Who is the best? Who is on top? Who is more special? When Jesus sensed that this was the subject of their conversation, he sat down.

Think for a moment about what makes you "sit down." What leads you to set aside whatever you are doing and look the other person in the eye? For Jesus, it may have been his concern that the very heart of his teaching and witness might be misunderstood, overlooked, or forgotten.

Jesus sat down, called the Twelve, and said to them, "Whoever wants to be first must be last of all and servant of all." This is important; this is critical. In a nutshell, this is discipleship.

O God, grant me ears to hear this word of Jesus. Beginning now, and throughout this day, give me courage to live it! Amen.

SATURDAY, SEPTEMBER 22 ~ *Read Mark 9:30-37*

The Gospel text for this week is a centerpiece for the whole book of Mark, a focal point for the portrayal of Jesus' fate at the hands of his enemies: he is to suffer and die before he is raised up again. It is the second of three prophecies in which Jesus foretells his own fate. (Mark 8:31-33 and Mark 10:32-45 are the other two.) All three of these passages share a common external structure as well: the anticipated suffering of Jesus is followed by evidences of the lofty ambitions of certain of Jesus' disciples.

In each case the inappropriate response to Jesus' prophecy appears to be completely unwitting. In the first instance, Peter simply expresses a protectiveness related to his own ambitions for Jesus (8:32); in the third, the prophecy appears to go over their heads (10:35 and following). In today's reading, confusion and fear drive the disciples to a different subject.

Different, but not unrelated. Greatness is the common denominator of both Jesus' words and the disciples' miscast responses. But the disciples can think of greatness only in terms of self-filling, while Jesus speaks of a greatness based on self-emptying. The disciples' gaze is rather high up in the clouds; Jesus looks upon the weakest, smallest, lowliest example around and demonstrates the meaning of true greatness.

"Whoever wants to associate with me, and even with God, is so invited," Jesus in effect says; and we all look up, dreaming of the possibilities of such greatness. Meanwhile, Jesus stoops down and takes a child in his arms.

Lord, reveal to my eyes and to my heart the truly great things, that I may seek them and, having found them, learn to love them. Amen.

Not one to mince words, the writer of James spells out some very plain matters in a very short space. Are you wise? This is how we will know: your good life will show works that are carried out with gentleness. On the other hand, if your hearts are occupied with envy and selfish ambition, then this is how we will know: disorder and wickedness of every kind will be in evidence. James calls this wisdom too, but of another sort.

And what exactly does "wickedness of every kind" mean? Exactly that: everything from disagreements to murder. It is difficult to imagine murder being an actual issue in the life of a congregation; but if the letter of James is anything, it is realistic. James knows well that when it comes to the struggle to become holy, compassionate, and wise, Christians are by no means out of the woods simply by virtue of their name. "Envy" and "selfish ambition" often find fertile soil in Christian climates.

But let us move to the next characterization—that of wisdom, which comes from above. This description, rather than the one we have just looked at, is the real heart of the text. It reminds us in many ways of the characterization of the blessed person in Psalm 1: fruitfulness—another use of the harvest metaphor—and a willingness to yield. The passage names other qualities: purity, peaceableness, gentleness, mercy, and the absence of partiality or hypocrisy. James teaches us that wisdom is far more than simply head knowledge; it gives texture to every dimension of life and service. And it is one thing more: a gift from above.

Meditate on the qualities of wisdom from above. Begin to seek these in prayer and in practice.

Intercessory Prayer

SEPTEMBER 24–30, 2012 • SUSAN H. BADEAU

MONDAY, SEPTEMBER 24 ～ *Read Esther 7:1-6, 9-10*

It started with Gerry. Fidgety, fast-talking. Then Kurt. Dignified. Brilliant. Also, Benski. Timid. Forgetful. Twinkling eyes. Veterans, all. Served our country bravely but now homeless, hungry, lonely. These men lived on the streets. They browsed in our bookstore, became our friends, and then like family. Soon we met Greta, Marcie, Laura. Young women on the brink of transition, living in foster care. Soon to cross into adulthood, and like Gerry, Kurt, and Benski, soon to be homeless, hungry, alone.

Some days I thought my own needs were too insignificant to bother my Lord with my petitions. Yet, as I thought about these people—cast-offs from society but brothers and sisters to me—I knew that their needs were worthy of God's attention. So, I began to approach God's throne on their behalf. They did not need half the kingdom. Just a chance to come inside. To have a home, a family, an inheritance. To belong.

I have been humbled and honored to grasp the fact that I can approach this throne of grace boldly on their behalf because I serve a King who longs to give good gifts, delights in sharing the kingdom. Like the king in Esther's story, God says to us, "What is your petition? It shall be granted you." God stands ready to open the doors of the kingdom for me and for my people too.

Heavenly Father, help us acknowledge the homeless, the orphan, the addict, the mentally ill as "your people"; may we boldly petition you on their behalf, knowing that you stand ready to say, "It shall be granted." Amen.

Director of Knowledge Management, Casey Family Programs, Summit Presbyterian Church; Philadelphia, Pennsylvania

It was a rare, quiet moment sipping coffee by the fire. The gaiety of Christmas morning in a house filled with children was past, New Year's Eve festivities lay ahead. Upstairs, tots and teens slept.

"Mom! Dad!" the peace shattered. "Adam won't wake up!" A month filled with holidays, feasting, and rejoicing was abruptly transformed. We plunged into sorrow and unspeakable grief. Our beautiful eleven-year-old son had died. Adopted five years earlier from foster care, Adam was cranky and easily frightened. He had a terminal illness; we knew this day would come. Yet we lived as though it never would. Each day we cared for Adam we prayed for relief from his twin enemies of pain and suffering inflicted by this fearsome disease. We asked God to heal his disease-riddled body and deeply scarred soul. Now his life had ended.

I felt angry and overwhelmed. Why hadn't God heard our prayers? Why had Adam left us so soon? Why, especially now, during the holidays, which would forever be marred with memories of death and pain?

A family member quietly massaged my tense neck. Without words, his comforting presence helped me remember Adam's golden smile, inherent sweetness, and gentle spirit. I knew then that our prayers had been answered; the enemy had indeed been defeated. While we would mourn and grieve, we would also be comforted. Like the Jewish people in Esther's time, our Adam and our family had received the much-desired relief from the enemy of disease and pain. I decided to prepare for New Year's Eve after all. God wanted to show us how to turn sorrow into gladness and a time of mourning into a holiday filled with feasting and rejoicing.

Lord, may we be your instruments of comfort to those in our midst who face a season of mourning. Amen.

Intercessory Prayer

WEDNESDAY, SEPTEMBER 26 ~ *Read Psalm 124*

It was four in the morning. The sun and my entire family was still asleep, as I walked along the beach praying. We had come to the shore for a brief respite after hearing troubling news from our daughter. Depressed, feeling abandoned and angry, I longed for the waters to engulf me, for the waves to sweep over me and carry me to a distant shore. I expected to be alone.

Yet, shell seekers were already on the beach. Watching them, I noticed a pattern. They would pick up a shell and look at it closely. They kept a few but tossed most away. I realized that they were seeking whole shells. They examined the shells for cracks and holes, casting the broken ones back, saving only those deemed perfect.

I started to pick up shells too. As I held one delicate, slightly broken shell in my hand, while watching the pounding waves crash and break against the shore, I was amazed. *How did this fragile shell survive at all?* I wondered. *Why wasn't it pulverized by the power of the water?*

Psalm 124 immediately came to mind. "If it had not been the LORD who was on our side," I recalled, "over us would have gone the raging waters." I looked at the broken shell anew. It had been tossed and slammed; yet, here it was, glistening and beautiful.

Each of us is like this broken shell—delicate, strong, extraordinary. With hopefulness, I prayed for my daughter. As she faced the crashing waves of life, I prayed she wouldn't fear being swept away, but that she would remember our help is in the name of the same Lord who made heaven, earth, and every drop of water in the ocean. And God is on our side.

Dear Lord, when the troubles of life threaten to engulf us, turn our eyes toward you and remind us that you have saved us from the raging waters. Blessed be the Lord. Amen.

The prayer of the righteous is powerful and effective." For many, this verse offers hope and encouragement but not always for me. Are my prayers effective? Am I righteous? I struggle with prayer and, unlike Elijah, I cannot often point to concrete results when I pray for the rains to stop pouring into the lives of my children or others.

"Pray without ceasing," we are taught. Yet I find it hard to pray for more than five minutes without becoming distracted. As I study prayer in the Bible, I am struck by other words and phrases associated with prayer: *continually, always, devoted to, at all times, night and day, earnestly.*

If I were more righteous, more devoted to prayer, I wonder, *would that prevent one teen from becoming pregnant or another from using drugs? Would it save one child from an abusive relationship or bring the prodigal home?*

The author of James speaks of the power of prayer and its potential for healing. He seems to draw a distinction between prayer as gift and prayer as tool. With prayer as gift, we may approach God on the behalf of others. We do not whip prayer out of our pocket to make God do our bidding. We pray as gift and "the Lord will raise them up."

I passionately devote myself to the work God has given me—helping youth in foster care. Three colleagues recently thanked me for "making my life a prayer" for vulnerable children. I may not always see the blue skies following the rain, but I can trust that prayers offered in faith can bring restoration and healing.

God, may I pray for all those in my care, trusting in your word that such prayers will bring healing and restoration to your precious children. Amen.

I have two sons in prison. This is not something I brag about at parties or include in my Christmas newsletter. Regardless of their crimes, they are my sons and I love them deeply. I pray for them daily, asking God to guide their steps back to the path of light and truth.

Each of them broke my heart. After years of teaching and guiding my sons, praying for them, involving them in church, providing them with tools for making wise choices, their decisions to stray feel like proof that I have failed in my God-given assignment as a mother. I feel their actions reflect poorly on me.

What arrogance! If their errors reflect on me, do mine likewise reflect on my heavenly Father? Are my sins proof that God failed as a parent to me? No! For "all have sinned and fall short of the glory of God" (Rom. 3:23). Straying from truth, choosing our own path, failing to listen to the still small voice inside—these are human failings, reflections of our deep need for God's mercy, forgiveness, and grace.

We all have our own prisons. While the sins of those in prison are laid bare for public viewing, our own private sins just as surely separate us from God. I have not assaulted, but I have hated in my heart. I haven't done drugs, but I fight my own demons. Yet daily God forgives me and draws me back. When I stray from the truth, God sends angels disguised as friends, family, even strangers to bring me back from my wandering, saving my "soul from death." What a wondrous service the community of God renders to one another!

Father God, thank you for sending people to turn us back to your path when we stray. May we also seek and find your lost children, turning them back to you. Thank you for your unending and amazing grace! Amen.

We adopted Dylan when he was four years old. He was blind, had cerebral palsy, developmental disabilities, and other challenges. Yet, we all appreciated his sweet, gentle spirit and contagious laugh. He loved music, family, camping trips, church, Christmas, Phillies games, and sweet potatoes.

Dylan's medical challenges worsened over time. In early August, he was hospitalized, seriously ill and experiencing unbearable pain. He left the hospital with hospice care coming to our home. We had lived through the death of one child, but Adam had died quickly and peacefully; we did not have a prolonged end-of-life journey with him. This was new territory.

From the moment Dylan got home, he was peaceful and pain-free. With few exceptions, he stayed this way until his death a week later. The few exceptions involved two endless days when we watched him endure fear, anxiety, and excruciating pain due to an unanticipated change in doctor's orders. We felt helpless in the face of this crisis, so God sent an angel to stand with us, ministering to Dylan, casting out the demons of fear and pain, and giving him a song of peace.

Was this miracle worker a doctor? pastor? faith-healer? No, Abby was an ordinary woman, a woman from a different faith tradition than our own and yet so profoundly sent by God to minister to us. We had prayed continuously for Dylan, and God answered our prayers in a most unexpected way. Abby bore "the name of Christ," and Dylan and our family reaped a reward beyond our imaginations, expectations, and fears.

God, may we not hinder those who would perform miracles in your name, even when they do not appear to be your followers. Give us gratitude for every cool cup of water you supply to us, and may our thirsty souls be truly quenched. Amen.

Every child needs to be received into the loving arms of a nurturing family. This message is the salt God uses to fill my salt shaker. Like salt, this message can be a seasoning or a preservative for those who work with children, or it can sting as salt in a wound for those who cause children to stumble. Helping children become part of families is as invigorating to my spirit as a dip in the chilly salt waters of Maine. Yet, the deeper I went into policy and advocacy, the less certain I became about the effectiveness of my efforts. Was my salt becoming unsalty?

Jesus addresses his disciples about their commitment to ministry. They are to examine themselves and assess what stumbling blocks might prevent them from energetic service to God. The examples Jesus gives of removing those stumbling blocks seem extreme. Yet he makes it clear that nothing is to divert us from our main task as disciples. Only then can we remain salty.

Recently I consulted on the case of a teenage boy. I drove to Henry's group home. I spent hours there, late into the evening, and something remarkable happened. My salt regained its saltiness. My time spent with Henry released the zest and life-preserving power of my salt. New ideas tumbled forth and opportunities for breaking down barriers and solving problems emerged. Henry's hope was renewed.

A few months later, I learned that these efforts had paid off. Henry was at last home with a family that will be his permanently. Henry's life was forever changed by events set in motion on that one rainy night. The events of that night changed my life too. My stumbling block of self-doubt dissolved in my renewed commitment to my ministry in the divine reign. My salt was made salty again, and what a blessing that is!

Lord, may I examine my life in the light of your love. Help me identify any obstacles to my wholehearted commitment to your reign. Amen.

Trust and Obey

OCTOBER 1–7, 2012 • STEVE PHILLIPS

MONDAY, OCTOBER 1 ~ *Read Job 1:1; 2:1-8*

Biographies give us insight into leaders and famous people of the past such as Abraham Lincoln or Saint Francis of Assisi. Few biographies have ever started with a more jarring pair of sentences than the story of Job. In some ways, knowing this familiar story makes it more difficult to grasp that Job "was blameless and upright."

The book of Job offers yet another attempt to understand why good—blameless and upright—people experience devastating situations and grievous suffering. To catch us up on the story in the intervening verses, we recall that Satan tells God that Job is faithful only because nothing bad has ever happened to him. Job seems to be God's favorite who is blessed and protected. So God allows Satan free rein in Job's affairs. He loses all his livestock and his children in one fell swoop. Scripture says he "fell on the ground and worshiped" (1:20). God's only request in round two is that Job's life be spared. Satan ups the ante, inflicting Job with a terrible skin disease, rendering him unclean.

We too face trials. Perhaps we second-guess ourselves and our relationship with God. We may wonder about God's love and care for us when maladies strike or crises hit. However, we know what lies ahead for Job, and we take comfort and strength from his patience and steadfast faith in God despite his circumstances. We don't know what is around the corner in our own lives, but we can stand firm in that same steadfast faith.

Lord, give us the ability to hold fast to our faith in both good and bad times. Amen.

Sports Director for WBIR-TV, member of Sevier Heights Baptist Church; living in Knoxville, Tennessee

The appeal of the book of Job to those who are enduring trials is more than just the happy ending. Job teaches us patience and righteousness in a grossly unjust situation. Today's scene opens with Job sitting in a heap of ashes, scraping his skin with a piece of pottery, with no livelihood and no children. His situation looks bleak indeed.

Perhaps you too have found yourself at the bottom looking up; perhaps there came a time when you had nothing left to lose. Today's verses can be instructive to Christ followers who find themselves in just such places. Interestingly enough, Job's wife offers the very solution that Satan desires: "Curse God, and die." Curse God and break the third commandment—at least then you'll be out of your misery.

Job's moral character and integrity hinge on his relationship to God. He is indeed blameless and upright. He points out to his wife that if we willingly receive good from God, we must also suffer the bad. For Job, the God of all creation holds within God's power all that is. In all the suffering that will follow, Job humbly accepts his situation, even rejecting his wife's "foolish" advice. "In all this Job did not sin with his lips."

All of us who love and worship God will face temptation. And the greatest temptation when nothing is going right is to "curse God." From Job's perspective, the best choice is to hold fast to your relationship with God in good times and bad. Test all advice, even from those you trust, against what you know of God and God's work in your life.

Father, I claim your promise that you will never leave me. Strengthen me that I may not sin against you when life's storms come my way. Amen.

Before John Grisham became a best-selling author, he practiced law in his native Mississippi. His courtroom work added detail and texture to his many novels.

Grisham's law background also attracted him to the story of Ron Williamson in Ada, Oklahoma. Williamson and his friend Dennis Fritz had been falsely accused, charged, and convicted of a 1982 murder. After serving eleven years in prison, their names were finally cleared. Grisham's first nonfiction book, *The Innocent Man*, details that story.

The death penalty was ruled unconstitutional in the United States in 1972. Since 1973 Williamson and Fritz are among at least one hundred thirty-eight people who have been exonerated and set free. Being falsely accused, even in serious crimes, is more common than we might know.

The psalmist, like Job, is a person of integrity who has led a "blameless life." He faces false accusations and appeals to a higher authority; he takes his case before God. Like a confident defense attorney, he states his love for and trust in the Lord. "Test me, O LORD, and try me, examine my heart and my mind" (NIV). The psalmist then lays out his case: your love is always before me; I walk in your truth; I don't hang out with liars and hypocrites. He turns to God and expects help from that source.

A defense such as the one the psalmist offers requires one critical element: truth. Would we be able to stand boldly before the Lord and proclaim our innocence, our love for God and for God's people? Would we be able to accept God's answer?

God, examine my heart and my mind, that I may praise and honor you before others. Amen.

Undercover Boss is a TV show where top executives from large companies agree to forego their corner office to spend time on the ground level of their business. The executives discover inefficiency, unresolved issues, and problem employees in almost every situation. However, a great many executives are stunned by the pleasant attitudes and hard work of some of their employees who make a fraction of the executive's salary. Once the "undercover boss" is revealed, the workers have a newfound respect for how much their boss cared for them individually, cared about their situations, and cared about the company.

The inconveniences those CEOs experienced and the benefit to their employees and companies pale dramatically against the story of Jesus Christ. While God for centuries had spoken and conveyed the divine will through the prophets, the Creator of the world takes a bold and unique step by coming to us as an infant and living among us for more than three decades. Jesus wasn't undercover, though he was unrecognized and disregarded by most. Despite the fact that messengers announced Jesus' coming, people couldn't or wouldn't lay aside their own struggles to observe the One in their midst.

The writer of Hebrews assures us that God values the Son so much that God made Jesus the "heir of all things," "superior to the angels" (NIV). Jesus' work among us, his obedience to the Father's plan, and his death on the cross opened a way for us to be cleansed of our sins.

Jesus finished his task of sustenance and purification and then took his rightful place alongside the Father, where he sits today advocating for those of us still working here on earth.

O Lord, we praise you and thank you for loving us and providing a way for us to be in your holy presence. Amen.

The Pharisees represented one of the largest, most powerful religious groups among the Jews at the time of Jesus. They find Jesus' growing number of followers alarming and his open criticism of them unacceptable. So they craft cleverly worded questions from which they believe there is no escape. In today's encounter, their concern is more with eliminating a threat to their power than with the issue of divorce. The Pharisees "test" Jesus by asking, "Is it lawful for a man to divorce his wife?"

There were two schools of thought in that time on the interpretation of Mosaic law on divorce. One side emphasized the phrase "finds something indecent about her" (Deut. 24:1, NIV), taking it to mean marital unfaithfulness. The other gave greater meaning to the preceding phrase "becomes displeasing to him." That interpretation would allow men to divorce their wives over trivial matters.

Jesus answers their question with another question that leads to deeper understanding. He moves from Mosaic law back to Genesis, examining the basis of relationship as originally established by God. The emphasis shifts from divorce to marriage: "They are no longer two, but one flesh. Therefore what God has joined together, let no one separate." Jesus affirms the lifelong joining of two people into one flesh. Marriage is a gift of God's good creation.

We walk a dangerous path when we try to conform God's Holy Word to our desires rather than having the Word conform us to God's image.

> *Lord, help us to search our hearts as we study your Word, that we would trust and obey and that our worship would be pleasing to you. Amen.*

Children have not always been considered the gift from God that Psalm 127:3 tells us they are. While most cultures celebrate the birth of a child, that usually gives way quickly to putting them to work or finding them a nuisance.

We decry the sweat shops that employ children at an unlivable wage in desperate conditions in developing nations; yet it has been just over seventy years since virtually the same thing was done in the United States. The Great Depression made jobs so scarce for adults that resistance to child labor laws was dropped, and the issue was addressed by federal law in 1938. The condition of the first-century child was certainly no better.

Research consistently confirms that most of our morals, beliefs, fears, and behaviors are set during childhood. Ministry to children is six to eight times more effective than to any other age group. Jesus' ministry focused on those whom society did not value, which makes it surprising that his disciples try to chase away those who bring their children to him and makes Jesus' indignation with his disciples understandable.

Jesus reminds the disciples the kingdom of God is specifically for those who are vulnerable and without status in society. Children, unencumbered by pride, ego, peer pressure, and preconceived notions, receive the kingdom without added filters.

All of us are to receive the kingdom as children, regardless of age. Children and others who are marginalized bring nothing to the table. They have no resources, but they gladly welcome arms that embrace and bless.

God, we thank you for all those who are vulnerable and for your love and care for them. Help us to come before your throne with that same openness to receive your kingdom blessings. Amen.

William Seward was the Secretary of State for Abraham Lincoln and Andrew Johnson. He had a vision of expanding America's influence, which led to negotiations with Russia to purchase Alaska for $7.2 million, an exceptionally large amount in the 1860s. Alaska was known only for snow and ice at that time, and the purchase was immediately nicknamed "Seward's Folly."

Gold and oil were discovered in Alaska after Seward's death. Now, Alaskan oil revenues exceed $7 million every two and a half days. Imagine the escalation of tension in the Cold War if Soviet troops had been stationed just 500 miles from the U.S. mainland without the buffer of Alaska. Seward's vision has greatly benefited the United States.

It was God's vision to create the world and place everything under the stewardship of humankind, from the Alaskan oil fields to the beaches of the Gulf coast, and around the globe. Think of the amazing love behind that gift.

The writer of Hebrews tells us more of God's vision: "We see Jesus," and in that seeing we bear witness to God's great love for us. Through Jesus, we are adopted into God's family through his blood. Jesus, the "author" of our salvation, will one day unashamedly call us his brothers and sisters!

Whatever others may say or think about our following the Lord Jesus, we can rest in the knowledge that our God has a vision, and it includes our being made holy through Christ's suffering and being brought into the family of God.

Lord, thank you for your awesome love, for the sacrifice of Jesus, and for your promise to make us part of your holy family. Amen.

Approaching God Boldly

OCTOBER 8–14, 2012 • BETH PORTER

MONDAY, OCTOBER 8 ~ *Read Job 23:1-7*

The story of Job invites us into the mystery of a God who tolerates bad things happening to good people, but who is ultimately discovered to be faithful, just, and wise. Job's pain is caused by the terrible losses and afflictions he has suffered and accentuated by his visiting "comforters" who do not believe in his innocence. But a greater cause is his frightening experience of God's absence.

Job may seem shockingly frank in speaking about his experience of God's absence. It can be instructive for us to realize that in Judaism there was and is still today a place for doubt. Judaism recognizes doubt as a necessary element in faith; it is okay to argue with God. We Christians have tended to regard doubt as weakness and criticism of God as blasphemy. This understanding can lead us to be less than honest about our experience. God meets us in our honesty, and God can handle our criticism.

The Jesuits, respected spiritual guides, point out the ebb and flow in our lives between spiritual desolation and spiritual consolation. In times of desolation we try, as Job does, to remember God's past faithfulness and take comfort that consolation will return. If he could find God, "he would give heed to me," Job reassures himself. Times of desolation can provide opportunity for spiritual growth and times of consolation for consolidating that growth by going forward in action.

Loving and just God, help me to speak honestly and trustingly to you when I am in anguish and doubts arise. Amen.

Serves in interfaith ministry on the pastoral team of L'Arche Daybreak; Coordinator of Educational Initiatives for L'Arche Canada (communities for persons with intellectual disabilities and the friends who share life with them)

In the Passion narratives of Matthew and Mark, Jesus quotes the opening cry of Psalm 22, "My God, my God, why have you forsaken me?" Hanging vulnerable on the cross awaiting death, Jesus also thirsted and all his bones were indeed "out of joint." Jesus' cry may seem to convey despair, but Jesus would have known the whole psalm. In Judaism, then as now, a prayer's first few words signify the whole. Jesus would have known that this psalm intersperses assertions of God's past faithfulness with its descriptions of terrible suffering. Today, we read only the first half of this psalm, which eventually concludes with a ringing proclamation of deliverance.

My L'Arche friend Michael has a big heart and loves deeply. When Michael prays, I sometimes think of the Psalms, where the whole panoply of painful and joyful experiences in the human journey of faith is made available to us. When his brother, Adam, and his beloved friend, Henri Nouwen, died in the same year, Michael's heart was broken twice over. He cried out his sorrows to God, weeping profusely. He emerged from this time with a consoling new insight—he had many brothers and sisters in L'Arche. Years later, he continues to call some of us "Sister" or "Brother." I doubt Michael would have reached this resolution without going through the process of talking and complaining to God so freely about his loss.

Profound suffering comes to most of us. As Christians, we can be reluctant to tell God or others just how bad we feel. Complaining or questioning God's goodness might scandalize others or weaken their faith. And are we not supposed to be thankful in all things! But the psalms are given to us so that we can be real with God in our own prayers. God can then be real to us.

Pour out your heart to God in a psalm of your own creation.

The reading from Hebrews reminds us that the word of God is "living"—ever relevant and life-giving. Praying with God's word can help us recognize and separate the dross of unspiritual thoughts and habits that obscure the work of God's Spirit in our lives.

As we mature in our faith, sooner or later we will hit a wall. We are disappointed in ourselves and find our spiritual life unfulfilling. The man in today's Gospel passage perhaps had reached this point. Providing we don't flee into distractions, this is a time of great spiritual opportunity.

Jesus looks at the man and loves him. The man is searching, which makes for a potentially converting moment. Jesus has listed for him the easier, mainly negative, commandments—ones the man has faithfully kept. In inviting him to sell his possessions, give the money to the poor, and follow him, Jesus bids him embrace the great commandment to love God with his whole being and not put anything, any idol—material or otherwise—between himself and God.

For us truly to hear Jesus' words here is to allow God's word to separate our desire for security or others' esteem or whatever our "possessions" might be from the desire of our spirit to live fully in communion with God. We can only move toward the latter if we boldly and trustingly approach the throne of God's grace, as the writer to the Hebrews urges.

Jesus' invitation proves to be more than the man is ready for. I wonder what he expected Jesus to say and whether, in time, he did find the grace to follow him.

Loving God, help me to respond with trust and generosity to your invitation to grow in communion with you. Amen.

Post-Holocaust theologians have struggled with the apparent silence of God during that horrendous period. Why did God not intervene? Martin Buber, drawing from Job, suggested that God hid his face during the Holocaust—that God could not bear to look on such dreadful brutality and terrible suffering.

Job expresses his anguish about God's felt absence in the midst of his suffering. He believes if he could just find God and talk his situation over with God, the Holy One would listen and confirm his innocence. Job has not lost his faith in God's justice, and he reminds himself of God's past faithfulness. But it seems in his time of great need God is hiding, leaving Job in dread and desirous of death.

In the midst of terrible suffering there are no facile answers. In our sophisticated society, many people still harbor quite unconsciously a kind of Santa Claus idea of God. If they ask God, God will make everything right! When troubles do not disappear, this idea of God disintegrates, leaving them disoriented and frightened. They may even lose faith in God entirely. But of course they needed to lose faith in the kind of God they were believing in. God allows the laws of the universe to work and does not pull the strings in our lives as though we were puppets.

For the person whose life is fully given to God, the divine absence can be the profoundest of sufferings. The only response available is to persevere in this "dark night of the soul," as Christian mystics have called it. In retrospect, they may see that this dark period strengthened their faith and may intuit, as Job seems to, that God was somehow present in the darkness. Job, in his faithful suffering, does us a great service in raising questions he cannot answer and pointing beyond himself to the One who can.

Dear God, deepen my faith that you are ever close to me, even when you seem hidden. Amen.

My friend Michael talks with difficulty. When we pray together after dinner, he utters his prayers slowly and simply—and sometimes commandingly: "God, my mother is s-s-sick . . . C-Can't WALK! You better do something, God . . . You better DO s-something!"

Michael's boldness reminds me of the exhortation in today's passage from Hebrews to approach God's throne of grace "with boldness." The theme resonates throughout the readings for this week. In their suffering or emptiness, Job, the psalmist, and the man in Mark's Gospel all boldly seek God.

Today's passage suggests that our bold seeking of God's grace comes as a response to having allowed God's word to judge our innermost thoughts and intentions. In exposing ourselves to God's word, we come to see our shadow side: thoughts of which we are ashamed come into the light. The reference to the sharp two-edged sword describes an experience that will be painful but precise and will reveal small details we have not noticed—greed or pride or other sinful attitudes that may accompany our good deeds. We may feel inclined to draw back from God, but the writer reminds us of sympathetic counsel: "a high priest . . . who in every respect has been tested as we are." With the support of Jesus, we "approach the throne of grace with boldness," confident of God's mercy and grace.

The image of the high priest returns me to Michael who, in his simple, profoundly heart-felt and direct intercession, seems to adopt the role of high priest on behalf of his mother who is very ill. Perhaps he models for us the possibilities for our own intercession for others.

Loving God, help me to seek your grace boldly in my own need and for others. Amen.

Why do the rich have a hard time entering God's kingdom? In Jesus' day, the rich were thought to have a spiritual advantage—they could give alms and meet other religious and community obligations. But often they held the poor in low regard and tended to despise them.

Similar attitudes prevail today. We may not struggle with the challenge of material riches. But riches can take other forms that block our being in full communion with God.

When I came to L'Arche, where I share life with people who have an intellectual disability, I quickly found I was "rich" in ability. I was competent; people liked and trusted me; and I loved the people I lived with and cared for. A need arose for someone to help in a rural French-speaking L'Arche community in Quebec, and I decided to offer my abilities there. In this different environment, I discovered my French to be inadequate and was flatly rebuffed by one of the women I was to assist. I felt increasingly incompetent. Because this woman showed me my powerlessness, I was coming to detest her. I felt ashamed of my feelings and utterly disillusioned with myself.

In the community's chapel, I wept and poured out my heart to God. As I was confronted with my inability, poverty, and self-centered pride, God's knowing and forgiving gaze opened the door to spiritual growth that I would not likely have experienced when I felt rich. I needed this experience of my own poverty.

Plumbing the depths of personal poverty is a lifelong journey. Thankfully, even though the reign of God is less available to us when we feel secure in our possessions and abilities, we can take comfort in Jesus' words. While it is difficult for the rich to enter into God's reign, "for God all things are possible."

Gracious God, may we be open to your invitation to eternal life, however it presents itself. Amen.

SUNDAY, OCTOBER 14 ～ *Read Mark 10:28-31*

Jesus' promise of a hundredfold reward for everyone who leaves what is precious to them for God's call may remind us of the outcome of the story of Job, who eventually receives twofold of his lost possessions. It is a generous promise. Even if I leave some things, I will receive a hundredfold for doing this! There is, however, a disturbing surprise: Jesus adds the little phrase "with persecutions" to this promise.

The faithful person will suffer. The spiritual path holds great riches for those who choose it, but there will be a price beyond letting go of what we value. Today those with open eyes and hearts hear a cry everywhere to stand up for justice and what is right in a society where we too easily succumb to what is convenient and meets our own needs. To take a stand with the poor or homeless or others who need our help may well bring criticism and perhaps persecution our way.

Today's reading ends with another surprise: many of the first will be last and last first. It reminds us to cultivate a spirit of humility as we reach out to those in need. Who will be first? I recently attended a funeral for Dorothy, an eighty-three-year-old woman who was deaf, intellectually handicapped, and unable to walk. She spent most of her life in institutions but the last eleven years in a L'Arche home. There, she claimed a place by the window where she waited every day to wave a cheery welcome to visitors and her housemates. Dorothy might have seemed to qualify for a "last" position, but at her funeral it was clear that she was a "first." Many people turned out to celebrate her life and speak of how her cheery welcome had blessed them—this woman who might have seemed a nobody.

Loving God, help me to let go willingly of what is precious to me and trust you with the fruitfulness of my life. Amen.

Searching for Peace

OCTOBER 15–21, 2012 • LUONNE ABRAM ROUSE

MONDAY, OCTOBER 15 ~ *Read Job 38:1-7*

Suffering overwhelms Job. He lacks a sense of peace because of the traumatic experiences that come from Satan's attacks on his character. Weakened by grief and inflicted with harm to his body, Job gains little from friends who visit in silence and offer no hope; they speak of Job's sin. Human explanations of storms, tsunamis, wars, and economic crises are never enough to erase the human hurt. Suffering is too often unexplainable in the human context.

The experience of grief takes humans through stages described by Dr. Elisabeth Kübler-Ross as denial, anger, bargaining, depression, and acceptance. In searching for peace, human beings desire a place of acceptance—managing realities of loss and discovering the grace of God's love and acceptance. What is essential to human conversation with God in searching for peace?

"Then the LORD answered Job out of the storm." Prayer is speaking and listening, hearing and answering. Job hears God in spite of his self-disgust and affliction. Approaching God requires more than random mouthing-off or complaints. Embedded within God's response we hear an impatience for what may be called intolerable nonsense: "Who is this that darkens my counsel with words without knowledge?" (NIV). When we are searching for peace, wisdom comes in talking less and listening more.

We all stand on the same ground in God's sight. What shall we do? Swallow our pride and listen for God. God has some things to say.

God of peace, have mercy on us, your people who need you. Grant us peace with justice and righteousness. Amen.

Senior minister, Metropolitan Community United Methodist Church, New York, New York

Our search for peace invites us to a life of praise. Sometimes that praise becomes difficult for us. We relate more to Job than to the psalmist. God has created; however, we remember that in majesty and with greatness, God has crafted humanity. In Psalm 104, it is God who actively sets about the matter of creation: God wraps, stretches, lays, and makes. God, the master designer, architect, and engineer has implemented a master plan! "Praise the Lord, my soul" (Psalm 104:1, NIV).

Sometimes our life circumstances or physical location affects our ability to see the bold witness of God the Creator. JQ lived in New York. He came to the church office seeking pastoral help. JQ stated, "I have only been to church once in my life. I am here today because I was asking a man for money at the grocery store. He replied, 'I am going to give you this dollar and a word of wisdom. I was once where you are in life. Turn to God. The One who saved me can help you.'"

Hallelujah is often referred to as the highest praise. It can refer to a life turned around by the Creator of all. JQ said to me, "It has not always been second nature for me to walk with God. Today, it is like taking a fresh breath with each beat of my heart." JQ has found the peace of God. It is written: "If from there you seek the Lord your God, you will find him if you look for him with all your heart and with all your soul" (Deut. 4:29, NIV). Our search for God leads us to peace.

The powerful presence of God within us, especially to those given the grace of caring for others, is leading men and women to the peace of God and to worship. Hallelujah! In the highest of praise, we say, Hallelujah!

Praise the LORD, O my soul.

O LORD my God, you are very great (NIV).

Creator God, we are knocking at the door of worship. Have mercy on your people. Open the door, and let us in. Amen.

Earlier in Hebrews the author describes Jesus as "a great high priest . . . who has been tempted in every way, just as we are—yet was without sin. Let us then approach the throne of grace with confidence, so that we may receive mercy and find grace to help us in our time of need" (Heb. 4:14-16, NIV). Early Jewish Christians in search of peace were tempted to carry over old traditions and forms of religious practice. Hebrews 5 encourages "steadfastness and prayer" as a means of grace.

Chaos seems to surround the journeys of Jesus from birth to death. Still he is the Prince of Peace. He came to the garden to prepare to face hours of degradation and humiliation in his trial and crucifixion. Disciples learn from Jesus that suffering and self-giving offer the path to peace itself. We witness the mystery of Jesus' experiences from the Lord's Supper through the Garden to the Cross and the Resurrection! At the Supper he taught the way of forgiveness and reconciliation. In the Garden he taught forgiveness. On the cross, Jesus taught forgiveness. And again from the grave he taught forgiveness. Forgiveness became a priestly action for Jesus and for his followers.

We learn that Jesus shared the same world with his tormentors. We are not removed from trials and temptations. Christians live in the same world as non-Christians. One vital difference between Christian living and non-Christian living may be in knowing that Jesus intercedes for us and offers us peace. We also know that such peace comes for all God's children and brings justice and righteousness.

Jesus, our great high priest, teach us how to live right, how to pray right, how to die right, how to rise above circumstances and soar. Teach us, Jesus; teach us how to live in your peace. Amen.

Of Jesus' many attributes, we may forget that he is a friend. In friendship, he gave unselfishly for humanity. Given the title of Son of Man, a title with Messianic meanings, Jesus notes, "The Son of Man did not come to be served, but to serve, and to give his life as a ransom for many" (NIV).

The Gospel records James and John as having the ambition not to be like Jesus but to be positioned as Jesus. "'Teacher,' they say, 'we want you to do for us whatever we ask'" (NIV). Jesus listens to the request of the brothers then teaches his disciples the true character of honorable servants. In the human-to-God relationship, we give up rights of selfish ambition for the good of other flawed humans. Seeking to model the character of Jesus brings us into service of others, while ignorance of selfishness or intentional selfishness promotes the self-exaltation of flawed human character.

What a friend we have in Jesus. Jesus asks James and John: "What do you want me to do for you?" (NIV). How differently the dialogues might have gone had they responded: "Pray with us! Lord, will you pray with us? When you arrive in your glory, will you remember us?" Where do you find yourself in this scene? What words would you put in the mouths of the disciples?

The peace of God, which passes all understanding, fills my soul when in prayer I seek the essential elements of servanthood. Traveling through a world of crises and disappointments, I do not desire greatness or fame. What I would love to do on this earth is glorify God, and that can only be for me to do through Jesus Christ, who teaches us to pray: "Our Father, who art in heaven . . . "

Lord Jesus Christ, Son of God, have mercy on us, so that we may grow as your servants. Grant us your peace. Amen.

FRIDAY, OCTOBER 19 ~ *Read Psalm 104: 24, 35c*

When I reflect on this psalm, I think, *How marvelous is all creation!* It is too marvelous for my meager words. Such reflection causes an affirmation to flow within me: I love the divine parentage of God. There is none greater!

Psalm 104 speaks of the wisdom in God's created order. We see the rhythms of the days and seasons, the seasonal patterns of plants, and the life cycles of animals. Given our peace-filled understanding of life, we know that all God's creatures reflect an affirmation of the bounty of God's creation. The sounds of birds and crickets are as assuring as the music from human artists. In the midst of such affirmation come our daily devotions. Through devotions we acknowledge God and provide space for discernment. I bathe in the works and wisdom of God, knowing the Lord has ownership of all reality. Our very existence is in the grace of God.

What are your thoughts on the natural life that surrounds you? Take time in your daily activities to observe the wonder of being. Sit in silence and simply observe a tree or a small section of the earth. Give thanks for the goodness of creation.

Sing a song by any tune that raises praise to God. Meditate on a hymn such as "O Worship the King" or "Lift Every Voice and Sing." The songs of the psalmist inspire the hearts of men and women who feel deep gladness for the works and wisdom of God. The psalmist inspires many to bring into the world their own expressions of what the Lord has done in their lives. Within myself I reach down and sing: "Whatever it takes, no matter how long, I will keep the faith until victory is won. For there is no higher calling. There is no greater glory, then to travel this journey with you."(Author's original lyrics written in Zimbabwe, 1990)

Lord Jesus Christ, Son of God, show us mercy and grant us pure hearts as we worship you. Amen.

We can divide the book of Job into multiple scenes. In this scene in chapter 38 God responds to Job as a voice from out of the storm. Put yourself into this Bible passage. Become the character of Job. Imagine hearing the voice of God as Job heard it. Read and pray over the entire scene, then come back to verses 34-41 and listen carefully. What feelings are generated as you listen through the ears of Job? What thoughts do you have as Job? Ready? Action!

What words or phrases held your attention or caused you to stumble and stop your reading? Every vein in my body was on fire and in shocking pain on hearing the voice of God say: "Brace yourself like a man; I will question you, and you shall answer me" (Job 38:3, NIV). In my own reflection, I cried out, "Mercy!" I bowed and knelt in prayer. I trembled in amazement more than fear.

During my time of reflection, I acknowledged that God "set the earth on its foundations; it can never be moved" (Ps. 104:5). The book of Job confirms the wisdom of the psalmist. Today's verses remind us of God's ongoing involvement in the rhythms of the universe. Awe is my overwhelming feeling in response to God's questions in this text. How do you respond?

The spiritual enlightenment from the Word of God is revealing and inspiring. How do we receive the Word? How do we respond to the historic and ongoing revelation of God that we know in the Bible? I cry out for more and say, "Teach me, O Lord. Teach me to live as a child of truth. Teach me to live as a person of faith. Teach me to live in the hope of eternal salvation. Teach me to love as a humble servant. Teach me, O Lord."

Lord Jesus Christ, Son of God, have mercy on us sinners, and save our souls unto blessed peace. Amen.

Do not overlook the fact that Jesus consistently upset those in authority because his proclamation offered spiritual liberation. When you read this passage, notice the other disciples' indignation with James and John. Jesus uses their indignation as a springboard and teaches the disciples new principles in the spiritual kingdom: "You know that those who are regarded as rulers of the Gentiles lord it over them, and their high officials exercise authority over them. Not so with you" (NIV). Perhaps quizzical looks appear on the faces of the disciples in response to these words from Jesus. He continues to speak to them. His concluding words probably surprise the disciples even more: "Instead, whoever wants to become great among you must be your servant, and whoever wants to be first must be slave of all. For even the Son of Man did not come to be served, but to serve, and to give his life as a ransom for many" (NIV).

Several inclinations and conditions within group dynamics can disrupt the purpose of the mission. Individual ambition, self-exaltation, pride, ego, and acts of superiority are a few poisons that affect harmony, mission, and purpose within groups. A spiritual leader will navigate the group in the midst of discord and confusion, indignation and misunderstanding. Jesus offers the supreme example of leadership navigation, leading by his own example of humility and servanthood.

Confession: I have not lived a perfect life. I have followed many curves and crooked paths during my own navigation. Yet, in my search for peace, I pray that I am striving toward Christian perfection. I have made wrong decisions and choices and have asked Jesus to reroute my life. Like the disciples surrounding Jesus, I am continuing to learn to be one who serves.

Let us pray for gain through loss. Lord, in your mercy, hear our prayer. Amen.

Hindsight and Insight

OCTOBER 22–28, 2012 • RICHARD FISHER

MONDAY, OCTOBER 22 ~ *Read Job 42:1-6*

On this day in 1844 the followers of William Miller experienced the "Day of Great Disappointment." William Miller had convinced them that the scriptures clearly taught that Jesus Christ would return that day to earth to cleanse it from all evil and to bring his followers into his kingdom. Many sold their belongings and traveled to a designated site to await the Lord's arrival.

When the sun rose the next day in its usual fashion and life went on as before, the Millerites returned home deeply disappointed. Some eventually turned to other forms of religion. Others went back to the scriptures to see how they had miscalculated. And some used this experience to transform their understanding of God's ways.

In our scripture reading today, Job receives no answers. He stands before God's power and wisdom and declares his own inability to comprehend that magnitude; the parameters of divine justice and mercy extend beyond the bounds of human knowing. God and God's ways remain a mystery. Job will never again accept the easy formula that good things happen to good people and bad things happen to bad people. Life lived before God is more complex than that. Job responds, "Therefore I yield" (REB). His experience with God brings new insight: living under God's sovereignty means living in relationship with the One whose sovereignty offers abundant mercy.

Gracious God, thank you for enduring my persistent questions, for being with me when I cast old understandings aside, and for leading me into new insights and deeper trust. Amen.

Retired United Methodist clergy and part-time tour guide in the Black Hills of South Dakota

Joe was on top of the world. His business thrived. His daughter had been accepted for a study program in Japan, and his son was finally getting his life together. Then suddenly it all came crashing down. A chain store opened in his town and undercut his prices. Within a few months Joe realized that his business could not compete. His daughter had to come home for hospitalization. His son had debts he could no longer pay.

Unemployed and depressed, Joe experienced a reversal of fortunes. A public golf course offered Joe a job as the golf pro and house manager, which resulted in a twofold restoration. His daughter's health improved and Joe's personal sense of well-being elevated. Indeed, "the LORD blessed [Joe's] latter days . . . more than his beginning!"

Many of us may wonder about Joe's restoration—and Job's! God graciously restores Job's fortunes twofold, bringing his life full circle. But Job's restoration says more about God's mercy than God's justice. The restoration of fortune does not result from Job's righteousness any more than his suffering resulted from his sin. Job, Joe, and all of us come to understand that God loves Job as God loves us all. God blesses Job and intends to bless all people. God's ways are mysterious and beyond our understanding, but we acknowledge the God of Israel and of Jesus Christ as a God of compassion whose ultimate will for all persons is peace and joy.

For Joe and Job, doors had closed, but God offered new beginnings in ways that they could not have foreseen. Perhaps a door has closed in your life; await with eagerness your restoration from a merciful God.

Thank you, God, for being here when things fall apart and for opening doors to new opportunities to bless and be blessed. Amen.

I remember the first time I met Mabel. I was the new pastor in town, having just completed seminary and been turned loose on the world. She was my first pastoral call. I prepped myself and went, eager to display my pastoral skills.

I found Mabel in her hospital-style bed, lying flat on her back. Mabel could move neither her hands nor her feet. Multiple sclerosis had ravaged her body quickly.

After I introduced myself, she immediately began asking about my life: "Where did you grow up? Tell me about your wife. How did you decide to be a pastor?"

After some conversation, Mabel began to tell me about her life, focusing often on the goodness and kindness of family members. Though physically constrained, Mabel did not fear or doubt God's love when it was so clearly manifested by others through the many big and small ways that they expressed their love and care for her. She then asked me to record a poem of blessing to God. "I write poems in my head," she said. "I have a new one I would like to put on paper. Will you be my hands?"

Likewise, the psalmist records his poem of praise to God. He has prayed for help and received it: "I sought the LORD, and he answered me, and delivered me from all my fears." His situation has found resolution. He has cried to God and been saved. He experiences deliverance and salvation. Even the angel of the Lord offers protection.

Perhaps this divine protection and blessing prompted Mabel, a young woman stricken with a debilitating illness, to write poems of blessing in her head and to value the love and kindness extended to her by all who visited. In so doing, she herself became a poem of blessing, helping all to "taste and see that the LORD is good."

Thank you, God, for your many blessings. Help us to be a blessing to others. Amen.

Looking back over my life, I realize that I have been gifted by many priests who, from time to time, interceded for me. Some were clergy, but many were laity. Martin Luther called them "little christs," a concept that he referred to elsewhere as the priesthood of all believers.

Some of these priests helped me become a person of faith. Whether preaching with insight, teaching with understanding, counseling with grace, or mentoring with patience, they sparked faith in my life and challenged me to grow as a disciple of Christ. Others befriended me at crucial moments in my life.

None of these was the Christ. Each was a flawed human being. Yet, each came into my life at an important time to offer what I needed to rearrange the pieces of my life or to continue my journey with renewed insights or energy or to make mid-course adjustments on that journey. Because of them, I did not stay the same.

Hebrews mentions a number of drawbacks to the "former priests." They died, and their ranks would need replenishment. They labored "day after day," while Christ offers "once for all." The author wants to assure readers that Jesus Christ is superior to all priests and religious figures who came before him and who would come after him.

Yet, these people who come to us "day after day" to meet our needs and offer care remain important because they point beyond themselves to the real source of meaning, healing, and fulfillment. They point us to the Christ, the high priest who is "holy, blameless, undefiled, . . . exalted above the heavens." He fulfills all hopes and remains on our side for all eternity.

Thank you, God, for those persons who have pointed us to Christ and have thus helped us on our journey. Amen.

Bartimaeus, while blind, is able to "see" who is coming toward him on the road. His physical blindness seems to heighten his spiritual sensitivity. He cries out to Jesus. The crowd tries to silence Bartimaeus. They see with their eyes but not with their hearts and minds. The man's insistent cries get Jesus' attention, and he calls the man to him. Jesus restores his sight and states the words: "Go; your faith has made you well."

A man named Walt ran a small business whose existence was extremely tenuous. He sold and repaired appliances. He also sold fishing gear and ran a bait shop. Although his wife came to worship regularly and his children actively participated in Sunday school and youth fellowship, Walt never darkened the door of the church. From all appearances, Walt was as blind spiritually as Bartimaeus had been blind physically.

Before I came to serve that church, the bishop had indicated a desire to appoint an African-American pastor. Quickly this small all-white town became restless. Some members of the church passed petitions asking the bishop to reconsider the appointment. They came to Walt's shop to get his signature. He read their petition and handed it back unsigned.

Looking directly at them, Walt said, "I don't understand you people. Aren't you the church that teaches my children to sing, 'Jesus loves the little children, all the children of the world'? Why would you ask people to sign such a statement?"

In this encounter, Jesus Christ opened Walt's spiritual eyes to see the inclusive nature of God's realm. And the crowd, who had kept Walt on the sidelines, witnessed a miracle of sorts, certainly a healing of perception, a call to wholeness based on the faith of another. The church voted to confirm the bishop's appointment.

God, help us listen to the voices of people both inside and outside the church. May our faith make us whole. Amen.

Jesus is the lens through which we see God most clearly. As we reflect on Jesus' encounter with Bartimaeus, God's compassion and power come into focus.

On the road from Jericho, Jesus hears a man's cry for mercy. Jesus may have been preoccupied with thoughts about what he would face in Jerusalem, but he hears the man's cry. The disciples' cacophony of voices, discussing and arguing among themselves, almost obliterates the man's cry, but Jesus hears Bartimaeus. Nothing blocks out this man's cries from the realm of Jesus' awareness and concern.

When Jesus comes face-to-face with Bartimaeus, he asks him, "What do you want me to do for you?" Jesus does not assume or presume to know what Bartimaeus desires. Bartimaeus responds with his petition, "My teacher, let me see again." Jesus then grants the man's request. Is it any wonder that when Jesus tells Bartimaeus to go, Bartimaeus chooses instead to follow Jesus "on the way"?

It seems so simple, but it is so profound. In Jesus Christ we catch a glimpse of God. God has a vast, expanding universe to harmonize, yet God hears the cries of a lonely person standing alongside a dusty road on one little planet spinning through the darkness. In this brief encounter with Bartimaeus, Jesus reveals God's presence and power as God brings healing and wholeness to earth.

Recall a time in your life when you insistently cried out to God. When you sensed God's presence, how did you respond to the question, "What do you want me to do for you?" How has your faith made you well and encouraged you to follow Jesus on the way?

Sensitize us to the nearness of your realm of healing, harmony, and well-being, O God, that we might see you more clearly and follow you more nearly. Through Christ our Lord. Amen.

Today's reading is filled with phrases that describe God's gracious activity in our lives and phrases that shape our response to God. Take time to reflect on them: God's angel pitches a tent beside ours and stays beside us. God is not far off in some distant galaxy, light years removed from us. God is as near as the breeze that rustles the leaves, as close as the breath that restores oxygen to our bodies. God answers our pleas and delivers us from our fears. God rescues us from trouble and delivers us from our afflictions. God redeems lives that have been ensnared by evil and remains present in those lives. All of these actions celebrated by the psalmist highlight God's life-saving and life-giving work on behalf of God's people. "Taste," bids the psalmist, "and see that the LORD is good."

Those who have tasted and have seen the goodness of the Lord respond in worship. They bless the Lord, an action that involves kneeling before God in humility and praise. They boast in the Lord, knowing they have not rescued themselves. They magnify the Lord, spotlighting God's mighty deeds in the lives of God's people so that all might see and taste for themselves. They exalt the Lord's name with songs of praise.

The psalmist is a realist. He knows through experience that the faithful, like Job, must face and endure many afflictions and hardships. That is the nature of life. Faith does not place a protective shield around us. But faith does discover that God is with us, rescuing, healing, and restoring. Faith does discern that God works with us and through us in the midst of our challenges, creating something new and good. Taste and see!

Gracious God, I bless your holy name. You have been at work in my life long before I was even aware of you. And I trust that you will be with me throughout this day, working for good in and through me. In the name of Christ I pray. Amen.

Extraordinary Love

OCTOBER 29–NOVEMBER 4, 2012 • MARK GALLI

MONDAY, OCTOBER 29 ~ *Read Hebrews 9:11-14*

We're mostly interested in temporary fixes. They are quicker, cheaper, and generally can be done by do-it-yourselfers. Instead of remodeling the bathroom, we put vinyl over the rusty bathtub and paint over the moldy walls.

Similarly, we're often interested in a temporary spiritual fix to "purify our conscience." It's quick: one hour on Sunday. It's cheap: it doesn't demand our whole heart, mind, and strength. It's perfect for the do-it-yourselfer: we're in control of the whole process. But God is in the business of complete remodels.

In biblical days, folks had no choice but to practice a religion of temporary fixes—a high priest annually offering up animals to assuage the people's guilt. But no sooner had the janitorial crew begun to clean up after the sacrifice than the conscience would again feel the burden. It was understood that our sin, like a bloodstain on the priest's garment, would never come out.

But Jesus came as a "greater" and "perfect" covering for sin. He entered the Holy Place not repeatedly but "once for all." He came as a high priest "without blemish," purifying not just the brutal fact of sin but "our conscience" as well. He obtained an "eternal redemption," so that we now can move from mere religion into a relationship with "the living God."

We see a picture of an extraordinary God who has revealed an extraordinary love. We no longer have to settle for ho-hum religion with its oh-so-ordinary—and temporary—results.

Jesus, help me trust in what you have done—accomplished an eternal, once-for-all redemption—so that I can enjoy an extraordinary relationship with you, my living God. Amen.

Senior managing editor of *Christianity Today*, Wheaton, Illinois

This passage is often read at weddings to suggest the type of faithfulness a husband and wife are to have toward one another. But it has a much deeper meaning as well.

In Ruth's day, a widow found herself in a precarious position. Women in general financially depended on men, first their fathers, then their husbands. If her husband died, her husband's family would care for her, but it was hardly ideal to be a charity case for life. No, the hope was that one of the eligible men in the family would agree to marry the widow. This was a widow's only hope.

So when Ruth says she wants to stick with Naomi, she is giving up on that hope. Furthermore, she is attaching herself to another widow—hardly a person with the financial means to secure Ruth's future. Ruth's pledge to stick with Naomi until death illustrates an extraordinary act of love and devotion.

This act of human love foreshadows the love that God has shown us in Jesus Christ. It harkens to the Spirit's relentless pursuit of wayfaring people. When the words of the prophets failed to turn us around, Jesus came to us in the flesh, desperately grabbing our arm as we turned away, saying, "Do not press me to leave you or to turn back from following you! Where you go, I will go; where you lodge, I will lodge; your people shall be my people."

The difference is this. Naomi had a choice about Ruth's companionship. But we are subject to the choice of God, the divine choice to love us with an extraordinary love. This God in Jesus says, "I will never leave you or forsake you" (Heb. 13:5) and "I am with you always, to the end of the age" (Matt. 28:20).

Jesus, thank you for coming to us in the flesh and now in the Holy Spirit and promising to never leave us or forsake us. Amen.

The older we grow, the less enthusiastic we seem about the next political election. In our youth, we may have really believed that the election of this person or the passage of that initiative would save the day, but we've been disappointed too many times. Politics remains a crucial way to improve the "general welfare," yes, but we don't need the scripture to tell us to "not put [our] trust in princes."

Whether it's a monarchy, socialism, democracy, or whatever, few would argue that one role of government includes looking out for the oppressed, the hungry, the disabled, and the indigent—the various "constituents" the psalmist mentions. But between corruption, indifference, or sheer complexity, government can never fulfill its calling perfectly.

After years of experience with this disappointment, we may become cynical. But the psalmist sees a Lord above our earthly lords who really does fulfill the commission. This one "executes justice for the oppressed," and "gives food to the hungry," and "sets the prisoners free," and "opens the eyes of the blind," and "upholds the orphan and widow"—among others! This one is, of course, the God of heaven and earth—the one "who keeps faith forever" with all these suffering people and more.

The Lord will keep faith with some in this lifetime and with others in the life to come (more of that tomorrow)—but keep faith God will. Thus the ordinary course of things as we experience it has been transcended by an extraordinary love once again. No wonder the psalmist goes a bit over the top: "I will praise the LORD as long as I live; I will sing praises to my God all my life long."

O God, may I trust in your gracious governance not only over human history but also over my life. Amen.

ALL SAINTS DAY

O n All Saints Day many churches remember the faithful who have gone before us, but the scripture readings suggest an even greater liturgical purpose of the day.

This passage pictures a time when "the LORD of hosts will make for all the peoples a feast of rich food." The psalm for this day (24) extols the glory of Temple worship, where God resides as "the King of glory." Revelation describes "a new heaven and a new earth." And in the Gospel lesson (John 11:32-44), Jesus raises Lazarus to life, saying, "I am the resurrection and the life." The readings harken to the time when we shall enjoy resurrected life in the unmitigated presence of our God and King.

So on this day we remember the saints, not so much because of their faithfulness but because of the promise of eternal life in Christ—another sign of God's extraordinary love!

But our mundane experience suggests otherwise: "By the sweat of your face you shall eat bread until you return to the ground, for out of it you were taken; you are dust, and to dust you shall return" (Gen. 3:19). And this: "Vanity of vanities! All is vanity. . . . What has been is what will be, and what has been done is what will be done; there is nothing new under the sun" (Eccl. 1:2, 9).

However, in Jesus Christ there *is* something new under the sun. What has been (sin and death) will someday no longer be. We may be dust, but "this mortal body must put on immortality" (1 Cor. 15:53). That day we will say, "This is the LORD for whom we have waited; let us be glad and rejoice in his salvation."

Lord, thank you that the faithful who have gone before us already rejoice in your presence. May I know day by day this extraordinary hope for myself. Amen.

Jesus speaks about the two great commandments. Today we pay special attention to the first: "You shall love the Lord your God with all your heart, and with all your soul, and with all your mind, and with all your strength."

Had we not been reading each day about God's extraordinary love, this command would seem like a relentless burden. After all, who can say they love God with all their heart, soul, mind, and strength—with every fiber of their being? If this command requires dutiful obedience, then our life will be a frustrating business that only brings despair.

But no! In light of God's extraordinary love, this commandment is the only reasonable response. A small act of kindness, a response of a mere thank-you is appropriate. If someone buys us dinner, we naturally want to return the favor. When God gives every fiber of divine being, to the point of death, that we might enjoy the most extraordinary blessings, we naturally want to respond with every fiber of our being.

Thus this "commandment" is not a requirement or prerequisite for our gaining God's love but more along the lines of a guide for our response. When we discover the extraordinary lengths to which God has gone to embrace us, we naturally respond with profound gratefulness, and the question, "What can I do for you, Lord?"

When God replies, "Love me with all your heart, soul, mind, and strength," we answer, "Well, of course!"

We don't for a moment think we can do that perfectly, any more than a baseball player can bat 1.000. But each time he steps up to the plate, you can be sure he's going to try—not out of duty but because of the joy of the game.

Lord, thank you for giving me something extraordinary and wonderful to do with every fiber of my being! Amen.

Love by nature overflows. It's like turning on a garden hose that cannot be turned off. We start to water the flowers and then the grass, but the water keeps coming. So we wash the car and then hose down the driveway. Still more water! After a while there is nothing more useful to do, so we playfully spray our children, fill up a swimming pool, and finally just hook it up to a Slip 'N Slide. And the water just keeps on coming.

It's like Jesus said, "Give, and it will be given to you. A good measure, pressed down, shaken together, running over" (Luke 6:38). He was talking about grain, but the "running over" part applies to water—and to love.

When we are inundated with God's love, our first response is to love God with every fiber of our being. But the love just keeps on coming, and we've got to do something with it. So we start playfully spraying our neighbors! Before you know it, the whole neighborhood is outside, having a block party, running through sprinklers and playing games with water balloons!

Love as commandment—that is, love as a religious duty—is not love. To approach this verse as if it were one more thing we have to do to be good Christians misses the point.

No! Instead, this commandment, like the first one, is simply a response to God's extraordinary love, which overflows from God's own being. Father, Son, and Holy Spirit so love one another that their love spills over into the creation and redemption of the world. That love, in turn, spills over not only in our love for God but for people left and right!

Lord, thank you for friends, neighbors, loved ones, and even strangers—people with whom I have the opportunity to share your extraordinary love. Amen.

"Hear, O Israel, the Lord our God, the Lord is one." This feels like a pious beginning to something practical. But in reality it is the practical ground of the two great love commandments.

Originally, the phrase was used to refute polytheism—the worship of many gods. All through their history, the Jews were tempted by polytheism, the religion of the surrounding peoples. It was hard to imagine that one god could manage every detail of heaven and earth! So the repeated refrain in Israel's history is that the Lord is one and fully sovereign over all creation.

In the Christian era, as the church proclaimed that God had revealed God's self as Father, Son, and Holy Spirit, Jews began to charge Christians with worshiping three gods! Since the church viewed itself as the continuation of Israel, this was not only an affront but wrong. So the phrase "the Lord is one" found a new use: to protect the unity of the Trinity.

Today, we see a deeper meaning still. The context here is the two great commandments about love. This setting and that of the whole New Testament implies that "the Lord is one" has a strong relationship to another verse: "God is love" (1 John 4:16). In short, nothing God does is not motivated by love. God in both being and action is one.

The scribe in this passage confirms Jesus' assertions of love more than burnt offerings. When God seems to fail to hear our prayers or allows us to suffer or speaks a word of wrath or judgment and we remain assured that all is backed by love, then we "are not far from the kingdom of God."

O God, one in being, one in love; may I never doubt, even in the most trying circumstances, your unfailing goodness to me. Amen.

Risky Business

NOVEMBER 5–11, 2012 • MARTHA HIGHSMITH

MONDAY, NOVEMBER 5 ～ *Read Hebrews 9:24-28*

I grew up on a farm where generations of my family have lived and loved and worked for over one hundred years. It was a wonderful place to grow up; but even as a child, I knew that farming was risky business. One late frost, a July drought, or a rainy spell during hay season could wipe out everything. But every year, Dad took a gamble on the land; every year, he bet the farm.

God bets the farm too, putting everything into the piece of land we call Earth, taking the risk that God's investment might be wasted. But unlike the farmer who can try again next year (if the bank is willing!), God has made the supreme investment—one chance. That first and last chance is Christ who "has appeared once for all."

God in Christ has risked everything to save us. This great extravagance means we get a second (and maybe third, fourth, and more) chance. This may seem like a no-risk proposition for us. After all, if Christ has already done it all—that is, removed sin by the sacrifice of himself—what is left for us? Aren't we free and clear to do as we want?

The promise of faith is that Christ will save those who eagerly wait for him. Our role in this holy relationship is the risky one of active patience. We have to bet the farm on Christ's promise. We have to live in the world with courage, confident that sin has been defeated. In a variation of the old saying: We have to work as though everything depends on us and wait as though everything depends on God—which, of course, it does.

What is most precious to you? How might you offer that to Christ? Are you willing to take that risk?

Presbyterian minister, Deputy Secretary, Yale University; New Haven, Connecticut

The Great Recession that began several years ago pushed a lot of folks into a more cautious lifestyle—some by choice, many by necessity. The painful realities of foreclosure, job loss, and reduced retirement funds forced changes in priorities. We all may end up with a healthier view of life's essentials, learn anew to value prudence and responsibility over the possibility of easy money, and depend on ourselves and our own good judgment rather than always wanting something for nothing.

While the recession could afford us an opportunity for a commendable return to important values, it could also endanger our faith if we come to rely too much on ourselves. Self-sufficiency does not signal a holy life! All our effort is worthless if we think everything depends on us. As the psalmist knows, "Unless the LORD builds the house, those who build it labor in vain."

One of my teachers once said that the goal of the spiritual life is getting our fear properly focused. We fear being helpless, losing our retirement nest egg, having to depend on others, or having no one to depend on at all. Too many of us are up at the crack of dawn and then burning the midnight oil, "eating the bread of anxious toil" (Psa. 127:2). We wear ourselves out trusting ourselves more than we are willing to trust God. But the spiritual life requires us to take the risk of giving our independence and drive to God, taking a chance on the Holy One.

Our holy calling does not ask us to squander our resources but rather to live with an open-handed, open-hearted generosity and abandon, holding tightly to that which comes from God and willingly letting everything else go.

What kind of risk are you willing to take to open your life to God? In what areas of your life does your caution come between you and your relationship with God?

Women were especially vulnerable in ancient times. Considered the property of their fathers or husbands, they had no standing, no resources, no protection. A childless widow had no means of support unless her community generously supported her. Ruth and Naomi are two such widows on their own, trying to make their way in the world. They find themselves vulnerable but not victims. These resourceful women employed Ruth's gleaning in the fields and Naomi's use of the kinship laws to their best advantage.

Naomi knows that her kinsman Boaz has potential obligations to her. Having an obligation and collecting on it, however, are two different things, and Naomi and Ruth take a big risk to ensure their survival. They plan the seduction of Boaz, with Ruth going to him, sweet-smelling and silken, in the middle of the night. Although the scriptures are silent about the details, the rest, as they say, is history.

And we call this kind of history *salvation* history. Although it seems hard for most of us to believe, Naomi and Ruth are risking their lives. If Boaz had rejected Ruth, the women would be dependent on another relative who apparently had little interest in their well-being. If Ruth was discovered lying with Boaz in the dark, her reputation—about the only thing of value that she had—would be in shreds.

But the real risk they took came when they listened to the whisper of God—God who sent them to Bethlehem, God who sent them to Boaz, God who had and still has a view of life that encompasses past disappointments, present danger, and the unknownness of the future. The two women may have felt they were risking all they had. In truth, they were risking all that God had.

How do you listen for the silent whisper of God in your life? What risks are you willing to take in reply?

God takes a risk on the most unlikely situations, hanging the whole of human history on two homeless widows—one old and past the age of children, the other a foreigner. God moves in persons' lives as an unseen, unheard presence, calling us to risk all just as God risks all.

The women's risk pays off; they secure their futures when Boaz takes Ruth as his wife. Boaz also took a risk. He joins himself to a woman who has already been married, who is not of his country or brought up in his faith.

The people in the story—Naomi, Ruth, and Boaz—venture into a risky relationship, but the birth of a son seems to confirm the wisdom of taking a chance. As the village women know, Obed is a sign of God's blessing, one who will restore Naomi's life, keep her in her old age, and affirm the precious worth of a daughter-in-law—more than the two sons she had lost and five more beyond that.

We know that this baby, born of an unlikely union, is the ongoing link to another baby, one who would come from the most unlikely union of all, that of God and humankind. Through Obed, God builds the house of David, a house big enough to include the outcast, the foreigner, the sinner, the victim, the heartbroken: "And Salmon [was] the father of Boaz by Rahab, and Boaz the father of Obed by Ruth, and Obed the father of Jesse, and Jesse the father of King David" (Matt. 1:5-6).

It is a risky business to trust the salvation of the world to the destitute and defenseless. It is a risky business to leave it all in the hands of women and children. But that is exactly what God has done.

Reflect on where God is taking a risk with your life. How will you respond?

In our family, the generation after mine has no sons. Instead, we have been blessed with three girls who have grown into wonderful young women. Like the sons the psalmist celebrates, they too are "a heritage from the LORD"; they too bring happiness to their families.

In ancient Israel, sons were considered a special blessing. They were the ones who inherited and controlled family wealth and property. A son meant that the family name and influence would continue through another generation; a son was a defense against the assaults of old age. These views were deeply embedded in the culture of the time, and they continue as strong feelings even today.

The psalmist clearly rejoices in the blessing of sons and a lot of them, but this second part of the psalm is perhaps best understood in light of the first part. Persons of faith know that unless God guides our life, everything else is ultimately futile. A houseful of boys does not guarantee that all will be well. But a house where all are loved and valued is a house where miracles happen, where grace abounds, where God is at work. Ruth was more to Naomi than seven sons because of love. From that love, God was building the house of David. God's heritage was a son for Ruth, yes, but God's gift was also courage for Naomi and Ruth.

Courage is an element of trust, and trust is an element of faith. Faith is the underpinning of holy risk. In the face of doubt and despair, in the presence of foes and fears, the faith that is our heritage from God, God's great gift and blessing, provides courage and confidence.

The psalmist says sons keep a man from "shame when he speaks with his enemies in the gate." Who are your enemies? Where do you meet your fears? What gives you the courage and confidence to risk speaking up in those situations?

Jesus is harsh with those who value the trappings and public practice of piety. In his view, they are hypocrites, more interested in appearances than reality. In Greek, the word for hypocrite means "actor." Jesus had no use for those who only wanted to playact at faith, dressing up in fancy clothes, claiming the box seats, and sitting at the head table all the time. For the scribes, appearance is everything. They cannot see their own blindness. Jesus implies a willingness on their part to do anything, including preying on others, to maintain their status. And because they cannot risk losing their power and prestige, they find themselves in danger of losing everything.

The challenge for many of us is that we are more aligned with the scribes than with the widows, whether we like to admit it or not. We may not seek out the limelight for ourselves, but sometimes our work in and for the church gets too focused on perpetuating the institution, keeping the lights on and the grass mowed and the silver polished. We get comfortable sitting in "our" pew and getting together for church suppers with people we like, who are like us. That is when we need to listen for Jesus saying to us: "Beware!"

Like the scribes, we too are at risk if we forget that it is not the institution but rather its mission in the world that matters. As the psalmist reminds us, "Unless the LORD builds the house, those who build it labor in vain" (Ps. 127:1). Unless God guides the church, our actions are useless. If we are so concerned with appearances that we forget the substance, or worse, abuse the gifts God in Christ has given us, we have missed the point. If status rules, either personal or ecclesial, we are lost.

What are you afraid to give up? How does it stand in the way of your relationship with God?

In the midst of great wealth and ostentation, the poor widow comes with her offering. She holds nothing back, giving everything in a moment of stunning abandon, throwing caution to the wind as she puts her coins in the offering.

To anyone watching—except Jesus—her two cents' worth is worth nothing. Jesus, though, understands that the value of a gift is relative, not absolute; that a large amount means nothing if given for show and costing the giver nothing. The widow's sacrifice comes from what the poet T. S. Eliot calls "a condition of complete simplicity, costing not less than everything."

Some might think the widow wasted her money. On its face, it is a foolish gift, too puny to make any difference to the Temple and yet too precious to her to give up. In addition, she gives all she has to a corrupt system to support the very ones who devour her and her kind. Her extravagant gesture seems to be in vain, resulting in nothing except more poverty for her. It seems like a lost cause. But what she does is truly Godlike. God also gave everything God had, offering it to our corrupted creation, giving what was most precious to people who might not even notice.

To give from abundance when we have more to spare is easy; to give as though our lives depended on it is different. It is giving from our poverty that God wants from us, but this is a risky business. It takes all we have to live this way, and we can only do it if we understand that God in Christ has already taken the real risk. All we have to do is respond in kind and know that our willingness to take a holy risk will not be in vain.

What are you withholding from God? Can you take the risk of trusting more fully in God's extravagant love and so offer your own love in response?

To See as God Sees

NOVEMBER 12–18, 2012 • DAVID DAVIES

MONDAY, NOVEMBER 12 ~ *Read Mark 13:1-2*

The footnote in my Bible says of the stones, "Most of them were 37.5 feet long, 18 feet wide, and 12 feet thick." This confirms our human inclination toward positive impressions based solely on size. Certainly the size impresses the disciples. Like first-time tourists to New York City who pose hazards to themselves and others because they continually look up at the buildings, the disciples cannot stop looking up and saying, "Wow!" Jesus asks them if they see the buildings, *really see* the buildings. Not as large stones cleverly stacked on top of each other and artfully carved and decorated but as testament to the moral corruption of the tyrannical leadership of Herod, the Jewish king who willingly sacrificed the lives and livelihood of the people he ruled to build monuments to himself and his Roman friends.

The stones didn't just stack themselves up. Each stone had a trajectory that left lives crushed in its path. No such building can stand for long, and Jesus with prophetic vision sees its fall. Prophecy is not so much forecasting the future as it is declaring a moral vision. "Do you see?" Buddhist teaching holds that "right vision" is seeing acutely what lies before us unvarnished by our emotions or imaginations. Right vision is seeing the present so deeply that the connections of each to the other become clear. The disciples look at the stones and are amazed, awestruck, and perhaps proud of this national monument. Jesus looks at the stones and sees a monument to greed and power paid for with lives of workers and by deprivation of families in the countryside.

God, let me see today as much as I am able, the world as you see it, a world connected to you at its most intimate level. Amen.

Computer programmer and co-owner of Soul Desires Bookstore, Omaha, Nebraska

TUESDAY, NOVEMBER 13 ~ *Read 1 Samuel 1:4-11*

In Barbara Kingsolver's novel *The Lacuna*, at a point when the main character has found himself as grist in the mill of anti-Communist fervor gripping the United States in the McCarthy era, he pens these words in his diary, "Life proceeds, it enrages. The untouched ones spend their luck without a thought, believing they deserve it." That sense of deserving defines the attitude of Peninnah toward Hannah in our reading. Peninnah, blessed with children, not only perceives that she is deserving but also that Hannah, being barren, is not. In biblical times, as evidenced by many stories, children were wealth and worth in the culture of women. This is a story of the haves and the have-nots in a different economy. Peninnah, it seems, is not humble in her status but chooses to flaunt her good fortune: maybe dropping a comment about Hannah's bad luck here; listing accomplishments of her children there.

Perhaps unintended, perhaps intended, the taunts provoke and irritate Hannah. Today we might call Hannah depressed. Depressed to the point that she loses interest in life, weeps often, and finally determines that she must make a deal with God to bear a child. She feels certain that God has forgotten her, lost her in the churn of events we call history that must be so much more important to God. Hannah goes to God like an entrepreneur goes to a banker, asking for a loan to start a business but having no means of repayment except for the loan itself and her earnest intent to work hard. If she is given a child, she will dedicate the child to God, presuming it lives to adulthood. Some people make unreasonable requests out of their sense of deserving. Desperation drives Hannah to make her request that is unreasonable in any economy of the world.

Loving God, open my eyes during this day to the blessings of my life. Help me not assume them as a sign of my deserving or another person's lack. Amen.

Mistaken identity, taking on a false persona, or being perceived as someone other than who we are, has been the stuff of good comedy for millennia. Shakespeare used it in many of his comedies such as *Comedy of Errors* and *Twelfth Night*. Situation comedies on TV return to it often. It becomes the stuff of tragedy when the force of events causes a person to mistake his or her own identity, to lose it to the perceptions of the world. Hannah is on the verge of such a crisis, and what better time for the storyteller to use mistaken identity for a little humor. We can imagine Eli observing the unseemly behavior of Hannah and thinking surely she will stop, fall asleep, or just go away. He delays himself from acting several times; but finally adopting his most high priestly mien, he approaches and reprimands Hannah with stern voice and scowling brow in order to rid the temple of this besotted woman.

Eli's vision is impaired by his desire for proper behavior and a tidy temple. He soon sees the situation in a whole new light when he receives the view of the world from Hannah's perspective. She convinces him with the depth of her being, for in the scripture, Eli never is told the specifics of her vexation. Perhaps he intuits the problem; perhaps he just understands the depth of her sorrow and her need for God to hear. He fumbles in embarrassment, his voice drops its edge, and his face moves from hard stare to dropped eyes to melting compassion. And when he recovers, his moment of comedy transforms the tragedy with this blessing, "Go in peace; the God of Israel grant the petition you have made to him." Eli's comedic transformation also transforms Hannah. Her vision of herself, so close to being buried alive by the oppressive vision of the world around her, is restored; she sees herself once again as one whom God loves.

Loving God, help me today to see others and myself as beloved children of yours. Amen.

To See as God Sees

I don't need to tell you, Hebrews is a difficult book for us to read today. The author seems too concerned with much that is of little concern to us today. I tend to think of it as sort of an infomercial aimed at both Christians and Jews in the days following the destruction of Herod's Temple in 70 CE. The author is concerned with right seeing also. The Temple is destroyed. How is one supposed to live when the opportunity of legally prescribed sacrifice is gone, even if one didn't do it as often as one should? Jesus has died. How is one supposed to see Jesus, who was after all a commoner put to death by the state?

For me, Hebrews 10:1 defines the focus of today's reading: "Since the law has only a shadow of the good things to come and not the true form of these realities, it can never, by the same sacrifices that are continually offered year after year, make perfect those who approach." Hinting at Plato's cave analogy of shadows and reality, the author states that Jesus' offering to us is the reality that the shadows of sacrifice can only hint at. Shadow has no effect. Try as we might, no matter how much we move our shadow over the tiniest of pebbles or even a leaf, the pebble will not move, the leaf will not tremble. So it is with priestly sacrifice. No matter how often, day after day, the sacrifice is offered, it will not take away sins. The vision of Jesus the author proffers is not of a common man executed on a Roman cross but of a high priest who, through the sacrifice of his life and death, brought forth a new creation for all. A new world for those who will see it (the sanctified) where God remembers "their sins and their lawless deeds" no more. A new world for those who will see it where sin offerings are useless.

Loving God, help me today to see this world and live in it as a new world where there is no separation from you and your love. Amen.

If I may paint with a broad brush, we all live with the expectation of being able to make a sin offering for today's offenses sometime in the future. We give ourselves permission to indulge our own whims and pleasures or what Wendell Berry calls "the set of personal excuses we call 'individuality,'" telling ourselves we will make it right in the end. We often live a paraphrase of Augustine of Hippo's prayer, "God, make me pure, but not yet," in the hope and expectation that sometime down the road, we will be able to offer our version of a sin sacrifice to God and get things on the right track.

And then there are those actions about which we feel quite justified in causing pain and distress to others. In it all we follow the operating procedure that "it is easier to seek forgiveness than to ask permission." What shall we do in this new world that the author of Hebrews proclaims, a world in which there is no place to make our sin offerings? Not just the absence of a place to go but no need for those who can see that new world to even make a sin offering.

Honestly, when I think of stopping my guilty pleasures, I see a rather joyless world because it all seems to be about me alone giving things up. The author of Hebrews responds that it is about more than each of us individually. We are to approach one another with "hearts sprinkled clean from an evil conscience" and consider how to "provoke [what a fascinating word to use here] one another to love and good deeds." This new world of right seeing is not a world of each alone but a world in which we meet and see one another again for the first time.

Loving God, today let me truly live out "forgive us our sins as we forgive those who sin against us." Amen.

Jesus and the disciples have left the Temple, walked through the valley and up the hill on the opposite side, the Mount of Olives. The disciples have been mulling Jesus' prediction of the Temple in ruins and can contain themselves no longer. The moral vision of Jesus' statement having escaped them, their minds race with visions of the end of the world because to them, the Temple will fall only with the destruction of the whole world (just look at the size of those stones). They want to know what to look for so they can be prepared when the time comes. What follows (not just in these verses but for the rest of chapter 13 as Mark has compiled it) is one of the strangest amalgams of signs and not-a-signs any ardent apocalyptic could want.

In our reading, Jesus starts by saying we should not look for individuals who claim to be of God and who make dreadful pronouncements as signs. Looking farther up the hierarchy to nations, their striving and battling each other—those will not be signs. And farther up the hierarchy—the natural world and the devastation it can wreak through famine and flood and earthquake—those will not be signs. We can easily make the case that the immediate crisis is worse than anything that preceded it, the present leaders more evil, the people more debauched, the destruction more complete. The end is always just around the corner.

Jesus offers a right way of seeing that doesn't deny the pain and heartache but also sees the birthing of a new world among the carnage of the old. Worldly vision gives birth to false expectations that die with the passing of the latest crisis; right vision gives birth to hopeful anticipation that nurtures lives of compassion.

Loving God, may I see the signs of your new creation even in the midst of the pain and suffering of this world. Amen.

Vision is ultimately about perspective. Right seeing involves getting the right perspective. Renaissance painters are sometimes said to have discovered or rediscovered perspective in their use of the vanishing point. Things close at hand appear larger; more distant objects and people are smaller. This is really the natural or real-world perspective that people have always understood. A person on a hill across the valley looks small. Earlier artists based the size of the person, his or her visible space in the painting, on importance, the size of his or her role in the event being depicted—not in how far he or she was from the viewer.

In this psalm, God's perspective comes from high above even the heavens, home to the angels and forces controlling the events of the world below them. What looms largest in God's vision, however, is not what the natural perspective would dictate. That which is nearest, the heavens with all their splendor and power, are not large in God's sight. Even the highest of the human power pyramid, the princes and rulers, makers of history, do not loom large in God's sight. What looms large in God's vision are those who are so out of place and powerless as to seem to have been given no place at all in the picture, those who from a natural perspective are so insignificant as to be painted using a brush with a single hair—the poor, the needy, the barren woman. Being seen large by God, they are lifted up, raised up, given a home. They live in God's sight with a size and weight equal to the most powerful of the people. And there was joy among the people and praise of the most high God.

Loving God, thank you for seeing me in the obscurity of my innermost being. Let my heart be lifted up in joy and sing your praise. Amen.

Remembrance and Anticipation

NOVEMBER 19–25, 2012 • MARJORIE HEWITT SUCHOCKI

MONDAY, NOVEMBER 19 ~ *Read 2 Samuel 23:1-7*

This is a "between-the-kingdoms" week. We conclude the liturgical year with texts about the ancient kingdom of Israel, and we will culminate the week with Christ the King, or Reign of Christ, Sunday. But the "hallelujah" of Christ the King immediately gives way on the succeeding Sunday to Advent and the hush of awaiting the King. We are between the times, remembering the past, anticipating the future's renewal.

Second Samuel 23:1-7 fittingly begins this week of remembrance/anticipation, giving King David's last words as his life and reign draw to a close. The beginning verses name his long-ago anointing by God for the sake of ruling righteously. This "sweet psalmist of Israel" sings of God speaking to him and through him for the sake of righteousness. He gives a lyric comparison between the righteous ruler and the morning sunrise, when all things flourish through sunshine and rain. Righteousness is the essential condition for flourishing. Then, in keeping with many psalms, comes the imprecation: those who inhibit righteousness will be thrust away as thorns. This is necessarily so, for unrighteousness is the destruction of good. To value righteousness and flourishing is to be vigilant against that which would undo righteousness, leaving misery in its wake.

The text calls each of us to the reflective work of remembrance. Is God's word to us borne out by fruits of righteousness in a flourishing community? What elements in our own lives inhibit righteousness and need rooting out as thorns?

God of our years, become our courage so that we may evaluate our work in the light of righteousness. Amen.

Professor Emerita at Claremont School of Theology; living in Upland, California

Anticipation and remembrance indeed! This psalm is a Song of Ascents, a ritualistic recitation as worshipers climb the road toward the Temple, which was built at the highest point in Jerusalem. But if pilgrims used this psalm as they approached the Temple, they begin with a reflection on failure! David did indeed yearn to build a temple for the Lord, a "dwelling place for the Mighty One of Jacob"—but we know he did not build it. The task passed to his son, Solomon, who raised the Temple about which his father had dreamed. So the psalm begins with remembrance of David's frustrated hopes and ends with the anticipation of a promise that the worshipers now know to be fulfilled, for in this "Song of Ascents" they approach the Temple built not by David but by Solomon. That which cannot be done in one's own lifetime will surely be accomplished in a generation to come.

Our work, our ministry, is never ours alone, nor is it ever possible in one lifetime to "do it all." The liturgical year tells us so, for one cycle succeeds another, always the same, always different. The work we are given to do is the work we are given to do, all of us! We are joined to one another, within a generation and across generations, for the mighty work and worship of God through the beauty of holiness, righteousness, love. The never-ending work of ministry requires transgenerational community. What we long for, another may build. Remembrance and anticipation! Within the joining of the two emerges the ever-present call and empowerment for ministry.

How is your own present work related to the work of those who came before you? What are your God-given dreams that depend upon those who come after you? How does your own ministry provide a basis for the work of those who will come?

God of all times, grant us the long-view look as we deal with our passions for service, trusting your communal call for the building of your temple of righteousness. Amen.

Remembrance and Anticipation   337

Remembrance and anticipation have their basis in our temporal mode of existence, for we were, and we have a history; we (or our successors!) will be, and we look toward a future. In the joining together of remembrance of things past and anticipation of things future, we experience the intensity of the present. Our text suggests that our own mode of temporality is itself rooted in God, who is always and everlastingly the One who is Alpha and Omega, past and future in an everlasting Present. Our fragile times are encompassed by the infinite togetherness of all times in God. The unity of our times, however, is not the simple fact of temporality but the way in which our temporality can be infused with the reflection of the everlasting Alpha-Omega God through the creation of a kingdom that reflects in time God's everlasting righteousness, goodness, and love. We experience God's "time" in and through such a reign. We can participate in the creation of this kingdom of righteousness in and through Jesus Christ who loves us and releases us from our sins, thus empowering us for kingdom-creating work.

Having suggested this, the text then calls upon an ultimate future: "Look! He is coming with the clouds; every eye will see him. . . ." This final week of Kingdomtide foretells the coming week of Advent: Jesus, the One who makes the kingdom possible in all our times. Anticipation is heightened, for no matter what the present state of our place in secular and religious history, there is always a coming that calls us beyond the present. The confidence in our anticipation is the sense in which that always-future-coming reflects the everlasting nature of the God we have always known in and through Jesus Christ.

Ever-coming One, teach us so to remember our past that we value its witness to your righteousness; teach us so to anticipate our future that we look for you in every call to ministry. Amen.

Thanksgiving Day, USA

Today's text interrupts our focus on past and future by delight in the present, caused appropriately enough on this day of Thanksgiving by a time of plenty. The pastures are green, the trees are bearing fruit, and the granaries are full—thanksgiving indeed! We are bountifully sustained!

Yet even this text employs remembrance and anticipation: remembrance of the sunshine and rain that yielded today's plenty and anticipation of sustenance in the winter to come through the ability to store food enough until next harvest. Present bounty remembers past labors and anticipates future well-being.

When Jesus taught us to pray for the coming of God's kingdom, he immediately followed "thy kingdom come" with "give us this day our daily bread." The plentiful food for which we give thanks sustains us for the work of the kingdom. And the prayer for daily bread is itself followed by prayer for spiritual sustenance: "forgive us our trespasses, as we forgive those who trespass against us, and lead us not into temptation, but deliver us from evil." Our spiritual food comes from receiving and giving forgiveness and watchfulness for ways of righteousness. Physically and spiritually sustained, we pray for and work toward the kingdom of God, where physical and spiritual food are plenteously available for all.

So we give thanks on this day for the double harvest—physical and spiritual food, physical and spiritual works that open us to the inbreaking God whose kingdom will indeed come.

Our Father in heaven, hallowed be your name. Your kingdom come. Your will be done, on earth as it is in heaven. Give us this day our daily bread. And forgive us our debts, as we also have forgiven our debtors. And do not bring us to the time of trial, but rescue us from the evil one. Amen.

The psalm is situated between remembrance and anticipation, memory and hope. The captives have just gained release from Babylon and returned to their homeland; they remember their years of captivity and now are "like those who dream" as the new future opens before them. Seventy long years it has been, so that most of those returning to Zion have never been there, having been born in captivity. But they remember the stories told them by their elders; they always knew that they were Israelites, not Babylonians. In this context, the psalmist exults: "Those who go out weeping, bearing the seed for sowing, / shall come home with shouts of joy, carrying their sheaves." Don't we also sow in tears—and anticipate that the God of the harvest will yet bring forth an abundance that answers the spiritual and physical needs of all?

Because we are in Christ and have absorbed his manifestation of God's reign, because we trust in the Spirit's power to enable us, we too anticipate the fullness of God's reign. We see it in part with every movement toward inclusive justice and kindness in our communities. And we experience its fullness as we enter into God at the end of our lives in unimaginable joy.

We who live between the times hold the memories of God's work in times past and anticipate the fullness of God's reign in times to come, even when those times surpass all times within God's own being. We hold the creative tension of memory and hope in each present moment. Out of this togetherness comes good cheer, courage for our given tasks, confidence in the power of God to weave us always together into strong community. We claim Psalm 126's promise that we shall indeed come with shouts of joy, bringing our sheaves with us.

God of all our times, we give you thanks for our personal and ecclesial memories; we give you thanks for grounding our hopes. Amen.

If we live in the tension between memory and hope, how does this affect the way we live our daily lives as Christians in this present time? Today's text gives us practical guidance: we are to give—and to live—prayers of intercession and thanksgiving for all. We are particularly called to prayers of intercession and thanksgiving for "all those in authority" (NIV) so that good governance may give us conditions of peace and well-being. The resultant tranquility, quietness, godliness, and dignity set the context within which we live and preach the gospel. We sometimes think that times of trouble are the times when people will listen and respond to the message of God's saving love, but this text suggests the opposite. Against a backdrop of peace, there is the freedom to preach and to teach about the redemptive love of God in Jesus Christ. Political stability and conditions of peace allow us to respond to the call of God's peace, God's love, God's undergirding of all life with the transforming energy of Christ.

God's kingdom is a depth dimension to our lives together. It is an attunement to the call of God in the midst of ordinariness, an awareness of the roots of peace in the love of God. God's kingdom is a future that pervades our present, changing the quality of our lives in conformity to the great love of God.

One of the functions of memory is its shaping of the present, just as one of the functions of hope is its directive power to shape the present. The kingdom of God, shaped through remembrance and anticipation, infuses the way we live our lives in the present. And this is "right and acceptable in the sight of God our Savior."

And so, beloved God of the kingdom, we offer our prayers for those who govern their respective lands, that they will be enabled by your grace to transcend the temptation to govern for personal gain and instead govern justly and righteously, creating an image of your peace. Amen.

THE REIGN OF CHRIST SUNDAY

What kind of a king is this? We know well that contemporary "kings" strive for thriving economies generated by consumerism. We are encouraged not only to spend all we have but to spend more, using credit cards to spend beyond what we can afford. Today's text from the Sermon on the Mount provides a stark contrast to contemporary culture.

Christ our King counsels a lifestyle of simplicity and trust. Look around you at the simple beauty and plenitude that God has so generously given; let go of the cultural inducements to "need" this, "need" that, endlessly buying in the temples of the economy. Live simply, trusting God to supply all our needs—in the "supplying," God redefines our needs. As we learn to trust God's generosity in this kingdom of God, we will learn to be generous ourselves.

Sometimes we are tempted to reject "kingdom" and "king" language as being too hierarchical and patriarchal. What we lose in rejecting the concepts is the sense in which passages like today's overturn our usual concepts of governance. In this final day of the liturgical year, we anticipate the message of Incarnation in the year about to begin. There the Christ we today name as King is born in a manger; the highest of all appears as the lowliest of all. To name and follow Christ as King is to redefine governance from a consumerist to a community model. To jettison the metaphor is to lose the continual challenge to all our human forms of governance.

We close the liturgical year; we begin the liturgical year. We culminate the old with memories of majesty reinterpreted; we anticipate the new with hope of ever new ways to discover Christ the King among us.

God of our memories, God of our hopes, make us ever attentive to your presence in our midst. Amen.

God's Promise

NOVEMBER 26–DECEMBER 2, 2012 • PAMELA D. COUTURE

MONDAY, NOVEMBER 26 ~ *Read Jeremiah 33:14-16*

Advent begins with God's promise: the long-awaited descendant in the lineage of King David, one whom Christians will name the Messiah, will arrive soon! Interpreting who Jesus is after his death, Christians identify Jesus as the one anticipated by scriptures such as this one from Jeremiah.

The promise of a Messiah begins the liturgical year, a time of multiple and complex emotions. Historically, the church has bedecked its worship spaces during this time in purple, a color representing the self-examination and somber preparation historically associated with Advent, a color also anticipating the presence of royalty.

This mix of emotions recognized in the liturgical symbols of the church takes contemporary form as people experience Advent differently. In North America, Advent tends to hasten the pace of our lives, adding holiday decorating, social events, and gift buying to the ongoing activities of family and work. Crowded schedules and heightened gaiety leave little room for those experiencing death, loss, separation from loved ones, shame, or guilt. And when the pace offers no room for somber emotions, the joy of preparation that is grounded in love, friendship, and gratitude may become a burden rather than a deep spiritual experience.

As you move toward Advent, where will you find your space for self-examination and for mixed emotions?

God who knows all things, increase my self-knowledge as I prepare for the coming of the Messiah. Amen.

The Geoffrey and Jane Martin Professor of Church and Community at Emmanuel College of Victoria University, Toronto, Canada

In order to live, we must trust life, make plans, develop expectations, imagine the future. Luke's opening verses reinforce emotions other than trust when nature and nations run amok. Sudden, unexpected death also explodes that trust. When we rely on continued contact with others and that expectation is fulfilled, we may quietly ponder the mystery of the reminder to live each moment as if it were the last. When a moment arrives that lifts us over the brink of the last—the last meeting, the last conversation, the last expression of love, the last hug—our disbelief may jolt our awareness beyond comprehension.

That jolt struck this week when I learned that my close friend, Dr. Mireille Mikombe Seya, a female physician who was headmistress of the Lupandilo School of Nursing in the Democratic Republic of Congo (DRC), had died in childbirth. A woman of deep faith, Dr. Mirielle's life demonstrated the truth of watchfulness. A 2005 graduate of medical school, she had already tended children, saved lives, creatively developed a gynecological and obstetrical practice with poor women, taught students, and envisioned a world safe from violence against women. In two years redeveloping Lupandilo she had accomplished a decade's worth of work, raising morale and creating hope. She lived every day as a gift from God, placing her faith in God's presence. Such a life and death models living watchfully.

Well lived, our lives organically integrate the care we have for the immediate others in our lives: our partners, family, close friends, and the work God has given us to do for anonymous others on behalf of the community, the church, or the world. The exhortation to watch calls us to discern the way we use our time, today. "Stand up and raise your heads; . . . redemption is drawing near."

God of time, may we discern your guidance for the blossoming of the love and talent with which you have graced us. Amen.

Death gathers community—people who have not been in touch with one another reach out, see one another for the first time, share memories. Death also fractures community—underground grudges reappear, latent disagreements become charged with emotion.

The death of Dr. Mirielle, a noted leader in the Congolese Methodist community but also well loved by persons in the United States, has created a flurry of e-mail and phone calls. Some of these communicated condolences, the social graces of community that we extend toward others at such a time when we need to reaffirm our connections. Others of these presented wrenching theological questions about God's presence in life and death. Some wrestled with the disparity of health care in our countries. Searching questions cause us to ponder the depth of our relationship with God and the breadth of the emotions our scriptures help us express.

The gathering of community around death creates a time when we give thanks for the presence of family and friends—living and dead—who give meaning to our lives. It is a time when we need our trusted friends the most! And during those times our companions may need to carry the hope of faith for us when we cannot carry it for ourselves or we for them. When our trust is shattered, we need the faith of one another—we need those who give thanks for us—to help us reconnect our relationship with God. Together, we face the doubts and fears of faith that rumble in the depths of our souls, waiting for some event to push them to the surface. Faith and trust are slowly restored in the presence of those persons who can hear and accept our deepest questions and anguish.

Life-giving God, may we be part of communities that bear witness to the restoration of faith. Amen.

The apocalyptic literature of the New Testament anticipates a time when, following great suffering, the Son of Man brings God's reign to earth. Those of us who live in countries with relative stability may look at events that shake our world and wonder what those events mean for the end times. Others of us live with ongoing political insecurity. When death and disease define the environment in which people live, they often demonstrate the perseverance of faith in ways that are unfathomable to those of us with easier lives. Regardless of the context in which we live, we wonder what the reign of God might mean in our lifetimes.

This week, as I meditate on Advent scriptures and grieve my friend's death, the United Nations has reviewed progress toward the Millennium Development Goals, including those seeking to improve maternal health. Amnesty International has announced that 6800 women have died in childbirth this week, one every ninety seconds. My friend was one of these women. I do not need to look beyond my own computer screen to find a groaning world. Maternal death is only one of the extreme injustices suffered by the people of poor countries.

The image of Son of Man arriving to a world in distress immediately introduces theological themes of incarnation, God inhabiting flesh. The idea of the Incarnation is imagined in the famous line "Love came down at Christmas" by Christina Rossetti. In the Incarnation, God seeks to be like us, so as to respond to our human condition. In response, we seek to grow in the image and likeness of God, loving more fully. In such love, despite the tragedies of the world exemplified by preventable maternal and child death, we may find a glimpse of the reign of God.

Son of Man, God of love, fill us with compassion for you and for one another. Amen.

The psalmist commits his soul to God and declares his trust. In light of the personal losses and social conditions that fall far short of what we would associate with the reign of God, it may be difficult for us to truly do the same! Every religious life that opens itself to the conditions of the world must confront the question: how can I put my trust in God? As long as trust in God means relying on God for our own particular, desired outcomes, we will be disappointed.

Lifting our souls to God and trusting in God leads us into an ever-deepening relationship in which the mysteries of life unfold. As we trust, we let go, look expectantly to the future, without setting requirements for what that future must hold. Instead, we trust the unfolding of the Creator's gift of life. We trust that our own small portion of human experience is already known by the immanent God, the God who has experienced all that humanity experiences as God incarnate, God in human flesh. We are humbled to lift our souls to the transcendent God, the mysterious, all-embracing, creative God whose purposes are wider and broader than we can see.

Placing our trust in this God allows us to face squarely the personal losses and social injustices that are often the source of our doubts. Yes, we continue to have our personal hopes and our particular way of fulfilling our vocation for love and justice. But these are tempered by the larger vision, the mysterious leading of God.

Advent is a time for an examination of those things that hold us back from fully trusting God; letting go and living in the comfort that comes from lifting our whole being into God's arms.

Holy God, reassure us by making yourself known in ways broader and wider than we can hope and dream. Amen.

W aiting for God" has a checkered history in Christian spiri- tuality. In some traditions human beings are expected not to take initiative until God clearly acts first. Other times people who benefit from the status quo have told those suffering from the status quo to "wait"; their time is not yet.

Between passivity and oppression lies a purposeful, active form of waiting. In waiting, the psalmist tells us, we learn the ways of God and we prepare ourselves for what comes next. Such waiting does not abdicate human responsibility for future vision—rather, waiting solidifies the vision of how human beings might participate in God's reign and produces confidence in action and commitment to the sacrifices required.

We are a global church; we have relationships across the world; we have technological means of awareness. Now, as a global church we can actively wait together. Our global rela- tionships may make us more mindful of the importance of knowing God's ways and finding God's path to salvation. Seek- ing right relations with brothers and sisters across the world who struggle in very different circumstances than we do may mysteriously open opportunities for us to see God incarnate in the world and thus more real in our lives. In the United States a now-antiquated adage compares soldiers and mothers: soldiers risked their lives on the battlefield, mothers risked their lives in childbirth. In first-world countries every premature death in war and childbirth matters to those left to grieve, but these deaths are comparatively few; in developing countries every premature death in war or childbirth matters to those left to grieve, and these deaths are many.

This Advent let us commit to a vision of making that adage as obsolete in the two-thirds world as in the first, and let us discern God's way toward God's reign.

God, you have given us vision. We await you. Amen.

First Sunday of Advent

What is the sin of youth, from the perspective of age? I hope the sin of my youth is narrowness of vision: at times the sin of avoidance, of backing away from the overwhelming needs of the world; at times the sin of self-righteousness, of knowing exactly what others could do to right all ills. I hope the advantage of age is humility: a wideness of heart that beckons more complexity into my soul than ever before; a resilience of spirit that sustains my work in the midst of discouragement; a compassion that allows me to commit to critical visions, knowing they will only be partially accomplished.

Providing the fertile soil for all humility is the knowledge of the steadfast love of God—a love I can perceive with all of my senses, a love I can proclaim to others when everything seems to be crumbling, a love that guides actions when they accompany or replace words.

The knowledge of this steadfast love makes Advent self-examination possible. It is what the Son of Man brings to a troubled world; it is what comforts us while we watch and wait; it unites us in life and death.

May we already know this love, even while we trust it to arrive in the form of a vulnerable mother and baby.

Swell the love in our hearts, dear God, that we may more perfectly see ourselves, know you, and find your way. We pray in the name of the mother and the babe who bring this season to us. Amen.

Preparing the Way of the Lord

DECEMBER 3–9, 2012 • M. ROBERT MULHOLLAND JR.

MONDAY, DECEMBER 3 ～ *Read Luke 1:68-71*

Zechariah's words would have engendered either skepticism or hope. The Jewish people suffer under oppressive Roman domination of their promised land. They yearn for God's intervention in the form of a "mighty savior" who will deliver them from Roman enemies, liberate the promised land, and restore them as a kingdom under a descendant of David. This hope, however, was repeatedly dashed as the Romans brutally squelched numerous attempts at liberation led by self-proclaimed "messiahs." Is Zechariah the real thing?

Many people today suffer from various forms of oppression that deny the wholeness of life for which God created them. For some the oppression results from an economy fueled by greed. For others oppression takes root in societal and systemic structures of self-interest in which injustice and discrimination are inherent. Yet others find themselves imprisoned by attitudes and behaviors that hold them in bondage. The world offers a multitude of purveyors of hope for deliverance from such oppressions. These "messiahs" play upon the deep hunger of the heart for wholeness of life, but they consistently fail to deliver.

Why, then, should we heed the promise of deliverance and of hope for a transformed life? We shouldn't if by "deliverance" we merely seek a self-referenced escape from the circumstances of our life or if by "transformed" we desire God to allow us to be and do what we want to be and do. However, if we are willing to consider a radical way of being in the world and dealing with life circumstances and relationships, then the promise is for us.

Lord, help me be your person in the world. Amen.

Professor Emeritus of New Testament, Asbury Seminary; Wilmore, Kentucky

John's proclamation of "repentance for the forgiveness of sins" as the means of preparing the way for the Lord sets the promise of deliverance in a whole new light. It suggests that deliverance is less liberation from the oppressive, destructive, and dehumanizing forces of the world than it is release from those dynamics of our being that hinder us from the fullness and wholeness of life for which God created us.

John's hearers believed that individual and corporate sin had precluded God's intervention to deliver them from Roman oppression and restore the kingdom to Israel. Jesus' life and ministry reveal that God does not so much intervene to transform the circumstances and conditions of the world as to transform persons and communities to be agents of transformation.

If we understand sin as a failure to be the person or community God created us to be in the world, then repentance is the acknowledgment and, especially, the rejection of that state of being. At the same time, repentance entails a commitment to become the persons or community God empowers us to be in the world. Deliverance becomes not an escape from the circumstances and conditions of the world but a liberation from the dynamics of our own being or community that have been subverted by the world. This liberation enables us to become the healing, transforming love of God for the world.

Repentance, then, is the radical prerequisite for preparing the way of the Lord in the world. Are you willing to repent of those structures of your being that hold you captive to destructive and dehumanizing ways of being in the world? In Jesus' words, are you willing to "lose yourself" for his sake?

Gracious God, stir in me desire to repent of being other than what you have created me to be—a person in your image for the sake of the world. Amen.

WEDNESDAY, DECEMBER 5 ~ *Read Malachi 3:1-4*

The people of Malachi's day, like those of Jesus' time, eagerly longed for God to come and deliver them from their oppressors. When this happened, God's presence would once again dwell in the Temple (Isa. 52:8), the covenant would be consummated (Jer. 31:31-33), the kingdom of David restored (Isa. 9:7; Jer. 23:5), and God's faithful would dwell in peace and prosperity (Ezek. 34:25-27). Even today people look for God to intervene and set things right. Into these idyllic visions Malachi thrusts a disturbing word—God's coming will not be pleasant and enjoyable; it will be like a refiner's fire! Even Jesus said he did not come to bring peace but a sword (Matt. 10:34).

Note Isaiah's experience (Isa. 6:1-7). As Isaiah encountered God he also encountered the reality of his own condition: "I saw the Lord, high and lifted up. . . . Woe is me, I am lost, for I am a man of unclean lips" (AT). When we experience God's presence we also awaken to those aspects of our being that run contrary to the image of God we were created to be. God's presence becomes a refiner's fire to burn out the dross and impurities in our being.

Experiencing God as a consuming fire (Heb. 12:29) is not a pleasant or enjoyable experience. The "dross" in our life is so much an integral part of who we understand ourselves to be that it seems as if God is seeking to destroy us. In actuality, however, God is simply seeking to refine us and restore us to our true self in God's image. The question is, are we willing to lose our false self in order to be restored to Christlikeness—our true self?

Refining Fire, burn out of me all that is contrary to your purposes for my life: all the selfish desires, all the impure motives, all the darkened perspectives, all the destructive habits. Restore me to your image. Amen.

Paul writes to a community who is "sharing in the gospel," using the term *koinonia.* Elsewhere he uses *koinonia* to describe believers' relationship with Christ, sharing the body and blood of Christ, and relationship with the Holy Spirit; in other words, a life in vital, dynamic relationship with God.

We see the transformed nature of this life in Paul's prayer that their "love may overflow more and more with knowledge and full insight." This love is agape, a radical mode of being that Paul further develops in 2:3-4: "Consider others above yourself, not looking to your own interests but to the interests of others" (AT). In other words, this transformed life is, like Christ, a life poured out for the well-being and nurture of others.

Such a life overflows with knowledge and full insight. The knowledge Paul notes here is experiential, not merely cognitive, and the "full insight" is the perceptual frame of reference that results from the intimate, vital, dynamic participation ("experiential knowledge") in the life of God in Christ. This life is pure, engaging others and the world without the destructive and corrupting poison of self interest. This life is blameless, not a hindrance to the wholeness and well-being of others.

The deliverance we have discussed this week results in liberation from a life that infects all its relationships and dealings with the world with the corrosive poison of self-absorption and self-interest. Do you desire such deliverance? Does your inner being long to be restored in the image of God? It is for such a transforming experience God promises deliverance.

O God, in this Advent season may the gospel be for me more than the story of Jesus' birth. May it be my rebirth into the Christlike life in the world for which you created me. Amen.

Zechariah's thanksgiving reveals that the purpose of God's deliverance is that we "might serve him without fear in holiness and righteousness before him all our days." Often overlooked is the phrase "without fear." All too many serve God out of fear: fear of God's judgment, fear of God's displeasure, fear of what others in the community of faith might think. True service of God is the result of a self-abandoning love-response to God's cruciform love for us. In fact, true service of God is the consequence of being in a relationship of loving union with God.

Zechariah points to this reality when he says "before him all our days." Loving service of God is a life lived in the Presence. Jesus notes this when he tells us, "Abide in me . . . because apart from me you can do nothing" (John 15:4-5) and illustrates the point by saying to those who were prophesying in his name, casting out demons in his name, and doing many deeds of power in his name (obviously "serving God"), "I never knew you; go away from me, you evildoers" (Matt. 7:22-23). Their "service" did not emerge out of a daily relationship with Jesus.

A life of loving service, grounded in loving union with God, is a radically different way of being in the world; in Zechariah's words, a life of "holiness and righteousness." Such a life, however, is not one of aloofness from the world or disdain for the world. It is a life that engages the world in ways that bring God's light into the darkness, God's life into the deadness, God's healing to the woundedness, God's wholeness to the brokenness, God's liberating grace to the destructive and dehumanizing bondages of the world.

O God, in your grace and mercy draw me into loving union with you that I may be one through whom your Presence touches the world. Amen.

Many today think of prophets as persons who foretell the future. Biblically, however, prophets were persons who represented God to their community. It might not be too far-fetched to say they were, in a sense, the presence of God for those around them. Often theirs was an uncomfortable presence challenging the distorted perspectives, condemning the false value systems, reproving destructive behavior patterns that impeded God's purpose for human wholeness in God's image.

However, Zechariah reveals another dimension of prophets. First, they "prepare [God's] ways." They are to be persons who, in the nature of their relationships with others and their life in the world, reveal to others the possibility of God's transforming presence in their own lives. Second, prophets give "knowledge of salvation." They are to be persons whose lives reveal to others the nature of salvation. Salvation revealed as deliverance from the distorted perspectives that warp human lives, release from the false values that deform or destroy human wholeness, liberation from the degraded behavior patterns that prevent fullness of life as a beloved child of God. Third, prophets incarnate God's forgiveness. They are persons whose love for others manifests something of God's cruciform love for persons in their deadness, darkness, woundedness, brokenness, and bondage.

All who claim Christ as Lord are called to be prophets of the Most High. Are you, in this Advent season, willing, like Mary, to allow Christ to be formed in you and brought to life in your world through you? Are you willing to become a prophet of the Most High?

Loving God, help me to be your prophet in my world. Amen.

SECOND SUNDAY OF ADVENT

Zechariah quotes Isaiah 40:3-5, the vision of God's restoration of Israel as God's covenant people. This provides insight into how "all flesh shall see the salvation of God." It comes through God's covenant people manifesting in the world the individual and corporate life of wholeness in God.

A world characterized by deep valleys of despair and hopelessness desperately needs the witness of a community filled with the unquenchable assurance that comes from a life "hid with Christ in God" (Col. 3:3, AT). A world distinguished by mountains of violence and injustice urgently needs the presence of a community whose humble life of other-referenced Love stands sacrificially against entrenched structures of injustice. A world misshapen by the crookedness of the false values of a pervasively self-referenced way of being crucially needs the example of a radically different way of being, that of a community whose values enhance and enrich human life and wholeness. A world diseased with the roughness of intolerance and prejudice critically needs the model of a community in which all are welcomed in the healing love of God and nurtured to wholeness in the image of God.

An essential part of our Advent journey of preparing the way of the Lord comes through our willingness to relinquish those aspects of our life as individuals and a community of faith that prevent us from being God's people in the world. We do this by allowing the refining fire of God's love to burn out all the dross of our self-referencedness and lead us into the transforming experience of a radically new mode of being. When we prepare the way of the Lord in this manner, we will become prophets of the Most High, individuals and communities of faith in whom the salvation of God becomes manifest.

O God, help me to prepare the way for you in my life and the life of my community of faith. Amen.

Rejoice Always

DECEMBER 10–16, 2012 • CANDACE LEWIS

MONDAY, DECEMBER 10 ~ *Read Zephaniah 3:14-20*

The long-awaited announcement has finally arrived. The good news is received like a family in the waiting room anticipating the birth of the first child. A good health report, a new friendship, a new job, a new grandchild are all good reasons to shout and sing aloud, joyfully praising our God.

As the third Sunday of Advent approaches, we prepare to light the candle of joy. Our scripture reading reminds us that we can experience joy in the midst of difficult and challenging circumstances. The prophet Zephaniah was called to warn the people of Judah of God's impending judgment if they continued in disobedience and refused to repent. As the people of Judah humbly sought forgiveness and returned to God, their path was illuminated and joy restored. Zephaniah proclaims a time of singing and rejoicing for the people of God.

Reflect upon the good news you have received of God's love, strength, power, and presence with you today. Release your problems, pains, and pressures to God and receive divine peace. God delights in you. God can quiet you with holy love. God rejoices over you with singing. Advent reminds us of God's desire to light a candle in the midst of our darkness and to restore joy and celebration to our lives.

Thank you, God, for your ability to remove fear and frailty from our lives and restore joy, celebration, and singing. In the midst of this sometimes dark and dreary world, continue to illuminate our paths that we might bring light to and share joy with those we will meet today. Amen.

New church strategist with Path 1 New Church Starts, the General Board of Discipleship; Nashville, Tennessee

Recently I served on a mission team to Ghana, West Africa. I recall a morning visit to a Methodist refugee camp. Expressions of joy and gratitude rang out as we gathered among students preparing for morning prayer. "Thank you, God, for fresh, clean drinking water springing up from this well. Hallelujah. Praise the Lord. Amen."

Tears filled the eyes of team members as we observed the celebration and shouts of joy acknowledging God's faithfulness to the community of students. The students rejoiced over fresh water, which many of us take for granted. Further conversation revealed this well had experienced damage, rendering it unusable for a period of time. Fearless, faithful students who trusted in God's provision worked to restore the well. Isaiah 12:2 reminds us that despite our current life circumstances we too can trust God and not be afraid: "The LORD GOD is my strength and my might; he has become my salvation."

God strengthened the students to persevere. God strengthens us to persevere. Breaking through to a new water reservoir within the same well released songs of praise from the hearts of the students. Fresh water reminded them of God's commitment to save and sustain their lives. Digging deeper had released water flowing with great strength.

Advent invites us to dig deeper. New discoveries await us beyond the commercialized Christmas stories and celebrations. As we dig deeper we might find a new reservoir of appreciation for God's saving grace coming into our chaotic world in the form of a baby born in a manger. Digging deeper can release the gratitude and appreciation in our hearts for God's gifts of mercy, peace, and daily provision. May we joyfully celebrate God's power manifested throughout our world!

We come with songs of joy and celebration, Gracious God! Amen.

WEDNESDAY, DECEMBER 12 ~ *Read Isaiah 12:4-6*

The prophet Isaiah encourages God's people to "give thanks to the LORD, call on his name; make known his deeds among the nations; proclaim that his name is exalted." I wonder how people shared good news among the nations in Isaiah's day. Maybe as they gathered in the marketplace or city centers, God's people rejoiced and sang in circles of prayer, lifting up praises to Almighty God. As others moved throughout the marketplace, they would pause and take note of the people of God singing, praising, and exalting the name of God.

We can experience the fullness of this text as we make others aware of God's activity in our lives and in the world around us. Modern technology allows us to share information quickly. Today good news spreads rapidly whether calling, e-mailing, texting, or posting on a favorite social networking site. Consider the various ways we can pass on the message of Advent with the nations of the world today. We can start by sharing a brief testimony or praise report with someone in line at the grocery store or coffee shop. We can post a message online reflecting our gratitude as we experience God working daily in our lives. Technology allows us to share with the world.

This Advent we too can shout aloud and sing for joy and tell others of the greatness of God among God's people. Decide today to tell someone about the joy you experience in your relationship with Christ.

God, our modern, digital, technology-filled world enables us to make global connections with ease. Thank you for a new awareness of the ways in which we can share with others. Give us courage today to tell others about your greatness in our lives. Amen.

When the doctor's assistant called my name, I momentarily allowed anxiety to grip my heart. I dread appointments when test results will be received. I expect the best and fear the worst at the same time. Prior to the physician's entering the room, I mouthed a silent prayer asking God to comfort and strengthen me. To my surprise, after the prayer I experienced a calming peace best identified as God's presence with me in the doctor's office. I found that presence hard to understand. I sensed that no matter what the results revealed, I would be OK because God was with me. Joy filled my heart and tears filled my eyes as I soaked in God's peaceful presence in the doctor's office. The physician shared the report of additional treatments required with optimism, reminding me of my positive future outlook. I smiled and graciously thanked the doctor as the joy of God's presence overflowed in my heart.

Paul reminds the Philippians that they too can rejoice in the Lord always. He confirms how easily we become anxious about life circumstances. Whether it's anxiety about a doctor's appointment, employment outlook, personal finances, or relationship problems—when anxiety and worry come, we can choose to dwell upon them or direct them to God. Philippians 4:6-7 says, "Do not worry about anything, but in everything by prayer and supplication with thanksgiving let your requests be made known to God. And the peace of God, which surpasses all understanding, will guard your hearts and your minds in Christ Jesus."

Choose to share with God in prayer any anxiety or worry you sense. Receive from God a peaceful presence that guards your heart when anxiety tries to return. Joy overflows despite life's problems because God is with us. As we prepare to light the Advent candle of joy, Christ's coming assures us of a positive future despite life's problems.

Gracious God, may I rejoice in you at all times. Amen.

Rejoice Always

FRIDAY, DECEMBER 14 ~ *Read Philippians 4:4-7*

We witness the commercialization of Christmas all around us. Holiday ads entice us to purchase more than we can afford. We overextend ourselves with shopping, cooking, events, parties, and people. Advent offers an alternative experience to a retail-driven, pressure-filled, consumer Christmas. Advent invites us to discover the joy that surrounds the coming of Christ. As we prepare to light the candle of joy, we intentionally remember and meditate upon God's gift of love given to us with the birth of Jesus Christ.

The epistle reading reminds us we have a say about what will fill our thoughts this holiday season. We can choose to lay aside worry and turn to prayer. Instead of allowing outside influences to consume us, we then will know the peace of God that "surpasses all understanding."

This shift in thinking offers an alternate perspective. Instead of thinking about the many unfinished tasks on my Christmas list, I can focus on what I have been able to accomplish and experience joyful rest and contentment. I can recall that "the Lord is near." Instead of thinking about how much money I do not have to purchase gifts, I can shift my thinking to a time of thanksgiving by creating a budget and living within my means. This shift in thinking brings with it a peaceful affirmation of God's presence with me throughout this holiday season.

Exchange stressful ruminating today for thoughts emanating from your relationship with Christ. God promises to guard our hearts and minds, giving us the priceless gift of peace that will remain with us as we pray our way through this Advent season.

Modern cars are equipped with warning lights. Warning lights alert us when something about our car needs attention. Ignoring the warning can result in expensive consequences. Asking questions in reference to warning lights allows us to respond promptly, resolve problems, and restore confidence in our car as reliable transportation.

The Gospel of Luke records the powerful, prophetic preaching of John the Baptist. For John's audience, John's messages sound like a bright-red warning light that flashes too brightly to ignore. His preaching convicts and penetrates minds and hearts. The people promptly respond by asking the question "What then should we do?"

John prepares the way for the coming of Jesus Christ. God's gracious love for the people allows John's preaching to precede Christ's ministry. God offers the people a chance by heeding John's warnings to hear the good news and to experience repentance and baptism. That results in a change of direction in their hearts, minds, lives, and actions. John challenges his audience not to make excuses and invites them into a new way of life filled with charity, justice, equality, and fairness for all.

Today's reading invites us into a time of self-reflection and self-examination of the warning lights flashing in our lives. We are to heed the biblical message without making excuses. Questioning ourselves, we too may see ways we have been uncharitable, unjust, or unfair toward others. As we seek to honor Christ, we too can "bear fruits worthy of repentance."

God, forgive us when we ignore your warnings. Thank you for being loving and long-suffering enough to send us your grace-filled message through Jesus Christ before judgment and consequences occur. May we produce worthy fruits this Advent season. Amen.

SUNDAY, DECEMBER 16 ～ *Read Luke 3:15-18*

THIRD SUNDAY OF ADVENT

Transitions in life and leadership are inevitable. We can compare life to a relay race: runners receive a baton, run their leg of the race, and pass the baton to the next runner. Usually the next runner is prepared, expecting the transition, and ready to run his or her assigned leg of the race.

John the Baptist is on the verge of a transition. He has run a good race, faithfully preaching and preparing the way for the long-awaited Messiah who will take up the baton. John baptizes many, challenging them to repent of their sins so they can receive the good news at hand. His ministry creates expectancy among the people as they look for the Messiah, spoken about throughout the sacred texts.

When people wonder if John is the Messiah, he humbly yet emphatically distinguishes his ministry from that of Jesus: "I baptize you with water; but one who is more powerful than I is coming; I am not worthy to untie the thong of his sandals. He will baptize you with the Holy Spirit and fire." John's answer leaves people anticipating the powerful impact Jesus' presence and preaching will have on their lives personally and on the world in which they live.

As we enter the third week of Advent, let's see and seize the opportunities to create expectancy about encountering Christ this Christmas among those who do not know Christ personally. As we speak of the power, presence, life, and love of Christ, let's pray that someone will receive the good news in his or her heart by faith.

Loving God, empower us to follow John's example of being a passionate, faithful witness of the good news of Christ. Our world longs to experience and encounter Christ. May we be bold witnesses this Advent season! Amen.

Waiting on God's Promise

DECEMBER 17–23, 2012 • JANET KNIGHT

MONDAY, DECEMBER 17 ~ *Read Micah 5:2a; 7:1-7*

Advent lectionary readings traditionally include Micah 5 because the Gospel writers saw in verse 2 a foretelling of the birth of Jesus in Bethlehem. However, biblical scholars generally agree that in verse 2 Micah is speaking of the past as if it were the future. God is represented as speaking to Israel using future tenses at the time David was being anointed king. Micah, writing between 737 and 686 BCE, then turns to the future in verses 3-5, foretelling difficult times for Judah until God chooses to raise up another king who will make Israel a united and safe nation again.

Perhaps in attending to these verses alone, we miss the greater message Micah holds for us—a message of confident, active waiting on God to act and of unshakable faith in God's ultimate goodness and mercy. Micah looks around and sees injustice and dishonesty everywhere: "Listen to me, you rulers of Israel, you that hate justice and turn right into wrong" (3:9, GNT). Instead of despairing, Micah waits confidently for God. And while waiting, he never ceases trying to make people see that injustice and dishonesty are not part of God's will.

What does Micah's example of active, confident waiting say to us today as we move through another Advent season when people are homeless, children are malnourished and undereducated, the elderly find medical care unaffordable, and our planet is in danger of dying?

God of hope, instill in me an attitude of active, confident waiting during this season of new beginnings. Amen.

Retired editor, *Pockets*, the magazine for children published by Upper Room Ministries; Nashville, Tennessee

What does God want of us? In Micah 6:8, the prophet tells us in no uncertain terms. And he tells the people of Israel that this is exactly what they have *not* been doing. "Your wealthy are full of violence; your inhabitants speak lies" (6:12). "The faithful have disappeared from the land, . . . they all lie in wait for blood, and they hunt each other with nets. Their hands are skilled to do evil" (7:2-3). And so, according to Micah, God will punish them. But even in that punishment there is promise—the promise of a leader who will rule not by worldly power but by the power that comes from the Lord. His rule will be the Lord's rule, a rule in which God will teach the people the just way. The great powers "shall beat their swords into plowshares, and their spears into pruning hooks; nation shall not lift up sword against nation, neither shall they learn war any more" (4:3).

What does God want of *us*—we who live in the second decade of the twenty-first century, so far removed from those people of seventh-century BCE Jerusalem. Or are we? The homeless walk the streets; many people have no adequate health care; a high percentage of our children live in poverty; our prisons overflow. All this poverty exists in the midst of great wealth and in spite of the fact that we have something the people of Micah's day did not: God's full revelation in Jesus, whose birth we are about to celebrate. Indeed, this Advent, this preparation time, is a good time to ask again: What does God require of us . . . of me?

Holy God, help me to do what is just, to show constant love, to live in humble fellowship with you. Amen.

I'd prefer not to read this kind of scripture passage during Advent. I would much rather read the wonderful Isaiah passages that hold so much promise—passages about preparing a road in the wilderness for the Lord (40:3) or people who have walked in darkness now seeing a great light (9:2) or the absence of harm and evil on God's holy mountain (11:9) or deserts singing and shouting for joy (35:1-2). But, "You have fed them with the bread of tears, and given them tears to drink in full measure"—I don't want to read that during the Advent season. Then I must ask myself, *How can I experience great joy over the birth of the Christ child if I do not understand and, indeed, experience for myself the cry for help and the need for deliverance?*

As we see in the Psalms, over and over again in its history Israel cried for help and asked for deliverance. Of the 150 psalms, just over one-third are psalms of lament—psalms that invoke God's name, cry for hearing and help, state the nature and cause of a particular misfortune, and pray for deliverance. Of these lament psalms, thirteen are community laments; that is, they are expressions of national sorrow brought on by a sense of the nation's sin. In this particular community lament, the people see a military defeat as a sign of God's wrath and so ask, "O Lord God of hosts, how long will you be angry with your people's prayers?"

What are our national sins? Misuse and overuse of natural resources? Unspoken yet pervasive racism? Far-from-equal distribution of wealth? Faith in military might? Consumerism? We must name our sin before we can cry, "O Lord God of hosts, how long will you be angry?"

Come, Lord Jesus, to all nations. Amen.

Elizabeth seems somewhat overlooked in the Christmas cast of characters. Her husband, Zechariah, steals the scene from her when he, not Elizabeth, receives Gabriel's announcement that a special son will be born to the couple. And although the scripture doesn't tell us so, Zechariah's inability to speak as a result of his unbelief probably remained as much a topic of conversation among the townsfolk as did Elizabeth's pregnancy.

But if we take time to ponder Elizabeth's words before moving on to Mary's beautiful song of praise and thanksgiving in verses 46-55, we see something special about Elizabeth. She recognized the long-foretold Messiah, even before his birth. Without proof of mighty and miraculous deeds, face-to-face with a young, unmarried, pregnant cousin who, like her, was "just ordinary folks," Elizabeth recognized the Savior of her people.

What does it take to recognize our Savior in such unlikely circumstances? Elizabeth must have been a woman of great faith, believing deep within herself that if the Lord had promised a deliverer, then the Lord would indeed send a deliverer. But Elizabeth had more than what might be called "blind faith." She possessed an openness to the Holy Spirit's activity in the world. Thus, when presented with evidence of the Holy Spirit's ultimate intervention in the affairs of the world, she herself was "filled with the Holy Spirit" and could say in wonder and humility, "Why should this great thing happen to me?" (GNT).

Elizabeth exemplifies confident waiting and openness to God's intervention. May that confidence, patience, and receptivity be ours this Advent season.

Think about where God might be intervening in your life. Ask God to give you the kind of faith, patience, and receptivity that Elizabeth demonstrated.

What if Mary had said no—"No, I do not want to do this thing"? We could hardly have blamed her. To say yes meant risking her very life. Or, if she was spared her life, she would have to live in disgrace. She might not have had a man to provide for her in a society in which most women had no identity and no possessions outside their father's house and later outside their husband's house.

But Mary, like her cousin Elizabeth, believed in a God who kept promises. And a long time ago that same God had promised Mary's people a deliverer, one who would rule "in the strength of the LORD." That God was a God who worked through common, ordinary people to intervene in history. That God was a God who gave strength and courage to those who allowed themselves to be instruments of God's will. So Mary said, "Yes, I'll do it."

Mary's yes was not a halfhearted, begrudging, resigned one. It was a joyful yes, a thankful yes, a faith-filled yes. The tenor of Mary's willingness is beautifully clear in her response to Elizabeth in verses 46-55. These verses are known as the "Magnificat," so named after the first word in the Latin translation, and have become one of the great hymns of the church.

We, like Mary, are ordinary people. But, like Mary, we can be powerful instruments to help bring about God's will, whether that will pertains to saving our planet, combatting racism, feeding the hungry, clothing the naked, ministering to the sick, visiting the imprisoned, or raising our children with a keen sense of peace with justice. Are we saying yes to God's call to us to be instruments of God's love and mercy? Do we respond to God out of thankful, joyful, faith-filled hearts?

Loving God, help us to say yes to you this holy season. Amen.

In words and cadence strikingly similar to Hannah's song in 1 Samuel 2:1-10, Mary depicts a God who champions the cause of society's powerless ones. Mary's words have been called revolutionary—and they are, but no more so than those of Hannah or the psalmist or the prophets Amos, Isaiah, and Micah. God's message has always been one of *shalom*, well-being for all people. That message is difficult to see when it becomes entangled in a people's understanding of their place in the world's power struggle, but the message is there nevertheless.

Hannah was an object of scorn because of her childlessness in a society that counted a woman's worthiness by the number of sons she delivered. Mary was young and pregnant out of wedlock. That this message of shalom is heralded so beautifully and so emphatically by two women centuries apart is perhaps indicative of its sustaining power. Similarly, faith in God's revolutionary message has its strongest voice today not in U.S. and Western European pulpits but in the base communities of Latin America and among the oppressed people of color in South Africa. Faced with a daily poverty most of us cannot conceive of and in constant danger of physical violence, these people can say, "How wonderful it is to live threatened with Resurrection! . . . and to know yourself already Risen!"*

God's revolutionary message has power for those of us for whom poverty, oppression, and extreme violence are not part of our daily existence. It calls us to a passion for justice for all the poor and oppressed of the world, a passion that may result in our sacrificing material wealth, power, or influence.

Consider the question: Where does God's revolutionary message call me?

---

*From the poem "We Dream Awake" by Julia Esquivel

SUNDAY, DECEMBER 23 ~ *Read Hebrews 10:5-10*

FOURTH SUNDAY OF ADVENT

How often have we heard the statement "Without Easter, Christmas would have no meaning"? Today's passage reminds us that there is more to Christmas than the birth of a special baby. It calls us to an obedience to God's will so complete that it becomes a dangerous challenge to the world's will and so results in the ultimate sacrifice. Ultimate because the sacrifice is that of a person's life, and ultimate because it is the full and perfect sacrifice that abolishes the need for the Old Testament system of sacrifice. Jesus offered himself in faithful love and obedience to do God's will, whatever that required. That sacrifice bridged humanity's alienation from God for all time.

So we can begin to understand the nature of God's promise to us. It is not a promise of military might or monetary riches or fame. It is a promise that the way to God is forever open. It is a promise of a God who will always be with us—Immanuel.

Each Advent gives us the opportunity to examine anew our response to God's fulfillment of the divine promise in Jesus. Centuries ago, Micah gave us one response: "to do justice, to love kindness, and to walk humbly with your God" (6:8). People around us are also responding to God's promise. Joyce Hollyday tells about the woman who runs the soup kitchen for the Sojourners Community every Saturday morning. Each Saturday she prays the same prayer that includes this line: "Lord, you're coming through this line today, so help us to treat you right. Yes, Lord, help us to treat you right."*

Dear Jesus, again we are about to celebrate your coming. Help us to treat you right. Amen.

---

*Joyce Hollyday, *Turning toward Home* (San Francisco: Harper & Row Publishers, 1989), 264.

The Word Brings Joy and Growth

DECEMBER 24–30, 2012 • ENUMA OKORO

MONDAY, DECEMBER 24 ~ *Read Isaiah 9:2-7, Luke 2:1-20*

God has given us an abundance for which to rejoice. The psalms declare that even the trees, the sea, and the fields rejoice in God's ongoing work of salvation. Isaiah prophesies of the people's rejoicing when the Prince of Peace has been born. The Gospel speaks of humans and heavenly hosts praising God.

As a youth minister many years ago I took the youth to a live Nativity performance. Everything was going as expected. The baby Jesus was fussing a little bit, and the actress playing Mary managed to look both tired and thrilled as she rested on the hay. Then the spotlight switched to another scene: The shepherds were in the field when the voice-over of the angel came on the microphone to announce the good news. When the voice came to Luke 2:13, all the lights dimmed except a floodlight that suddenly revealed a dozen angelic-looking actors with life-sized wings, long white robes, and halos. All at once they began a chorus of beautiful harmonious praise, singing the words of scripture, "Glory to God in the highest heaven and on earth peace among those whom he favors!" That was twelve years ago. Yet, whenever I recall the experience, I find myself wishing I could relive it again and again each year. It makes me wonder each Christmas season how we individually and communally might order our lives so that the beautiful, unbelievable message of the angels might fill us with awe and gratitude, rejoicing in our stunned silence and in our humble prayers.

Lord, help us order our daily lives so that the news of your birth will find us awe-filled and grateful. Amen.

Former Director for the Center for Theological Writing, Duke Divinity School; Durham, North Carolina; author of *Reluctant Pilgrim* (Upper Room Books, 2010)

TUESDAY, DECEMBER 25 ~ *John 1:1-14*

CHRISTMAS DAY

Ason is born today to Mary, to Joseph, and to God the Father. A king is born today, a king of creation. A victor is born today. One who existed at the beginning of time, is present now, and will come again in glory. Many of us might easily reconcile the idea of Christ as son, king, and victor. Those designations make sense to us. But what do we make of Christ as the incarnate Word of God, the speech of God, what the Greeks call the "logos." What could it mean for our lives?

I had a preaching professor who would often start the class by asking loudly and determinedly, "Is there a word from the Lord?" He asked as though he expected an answer. You could tell that this man had spent his life immersed in scripture and lived as though he regularly received convicting and transformative words from God.

The Gospel of John tells us that Jesus is the Word that always was, and always is. Scripture posits countless examples of God's word bringing new life into existence, beginning with the Genesis account of creation. God spoke the word and created. God's word brings life where nothing existed or where there was death. God's word brings order to chaos, light into darkness, and freedom from the things that enslave us. God's word also brings grace, mercy, forgiveness, renewal, joy, peace, love, and resurrection. All these realities are born today in Christ and for all creation.

We need to train ourselves to listen for God's creating Word around us because God is always speaking new existence into our lives through Christ Jesus. When we experience the Word, we are called to invite others to listen for it as well.

Sustaining God, how can we make our lives a dwelling place for your Word? Reveal to us how you would like to take up residence within us this season. Amen.

Children of God are born to faithful women like Hannah and Mary, women who bear witness to strength and spiritual commitment. When we first meet Hannah in 1 Samuel 1, she is lost in earnest prayer to God. She promises to consecrate her child to God's service. God hears her prayer and blesses her with Samuel. Hannah is a first-time mom cradling the child she has longed for all her life. Hannah would love to raise Samuel into young adulthood. But Hannah also loves God and keeps her word. Hannah takes Samuel to the temple and entrusts him to God; she knows she can trust God with her most prized possession, her child.

Samuel has been in the temple for a few years. Scripture now describes him as a boy of age to wear the sacramental linen ephod that signifies his consecration to God. Samuel is in God's hands. But Hannah is still Samuel's mother, and she continues to nurture and love him in all the ways she can while honoring her love and commitment to God. She visits Samuel each year as permitted and sews him clothes. Samuel knows that his mother loves him. God knows that Hannah loves her Lord.

We read this story and we acknowledge what Hannah also knows: God loves Hannah, and God loves Samuel. Because of Hannah's faithfulness, God has entrusted her to be part of God's work in the world. Mary, another faithful woman, was entrusted with playing a part in God's work in the world. This season is about the Christ child, the savior of the world. And yet it is also a season about how God has chosen to make God's work possible through the bodies of faithful people; faithful women who seek God out, who persevere in faith, who hone lives of spiritual discipline, and who speak openly with God and expect God to hear them.

God, make us bold enough to speak to you, faithful enough to expect you, and trusting enough to give you our hearts. Amen.

Young Samuel is a priest-in-training for his people. Under Eli's guidance and instruction he has been set apart for God's purposes. His life looks different from that of other boys his age. All we have to do is look at Samuel's clothing: a linen ephod typically designated for holy men, and we can tell that this child is different. He sets about the things of God. And yet, Samuel still receives annual visits from his devoted mother who each year makes him a new robe to fit his growing stature. He has been set aside for God's work, but he is still growing and maturing into his faith and his calling, both literally and figuratively. Verse 26 significantly reveals that even though people may look at Samuel and delight in him, God also sees Samuel and delights in his spiritual maturation.

Centuries later, another young child is a "holy-one-in-training." The Christ child is born; his life, death, and resurrection invite us to become reconciled children of God, men and women called and set apart for God's work. We too are to increase "in wisdom and in years, and in divine and human favor." We, like Samuel, have a source of inspiration. Christ is our guide and our instructor. He provides the way to our spiritual maturation. We delight in the infant child whose birth we celebrated yesterday. Yet this King of kings, this Son of God is our high priest, the one under whose care we have been graced. We cannot expect our lives to be transformed overnight. We have to sit with Jesus, study with Jesus, pray with Jesus, walk alongside Jesus; watch, learn, and mimic what we see. In this way we too will delight God as we grow in our faith. So let's stay by the manger—but not too long. We have much to learn from this holy one beyond the cradle.

Lord, increase our desire to grow in faith. We thank you that your love for us does not depend on our actions but that you still yearn for us to become more like you in all we do. Amen.

FRIDAY, DECEMBER 28 ～ *Read Psalm 148*

I've been writing since I was seven years old, and it has always brought me immense joy and satisfaction. It took me awhile to own and accept that this was how God made me and that it was okay to be a writer, to enjoy the work I feel called to do. Writing is one way that I praise God with my life. Psalm 148 is a hymn of praise that reveals how all of creation praises God by simply doing what creation was meant to do. Snow praises by being snow. Mountains and hills praise by being mountains and hills. God's creation seems most authentic when it simply lives into what God created it to be. As humans we were created to worship and praise God. Three days after Christmas the psalmist's words remind us Christians that the birth of Christ calls us to be people who dwell in relationship with God and whose lives witness to worship and praise.

So often we praise God when our lives are going well and we have something to celebrate. But Psalm 148 doesn't say anything about "praise God when you feel like it" or "praise God when times are good." It simply calls creation to praise God because God is; God creates; and God's "glory is above earth and heaven."

If we sought to live as people created to praise God, what might our lives look like? How do we praise God in all aspects of our lives? We all have unique talents and personalities. But we were also all created with the same end purpose of worshiping God. What would it look like if we discerned more intimately our unique path to praise God with the works of our hands; with our unique temperaments, quirks, passions, and talents? The mountain does not praise as the stormy wind, but it still praises and fulfills God's command.

Lord, you made us to praise you at all times. Help us discern our unique calls to praise you as we follow Christ this season. Amen.

The Word Brings Joy and Growth

This reading of Colossians 3:12-17 can make us feel spiritually inadequate and even hopeless. It sounds like so much effort to become who Christ desires us to be in him. We can spend our lives trying to cultivate just one of the virtues on this list! This letter is written to the growing church in Colossae. These people are already seeking to be faithful. They just need more encouragement and wisdom in discerning how best to grow in their faith, who to listen to, and how to develop stronger spiritual practices.

These verses gently and lovingly remind us that God does not call us to transformation by our own devices or by ourselves. They encourage us to allow God to have God's way with us over time. The word of Christ dwells in us richly; we are already chosen as God's holy and beloved, and we support one another in living lives that testify to that reality.

The image of clothing ourselves with compassion, kindness, humility, meekness, and patience invites us into active participation in what God desires to do in us. I read verse 12, and I cannot help but think of times when my extended family has gathered for the holidays and I have helped my little nephews and nieces get ready in the morning. At the tender ages of four and five, they already know what they want to wear! They are determined to pick out their own clothes, even if the selected color scheme makes me want to wear sunglasses! God desires to help us get dressed spiritually, but I also think God desires that we be determined about the spiritual clothes we would wear, regardless of how it looks to the outside world.

Lord, grant us wisdom to encourage one another to grow and practice spiritual disciplines. Remind us that you are at work among us and that you invite us to partake in that work. Amen.

When I try to imagine Jesus as a twelve-year-old based on this story, I think of one child I met while I attending seminary and volunteering with the youth group of a local church. I met Jonathan when he was twelve years old, and, boy, did this child hunger for God. He exhibited great curiosity about the Bible and always raised questions. Jonathan had, and continues to have, a heart for God. He's a sophomore in college now, and whenever he comes home for breaks we get together for coffee. He still asks the hard questions about living a life of faith. It is a gift to watch him grow in spiritual maturity.

Our only glimpse into Jesus' childhood centers on his learning and teaching in the Temple at age twelve. When we consider Jesus' growing-up years, we may want to know about his personality; what kind of trouble he got into; how he developed as a boy, a teenager, a young adult. I read this passage and immediately think back to Samuel's maturing in faith as noted in 1 Samuel 2:26. Jesus was human as we are. He too needed spiritual instruction and maturation. Yes, even as a child he voiced unbelievable questions and thoughts to the rabbis but he still was learning from spiritual leaders. No one forced Jesus to stay behind. He was drawn to the things of God, and that's how he grew in wisdom.

This passage makes me dwell on two things. First, how do we maintain a child's hunger and curiosity for the things of God? Second, who are the children around us who openly hunger for God and how do we encourage, teach, sustain, and help them grow in the faith?

Ask God to help you discern if you are equipped and called to disciple a child growing in the faith. Stay alert and open for how God might answer your prayer in the coming days, months, or even years.

Resolutions

DECEMBER 31, 2012 • TOM APPEL

MONDAY, DECEMBER 31 ~ *Read Matthew 2:1-12*

No doubt New Year's resolutions would be far less popular in the United States were they not motivated by the inevitable overindulgence that the holidays bring. We loosen our belts a notch after Thanksgiving, and before we have time to ponder a trip to the gym, we are bombarded by the Christmas rush and find our bank accounts deflated, our stomachs inflated, and suddenly, it's the beginning of a new year.

Whether or not you make resolutions, the example set by the Magi in this passage is certainly inspiring on New Year's Eve. Often, we forget the determination and sacrifice of these wise ones who take a trip that, in their time, is extremely perilous. We don't know how far they traveled, but we do know that their mode of transport is far less comfortable than flying economy and that the land they traverse is an unforgiving place of mountains and deserts.

Yet they journey—and for what? Not to trade goods and make their fortune and not to move their flocks and family to greener pastures. They want to give gifts and to worship Jesus, because somehow they know this is what they must do—this is their calling. These Magi remain faithful to this calling despite what must have been a costly and difficult journey topped off by a conniving king. New Year's Eve provides a catalyst to take stock of the year gone by and consider the one to come. Let us share the passion of the Magi who put aside everything to seek out and worship the giver of life, Jesus.

God, lead me this coming year in paths of righteousness for your namesake; may I journey with my eyes fixed on you. Amen.

Neighborhood organizer and writer, living in Nashville, Tennessee

The Revised Common Lectionary* for 2012
Year B – Advent / Christmas Year C
(Disciplines Edition)

January 1
New Year's Day
Ecclesiastes 3:1-13
Psalm 8
Revelation 21:1-6a
Matthew 25:31-46

January 6
EPIPHANY
(may be used for Sunday, Jan. 1)
Isaiah 60:1-6
Psalm 72:1-7, 10-14
Ephesians 3:1-12
Matthew 2:1-12

January 2–8
BAPTISM OF THE LORD
Genesis 1:1-5
Psalm 29
Acts 19:1-7
Mark 1:4-11

January 9–15
1 Samuel 3:1-20
Psalm 139:1-6, 13-18
1 Corinthians 6:12-20
John 1:43-51

January 16–22
Jonah 3:1-5, 10
Psalm 62:5-12
1 Corinthians 7:29-31
Mark 1:14-20

January 23–29
Deuteronomy 18:15-20
Psalm 111
1 Corinthians 8:1-13
Mark 1:21-28

January 30—February 5
Isaiah 40:21-31
Psalm 147:1-11, 20c
1 Corinthians 9:16-23
Mark 1:29-39

February 6–12
2 Kings 5:1-14
Psalm 30
1 Corinthians 9:24-27
Mark 1:40-45

February 13–19
TRANSFIGURATION
2 Kings 2:1-12
Psalm 50:1-6
2 Corinthians 4:3-6
Mark 9:2-9

February 20–26
FIRST SUNDAY IN LENT
Genesis 9:8-17
Psalm 25:1-10
1 Peter 3:18-22
Mark 1:9-15

February 22
ASH WEDNESDAY
Joel 2:1-2, 12-17 (or Isaiah 58:1-12)
Psalm 51:1-17
2 Corinthians 5:20b–6:10
Matthew 6:1-6, 16-21

February 27—March 4
SECOND SUNDAY IN LENT
Genesis 17:1-7, 15-16
Psalm 22:23-31
Romans 4:13-25
Mark 8:31-38

March 5–11
THIRD SUNDAY IN LENT
Exodus 20:1-17
Psalm 19
1 Corinthians 1:18-25
John 2:13-22

March 12–18
FOURTH SUNDAY IN LENT
Numbers 21:4-9
Psalm 107:1-3, 17-22
Ephesians 2:1-10
John 3:14-21

March 19–25
FIFTH SUNDAY IN LENT
Jeremiah 31:31-34
Psalm 51:1-12
(or Psalm 119:9-16)
Hebrews 5:5-10
John 12:20-33

March 26—April 1
PASSION/PALM SUNDAY
Mark 11:1-11, 15-18
(or John 12:12-19)
Psalm 118:1-2, 15-29

Liturgy of the Passion
Isaiah 50:4-9a
Psalm 31:9-16
Philippians 2:5-11
Mark 14:1–15:47
(or Mark 15:1-47)

April 2–8
HOLY WEEK

HOLY MONDAY
Isaiah 42:1-9
Psalm 36:5-11
Hebrews 9:11-15
John 12:1-11

HOLY TUESDAY
Isaiah 49:1-7
Psalm 71:1-14
1 Corinthians 1:18-31
John 12:20-36

HOLY WEDNESDAY
Isaiah 50:4-9a
Psalm 70
Hebrews 12:1-3
John 13:21-32

MAUNDY THURSDAY
Exodus 12:1-14
Psalm 116:1-4, 12-19
1 Corinthians 11:23-26
John 13:1-17, 31b-35

GOOD FRIDAY
Isaiah 52:13–53:12
Psalm 22
Hebrews 10:16-25
John 18:1–19:42

HOLY SATURDAY
Exodus 14:10-31
Isaiah 55:1-11
Psalm 114
Romans 6:3-11
Mark 16:1-8

EASTER, APRIL 8
Acts 10:34-43
Psalm 118:1-2, 14-24
1 Corinthians 15:1-11
John 20:1-18
   (*or* Mark 16:1-8)

April 9–15
Acts 4:32-35
Psalm 133
1 John 1:1–2:2
John 20:19-31

April 16–22
Acts 3:12-19
Psalm 4
1 John 3:1-7
Luke 24:36b-48

April 23–29
Acts 4:5-12
Psalm 23
1 John 3:16-24
John 10:11-18

April 30–May 6
Acts 8:26-40
Psalm 22:25-31
1 John 4:7-21
John 15:1-8

May 7–13
Acts 10:44-48
Psalm 98
1 John 5:1-6
John 15:9-17

May 14–20
Acts 1:15-17, 21-26
Psalm 1
1 John 5:9-13
John 17:6-19

May 17
ASCENSION DAY
Acts 1:1-11
Psalm 47
Ephesians 1:15-23
Luke 24:44-53

May 21–27
PENTECOST
Acts 2:1-21
Psalm 104:24-34, 35b
Romans 8:22-27
John 15:26-27; 16:4b-15

May 28—June 3
TRINITY
Isaiah 6:1-8
Psalm 29
Romans 8:12-17
John 3:1-17

June 4–10
1 Samuel 8:4-20 (11:14-15)
Psalm 138
2 Corinthians 4:13–5:1
Mark 3:20-35

June 11–17
1 Samuel 15:34–16:13
Psalm 20 *or* Psalm 92
2 Corinthians 5:6-17
Mark 4:26-34

June 18–24
1 Samuel 17:1*a*, 4-11, 19-23,
   32-49
Psalm 9:9-20
2 Corinthians 6:1-13
Mark 4:35-41

June 25–July 1
2 Samuel 1:1, 17-27
Psalm 130
2 Corinthians 8:7-15
Mark 5:21-43

July 2–8
2 Samuel 5:1-5, 9-10
Psalm 48
2 Corinthians 12:2-10
Mark 6:1-13

July 9–15
2 Samuel 6:1-5, 12b-19
Psalm 24
Ephesians 1:3-14
Mark 6:14-29

July 16–22
2 Samuel 7:1-14a
Psalm 89:20-37
Ephesians 2:11-22
Mark 6:30-34, 53-56

July 23–29
2 Samuel 11:1-15
Psalm 14
Ephesians 3:14-21
John 6:1-21

July 30–August 5
2 Samuel 11:26–12:13a
Psalm 51:1-12
Ephesians 4:1-16
John 6:24-35

August 6–12
2 Samuel 18:5-9, 15, 31-33
Psalm 130
Ephesians 4:25–5:2
John 6:35, 41-51

August 13–19
1 Kings 2:10-12; 3:3-14
Psalm 111
Ephesians 5:15-20
John 6:51-58

August 20–26
1 Kings 8:1, 6, 10-11, 22-30,
    41-43
Psalm 84
Ephesians 6:10-20
John 6:56-69

August 27—September 2
Song of Solomon 2:8-13
Psalm 45:1-2, 6-9 or Psalm 72
James 1:17-27
Mark 7:1-8, 14-15, 21-23

September 3–9
Proverbs 22:1-2, 8-9, 22-23
Psalm 125 or Psalm 124
James 2:1-17
Mark 7:24-37

September 10–16
Proverbs 1:20-33
Psalm 19
James 3:1-12
Mark 8:27-38

September 17–23
Proverbs 31:10-31
Psalm 1 (or Psalm 54)
James 3:13–4:3, 7-8a
Mark 9:30-37

September 24–30
Esther 7:1-6, 9-10; 9:20-22
Psalm 124
James 5:13-20
Mark 9:38-50

October 1–7
Job 1:1; 2:1-10
Psalm 26 or Psalm 25
Hebrews 1:1-4; 2:5-12
Mark 10:2-16

October 8–14
Job 23:1-9, 16-17
Psalm 22:1-15
Hebrews 4:12-16
Mark 10:17-31

OCTOBER 8
THANKSGIVING DAY, CANADA
Joel 2:21-27
Psalm 126
1 Timothy 2:1-7
Matthew 6:25-33

October 15–21
Job 38:1-7, 34-41
Psalm 104:1-9, 24, 35c
Hebrews 5:1-10
Mark 10:35-45

October 22–28
Job 42:1-6, 10-17
Psalm 34:1-8, 19-22
Hebrews 7:23-28
Mark 10:46-52

October 29–November 4
Ruth 1:1-18
Psalm 146
Hebrews 9:11-14
Mark 12:28-34

November 1
ALL SAINTS DAY
Isaiah 25:6-9
Psalm 24
Revelation 21:1-6a
John 11:32-44

November 5–11
Ruth 3:1-5; 4:13-17
Psalm 127 or Psalm 42
Hebrews 9:24-28
Mark 12:38-44

November 12–18
1 Samuel 1:4-20
Psalm 113 (or 1 Samuel 2:1-10)
Hebrews 10:11-25
Mark 13:1-8

November 19–25
THE REIGN OF CHRIST
2 Samuel 23:1-7
Psalm 132:1-12
Revelation 1:4b-8
John 18:33-37

November 22
THANKSGIVING DAY, USA
Joel 2:21-27
Psalm 126
1 Timothy 2:1-7
Matthew 6:25-33

November 26—December 2
FIRST SUNDAY OF ADVENT
Jeremiah 33:14-16
Psalm 25:1-10
1 Thessalonians 3:9-13
Luke 21:25-36

December 3–9
SECOND SUNDAY OF ADVENT
Malachi 3:1-4
Luke 1:68-79
Philippians 1:3-11
Luke 3:1-6

December 10–16
THIRD SUNDAY OF ADVENT
Zephaniah 3:14-20
Isaiah 12:2-6
Philippians 4:4-7
Luke 3:7-18

December 17–23
FOURTH SUNDAY OF ADVENT
Micah 5:2-5a
Luke 1:47-55
(*or* Psalm 80:1-7)
Hebrews 10:5-10
Luke 1:39-45

December 24–30
**FIRST SUNDAY AFTER
CHRISTMAS**
1 Samuel 2:18-20, 26
Psalm 148
Colossians 3:12-17
Luke 2:41-52

December 24
CHRISTMAS EVE
Isaiah 9:2-7
Psalm 96
Titus 2:11-14
Luke 2:1-20

December 25
CHRISTMAS DAY
Isaiah 52:7-10
Psalm 98
Hebrews 1:1-12
John 1:1-14

December 31
Isaiah 60:1-6
Psalm 72:1-7, 10-14
Ephesians 3:1-12
Matthew 2:1-12